# Dream
# and
# Reality

# DREAM
# AND
# REALITY

## *The Modern Black Struggle for Freedom and Equality*

*Edited by*
# JEANNINE SWIFT

Prepared under the auspices of Hofstra University

Contributions in Afro-American and African Studies, Number 142

**GREENWOOD PRESS**
New York • Westport, Connecticut • London

**Library of Congress Cataloging-in-Publication Data**

Dream and reality : the modern Black struggle for freedom and equality
/ edited by Jeannine Swift ; prepared under the auspices of Hofstra
University.
    p. cm.—(Contributions in Afro-American and African
studies, ISSN 0069-9624 ; no. 142)
    Includes index.
    ISBN 0-313-27758-3 (alk. paper)
    1. Afro-Americans—Civil rights.  2. Civil rights movements—
United States—History—20th century.  3. United States—Race
relations.  I. Swift, Jeannine, 1935- .  II. Hofstra University.
III. Series.
E185.615.D72   1991
323.1'196073—dc20        90-46701

British Library Cataloguing in Publication Data is available.

Library of Congress Catalog Card Number: 90-46701
ISBN: 0-313-27758-3
ISSN: 0069-9624

First published in 1991

Greenwood Press, 88 Post Road West, Westport, CT   06881
An imprint of Greenwood Publishing Group, Inc.

Printed in the United States of America

**Copyright Acknowledgments**

The publisher and author gratefully acknowledge the following sources for
granting permission to reprint:

Langston Hughes, "Freedom's Plow," lines 9-10, in *The Langston Hughes
Reader* (New York: George Braziller, Inc., 1958), 131. Permission granted
courtesy of Harold Ober Associates, Inc.

Langston Hughes, "Let America Be America Again," lines 62-69, in
*America in Poetry,* ed. Charles Sullivan (New York: Harry N. Abrams,
1988), 185. Permission granted courtesy of Harold Ober Associates, Inc.

# Contents

# Preface

*Jeannine Swift*

Since the earliest period of the forcible kidnapping of Africans to satisfy a growing demand for labor in this land, which eventually came to be called the United States of America, black people have fought against the tyranny of domination by white people. As Vincent Harding so thoroughly documents in his book There Is a River, that struggle began in Africa, continued on the ships, and has not stopped to this day.

In February of 1988 the centennial year of the birth of Marcus M. Garvey and the twenty-fifth anniversary of the Civil Rights March on Washington during which Dr. Martin Luther King, Jr., gave his powerful and famous "I Have A Dream" speech, Hofstra University gathered together scholars, attorneys, activists, and political figures in order to examine the present state of Black Civil Rights. Many of the great moves forward which occurred in the period after the March on Washington have been countered by steps backward since 1980. Increased and more open tension in northern cities have given witness to the fact that mutual respect between black and white people is far from achieved. We gathered at this conference "Dream and Reality: The Modern Black Struggle for Freedom and Equality" as a way to examine that reality in order to provide understanding and direction. As a nation, we cannot stand proud if we do not practice that "justice and equality for all" which we proclaimed to the world over two hundred years ago. The essays in this volume are a selection of those first presented at that conference. They have since been revised for publication.

# Dream
# and
# Reality

# 1 A Tale of Two and One-Half Decades

*Julian Bond*

Today we celebrate a history of shifting American attitudes toward race. Although Americans have always had a preoccupation with race, it is only in the recent past, and then only at the insistence of the victims of racism, that the nation began to take any kind of aggressive steps to inhibit and diminish the white supremacist impulse in the American character.

It was just forty years ago that the Swedish socialist Gunnar Myrdal released his classic study, An American Dilemma, issuing a challenge to Americans to try, if we could, to match our practices with our promises. It was only thirty-seven years ago that the U. S. Supreme Court declared in Brown v. Board of Education that segregation in the public schools and by implication in all of public life was against the law. "Not until the Supreme Court acted in 1954, did the nation acknowledge it had been blaming the black man for what it had done to him. His sentence to second-class citizenship had been commuted. The quest for meaningful equality, equality in fact as well as in law, had begun."(1)

If the depression in 1929 had convinced Americans they were obligated to protect the well-being of their fellow citizens, the Supreme Court's decisions in 1954 and 1955 began to convince reluctant Americans that they would have to share their bounty, their knowledge and their world. "For the American Negro," as Kluger notes, "no more would he be a grinning supplicant for the benefactions and discard of the master class. No more would he be a party to his own degradation. He was both thrilled that the signal for the demise of his class status had come from on high; and angry it had taken so long and first extracted so steep a price in suffering."(2)

A year after the Brown decision, a middle-aged department store seamstress in Montgomery, Alabama, refused to give up her seat on a city bus so a white man could sit down. Five years after Montgomery, four black young men, college students in Greensboro, North Carolina, refused to give up their seats at a dime store lunch counter which had been reserved for whites. These small acts of passive-resistance to American apartheid and the cumulative acts of tens of thousands more helped create a people's movement in the American South which eliminated legal segregation in little more than a decade.

There are those Americans today who will declare that yesterday's movement went too far. These are people who have either forgotten or never knew what yesterday was really like. The words of the late Dr. Martin Luther King may help to generate a sense of that place not quite a generation ago. To white clergymen in Birmingham who could not understand why this Christian minister was an inmate in their jail, he wrote:

When you've seen vicious mobs lynch your mothers and fathers
at will and drown your sisters and brothers at whim; when
you've seen hate-filled policemen curse, kick and even kill
your black brothers and sisters; when you see the vast majority of your twenty million Negro brothers smothering in an
air-tight cage of poverty in the midst of an affluent society; when you suddenly find your tongue twisted and your
speech stammering as you seek to explain to your six year old
daughter why she can't go to the public amusement park that's
just been advertised on television and see tears welling up
in her eyes when she is told that Funtown is closed to colored children and see ominous clouds of inferiority beginning
to form in her mental sky and see her beginning to distort
her personality by developing an unconscious bitterness
towards white people; when you have to concoct an answer for
a five year old son who is asking, "Daddy, why do white
people treat colored people so mean?"; when you're humiliated
day in and day out by nagging signs reading "White" and
"Colored"; when your first name becomes "boy" and last name
becomes "John"; when your wife and mother are never given the
respected title "Mrs."; when you are harried by day and
haunted by night, living constantly on tip-toe stance never
quite knowing what to expect next;  when you are plagued with
inner fears and outer resentments;  when you are forever
fighting a degenerating sense of "nobodyness" then you will
understand.(3)

This conference is an attempt to understand, to add up the accounts,
to measure distances travelled as well as the distances yet to come.
Without appearing at all over-optimistic, the job done so far has been
remarkable, no matter how great the task that remains undone.  Who among
us twenty-five years ago could have believed that a people's behavior and
their opinions could change so sharply?  "The reign of white privilege in
the United States began to end," Jack O'Dell has written:

When there was created a dual authority in the country,
there was on the one hand the established authority, the
citadels of institutionalized racism, the masters of war, the
apparatus of government, state, local and federal, and those
chosen to do the dirty work of suppressing our movement in
defense of the status quo.  This established authority acted
out a way of life that was rooted in custom and tradition and
dictated by class interest.  The other center of authority
was the civil rights anti-war movement which represented a
continuum of protest during this period.  This authority, the
movement, represented the people's alternative to the power
of institutional racism and colonial war.(4)

That movement, of course, bears major responsibility for creating the
present benefits that all of us--women, men, young, old, black, white
--enjoy today.  O'Dell has written that it is equally important to recognize that the Civil Rights Laws of the 1960s were passed after the fact.
"They did not create change; rather the struggle for expanded Democracy
participated in by tens of thousands of our fellow citizens produced a
body of legislation that confirmed the effectiveness of that struggle.
The laws were a crystalized form of expressing a new reality that people
would no longer abide by the rules and mores of racial segregation."(5)
    Mrs. Rosa Parks' protest in Montgomery helped to introduce the world
to a new leader, who reluctantly accepted the stewardship of Montgomery's
movement against segregated bus seating.  His eloquent voice soon propel-

led him to the leadership of a growing national movement, a position he held until his assassination in 1968.

The modern Civil Rights Movement was constructed on a series of actions and events which stretch back to the beginning of African slavery on American soil. From then until now, from Gabriel Prosser, Nat Turner, Denmark Veasey, through Martin King and Malcolm X, and into our time today, there has been a certain continuity in that struggle. Reflect on the movement's beginning in the cruelty of American slavery: sixty million live souls sailed from West Africa in chains; only fifteen million survived the holocaust of the Middle Passage. Once here the African quickly revolted against being another man's property; in Hispaniola in 1522, in Cuba in 1533, Mexico in 1537, a steady, bloody stream of revolt. Overcoming that awful heritage and remembering those revolts ought to be part of our current commemorations as well.

Martin King would have been fifty-nine-years old had he been able to celebrate his birthday in 1988. Had he lived, there is no serious doubt our world would be different than it is. Because he did live when he did, we live in a world a little better than we might have done, a world a little less filled with fear and hate. Had he lived he would undoubtedly look at the world about him with some considerable alarm. Black Americans can claim some considerable accomplishments in the years since Martin King died, but the movement he led on yesterday now appears to be in some disarray, and the gains he achieved now seem in imminent danger of being destroyed.

History is sure to record that this man and the movement he led were the premier factors in the twentieth-century struggle for economic and political justice. Martin King was born to a world nearly as rigidly segregated by custom and by law as is South Africa today. South of the Mason-Dixon line most black people were just two generations away from slavery, a paycheck or two away from abject poverty. As a people, southern blacks were politically impotent, educationally impoverished, and economically bankrupt. Among King's contributions were to give eloquent voice to the aspirations of Black America and to give life to a method of mass participation in the struggle for equal rights so that everyone, every woman, every man, every minister, homemaker, student, everyone could become an agent of his or her own deliverance.

The movement of Black America in King's lifetime passed through a series of climaxes. These were years of great legal struggles in the courts complemented by extra-legal struggles in the streets. In this period gains were won at lunch counters, at movie theatres, at bus stations, and at polling places; and the fabric of legal apartheid began to come undone. A movement which had its origins as a drive for elemental civil rights has today largely become a political and an economic movement; black women and men are now holding office and wielding power in numbers we only dreamed of before. Despite an impressive increase in the number of black people holding public office, despite the ability we have to sit and eat and ride and vote and go to school in places that used to lack black faces, in a very real way in 1988 we find our condition unchanged. A quick look at all the statistics which measure how well or how poorly a group of people is doing, the kinds of figures which measure infant mortality, median family income, and life expectancy, will demonstrate quickly that while our general condition has improved a great deal, our relative condition has actually managed to get worse. It is almost as if we were climbing a molasses mountain dressed in snow shoes, while others ride a rather leisurely ski lift to the top. Now the ski slopes are more treacherous, the molasses melting into mud, a Sargasso Sea of joblessness for many and hopelessness for many more. In such a climate, yesterday's goals and methods become suspect; the bus front seat may lose meaning for people whose longest trip is likely to be from the feudal system of the rural South to the more mechanized high-rise poverty of the North. The right to an integrated education may mean little to children bussed from one ignorant academy to another.

The classic civil rights struggles of the decade of the 1960s were carried forward with great success against state-sanctioned segregation and succeeded to the extent that they did because the victims became their own best champions and because they found a sympathetic ear in the national body politic. But as their demands became more insistent, as a foreign war began to drain our treasury and young manhood, and as our best and brightest were beaten down by bullets, a radical shift began to occur in the national consciousness. From the founding of the Republic, the hopes and aspirations of Black Americans have passed through a series of periods of national reconstruction. Each of these ended with the surrender of responsibility for the plight, first of black and now of black and poor people to the individual states, to a kind of laissez-faire benevolence that seems doomed to condemn us to perpetual economic half-citizenship.

We are today just short years away from the most recent of these periods of reconstruction, that heady period following the historic 1954 Supreme Court decision, and even fewer years away from the modern renaissance of black activism which began with the Montgomery bus boycott in 1955 and 1956 and grew to 1960 student sit-ins, which climaxed in the 1964 Civil Rights and 1965 Voting Rights Acts, when we began to believe that freedom, like the end of the war in Vietnam, was just around the corner. All these beginnings have now come to an abrupt end, not simply because the towering leadership figure of the era was struck down by an assassin's bullet or because another man was elected president of the United States. The circumstances of death for the most recent reconstruction are many and complex.

These remarks might well be subtitled "A Tale of Two and One-Half Decades." I want to address the future, what is in store for us, what the future may demand of us; but I also want to look at the past, and to do that I must try to talk with two voices: first, as a contemporary fellow passenger on what promises to be a tough and frustrating trip toward the twenty-first century, and second, as a witness to and participant in an earlier leg to that journey, a trip that has taken us from Selma to Saigon, from Bull Connor to Alan Bakke, from James Earl Ray to Bernard Goetz, from the old George Wallace to the new Ronald Reagan, from Lincoln Perry to Clarence Pendleton, from the Ku Klux Klan to Neo-Nazis and the Posse Comitatus, from Brown v. Board of Education to Grove City College v. Bell, and from a president born in Texas who had the courage to stand up for civil rights to a president born in the land of Lincoln who has opposed every piece of civil rights legislation put forward in the last half of the twentieth century. If we go forward any faster, it may be hazardous to our health.

Think back with me, those of you who can, just two years before the March on Washington in 1963. 1961 was a presidential inaugural year. A tired old general was mustering out a listless Republican administration; a vigorous young cold war liberal was preparing to lead the nation toward a new frontier. The inaugural speech of John F. Kennedy in January 1961 featured some of the more memorable pieces of presidential rhetoric in recent memory. It was, as they say, a well-crafted speech, its ideas marshalled for maximum emotional effect, its phrasing most articulate, its cadences rolling with measured eloquence. At the same time it was a most dangerous speech; for if it glistened with idealism, it also bristled with challenge. Whatever else it did, it somehow managed to capture the imagination of millions and helped to define the political motive and the moral outline of the several decades yet to come. Some of you will recall that president promising to go anywhere, to fight any foe, to bear any burden in defense of freedom. That promise, translated into public policy, produced the quicksand of Vietnam. But the speech also pronounced a clear call to dedication, to sacrifice, to the idealism of young and old Americans. That call, translated into public policy, produced the Peace Corps and domestic social programs for the poor. At the same time in the late 1950s and the early 1960s something else had begun to bud and blossom, as Black America began to revive a near-dormant revolution. We had borne our share and more of wartime's burdens and now were demanding a share of the precious and prosperous peace. In Montgomery, Alabama, a small black woman did just that. On her way home from work one evening, Mrs. Rosa Parks put in motion a movement which eliminated legal segregation in the United States in little more than a decade.

Recall if you will that nonviolent protest was nearly the only available avenue of expression to what was then a largely voteless people. The year Mrs. Parks was arrested in Montgomery, fewer than 3 percent of the eligible blacks in Mississippi were permitted to vote. In 28 counties in the southern states with black populations of 82 percent or greater, there was not one single black registered voter, although some of these counties had more whites registered than there were whites eligible to vote. Yesterday's protests forced the elimination of the racial barriers from public accommodations and the political process. They did so almost entirely because of the willingness of young and old, Black and White Americans to adopt the twin disciplines of nonviolence and hard work. Their bodies, then, were weapons directly aimed at the heart of the beast. Their votes, then, were a precious commodity available not just to the highest bidder or most pleasing psyche but to the candidate whose record and past performance held greatest promise for some delivery in the future. But since that period of great involvement and forward progress, some serious setbacks have happened to us all.

The sun set on the decade of the 1960s and rose to illuminate the new Nixon era. A national negative mindset quickly became crystal clear. Idealism and vigor were replaced with cynicism and narcissism. Our young people abandoned the war against racism and colonialism and turned inward, toward examination of their "id." As the decade ended, a major portion of the population had absolutely ended all connection with the struggle for equal rights and racial justice in America. The "Me" generation had homesteaded the New Frontier.

The 1970s was a decade of reaction and self-indulgence, of retreat from responsibility. In Washington the Great Society was replaced with malign neglect; a kind of lifeboat ethic sailed into the national consciousness, the notion that we were all passengers on a kind of global Titanic, a sinking ship without lifeboats enough to go around. Quite naturally, those who are first pushed out of the lifeboat constitute that increasing portion of the population which is quickly becoming absolutely irrelevant to the productive process, the uneducated young and the useless aged, far too many of whom have skins that are dark. Fortunately by 1975, the architect of avarice as social policy had been disgraced, dismissed from power; a carefree caretaker installed instead. In 1976, Black Americans went to the polls in record numbers to elect a man who clearly knew the words to our hymns; in less than a year, we began to wonder if he had ever known the numbers on our paychecks. Sadly, he lost office in 1980, and then in 1984 the people spoke again. They reinstalled the evil empire by reelecting an amiable incompetent, who clearly intended to take the federal government entirely out of the business of enforcing equal opportunity in the United States. He intended to eliminate affirmative action for minorities and for women. He intended to erase the laws and programs written in blood and sweat in the quarter century since Martin King had become the premier figure in the freedom movement and a majority of Americans, both black and white, had become single-minded in pursuit of human freedom. As was true more than a hundred years before, a president desperate for power entered into an illicit arrangement, not just with the unreconstructed South, but with the national unreconstructed mentality that believed then, as it does now, that private profit and public arrogance could be pursued at the expense of the people living on the economic edge.

With more than one hundred of its members having been under indictment, the Reagan administration is surely the most corrupt in the twentieth century. Conflicts of interest were a condition for appointment or employment. A band of financial and ideological profiteers descended on Washington and on the public treasury like a crazed band of right-winged locusts bent on destroying the rules and laws which protect our people from bigotry, from poisoned air and water, from greed. They broke the laws they were sworn to uphold, laws against theft, against corruption. But nowhere was their assault on the rule of law so great as in their attempt to subvert, ignore, defy, and destroy the laws that require affirmative action, that require integrated public education and a political process free from racism. When Congress and the Constitution said no, they said yes. They even perverted the language as they perverted the process. In their double speak, white men became the victims of discrimination, just as unemployed mothers and underpaid school teachers replaced financiers and monopolists as the new special interests, just as cut-throats, thugs, and drug lords became freedom fighters.

A constituency of the comfortable, the callous, and the smug was recruited to form a solid rank against the forgotten. We suffered through the national nullification of the needs of the needy, the gratuitous gratification of the gross and the greedy, the politics of penuriousness, prevarication, impropriety, pious platitudes, and self-righteous swinishness.    For the last decade, we have suffered under a form of triage economics, which has produced the first increase in American infant mortality rates in twenty years and pushed thousands of poor and working poor American families deeper and deeper into poverty. This administration constituted a clear and present danger to the hopes and dreams of Black Americans and to the dream that Martin King spoke of so movingly just a few short years ago. By August of 1984, the Census Bureau reported that the number of people living in poverty had increased over the previous four years by nine million, the biggest increase since these statistics were first collected over two decades ago. Today the poorest two-fifths of our population receives a smaller share of the national income and the richest two-fifths a larger share than at any time since 1947. If we are to believe with Thomas Jefferson that the common man is the most precious portion of the state, we find that precious resource in real danger of economic extinction today. Recently, the National Urban League reported that income levels for black families were down while poverty levels were up. Equally frightening ought to be the danger we all face from increased American interference in the lives of our neighbors in this hemisphere and in other countries around the globe. Criminal invasion in Grenada, sponsorship of subversion and terror in Nicaragua, encouragement of white supremacy in South Africa, these are the results of American arrogance ratified at the polls last presidential election day. What is so frightening about diminished life chances among Black Americans here at home and the heightened chance of the loss of all human life worldwide is not just that so many of our fellow citizens are not aware, but that so many are aware and simply do not care. The movement Martin Luther King led succeeded because it summoned a large part of Black America to group action and enjoyed the endorsement of major portions of White America as well. Rebuilding that coalition of conscience ought to be a priority for all of us.

We face many current difficulties for a variety of reasons too numerous to list here, but one is that we have failed to remember an important lesson taught us by the movement of yesterday. When we focus on Martin King, for example, we tend to focus on his devotion to Gandhian nonviolence--as well we might--and how in his hands passive resistance became militant aggression against American apartheid; or we focus on his insistence that the fruits of his labors ought be shared by all Americans, black, brown, and white, and his demand that the troops of his army ought be integrated too.  But we seem to have forgotten a more basic message that he brought us in Montgomery and Albany, in Selma, in Birmingham and St. Augustine, and in Memphis on the evening before his death.  That message was not original with King, but few leadership figures in the struggle for equal rights have expressed it so well before or since. For him, it began when Mrs. Parks refused to stand up. Until that moment most of us were little more than eager bystanders at the side of a tiny stage upon which was acted out the drama of human liberation. The actors were those few lawyers who could litigate the race problem or the occasional social scientists who could codify and graph and chart the dimensions of the terror of white supremacy.  The average man and woman found their participation limited largely to voting, where voting was permitted, or to making some small contribution in cash or kind to the work of that small band of civil rights professionals.    But when Mrs. Parks refused to stand up, when Martin King stood up to preach, mass participation came to the movement for civil rights.    The lesson of the Montgomery bus boycott and the Civil Rights Movement of the 1960s is not that these actions can be repeated and duplicated time and time again. One important lesson is that this is a struggle too important to be fought by leadership figures alone; instead there is a task here for each of us, both singly and in unison. There is, I believe, a sizable body of opinion in the United States which refuses to surrender yesterday's goals. But far too many of these people, our countrymen and women, young and old of many many races, creeds, and colors mistakenly believe themselves to be impotent, unable to influence the society in which they live.  Nearly three decades ago, black young people in the southern United States sat down in order to stand up for their rights; they marched and picketed and protested against state-sponsored segregation and brought that system crashing to its knees.  In later years another generation said no to an aggressive colonial war waged by their country in their name and put their bodies in the path of the war machine. Today's times require no less and, in fact, insist on more.  Yesterday's movement produced many successes in commerce and in politics, but if our progress from the back of the bus to the middle rungs of the corporate ladder remains incomplete, and if nearly a third of Black America has been left standing in the unemployment line or waiting in the welfare office, let us take heart.  If there is much to be done, there is much to do it with, and we have much more than those pioneers who brought us this far.  We have more than a century and a half worth of aggressive self-help and volunteerism in church and civic clubs, in neighborhood associations providing scholarships, helping the needy, financing the cause of social justice. We have an equally long and honorable tradition of struggle, and if yesterday's marches have faded from the headlines and from our memories, they still send forth the message that we move farther fastest when we move forward together.  We have a long history of cooperation between us and among us; of field slave helping house slave to poison the master, of doctors taking chickens for payment when money was scarce and need was great, of neighbor guarding neighbor's house and children, of teachers visiting parents to make sure scholarship sits on a strong foundation at home.  Time weakens these traditions as it does with any people, but there remains a great deal we may do for ourselves.

We ought to double our support for organizations like the NAACP and those other groups that guard our liberties and protect our rights.  If you are not a member or supporter, then you are part of the problem and not a contributor to the solution.   We can more actively monitor the schools our children attend, making sure the end of their education is not the beginning of a lifetime of unemployment. We can realize our full

political potential, registering, educating, and voting every citizen in
our community.   Those who stay home on election day are as useless as
wings on a frog and nearly as attractive too.   We can spend our money
with people who will spend it back with us, and we can realize we live in
an interdependent world.     We cannot contemplate freedom for ourselves
while blacks in Johannesburg cannot vote.  Our young men deserve a better
future than fighting senseless jungle wars in Central America.   We cannot
squander our national treasury on mutually assured destruction and on
Buck Rogers weapon systems while Americans are homeless and unemployed.
There are several unfinished items on the civil rights legislative agenda
too.   First is passage by the Congress and signature by the president of
the Civil Rights Restoration Act of 1988, to overturn the pernicious
decision in Grove City College v. Bell.   Next is action on the Fair
Housing Amendments Act of 1987, adding important enforcement provisions
to the Fair Housing Act of 1968.   There are others, including enforcement
of existing law--the Voting Rights Act, the Civil Rights Act of 1964, and
continued and stronger federal oversight in the far from finished process
of integrating public education.   Suffice it to say that today's agenda
is little different from that of yesterday; today's problems are separated from those of yesterday more by time than by substance.

There is fortunately ample opportunity for us all.   There are a host
of organizations dedicated to making Dr. King's dream come true.   Each of
these badly needs volunteers and contributions.   There are candidates who
need help to win; there are officeholders who ought be defeated.   There
are school children who need special help.   There are a host of others
who cry out almost daily for assistance.   There is a world waiting to be
won.    The year Dr. King was shot down on the balcony of the Lorraine
Motel in Memphis by James Earl Ray, the National Advisory Commission on
Civil Disorder appointed by President Lyndon B. Johnson reported that we
were two societies in the United States:   one largely black and poor, one
largely white and rich, moving further and further apart. These last several years have widened that gap.

To look backward at an imaginary ancient golden age is to surrender
our futures to private greed, to increasing concentrations of wealth and
power, to the continuing crisis to which the unchecked race for profits
submits us all.   Holding on to victories won twenty short years ago requires that no method, that no means ought to be discounted.    Even a
method less valued now--appealing to conscience, justice, and fair play--
ought to be employed.  A people in extreme distress cannot afford to turn
their backs on any method that may produce a motive for doing right.
Doing right, after all, is what this life is all about.

Let me leave you with some words from the past, from the late
scholar W.E.B. DuBois, who, around his twentieth birthday, tried to put
down on paper an antidote to the kind of political violence he saw about
him at the turn of the century and that we yet see about us today:

> I believe in God who made of one blood all the nations that
> dwell on the earth. I believe we all, black, brown, white are
> brothers, varying, through time and opportunity, in form and
> gift and feature but differing in no essential particular,
> alike in soul and in the possibility of infinite development.
> But especially do I believe in the Negro race; in the beauty
> of its genius, the sweetness of its soul, its strength in
> that meekness which shall inherit this turbulent earth.    I
> believe in service, humble, reverent service, from the black-
> ening of boots to whitening of souls, for work is heaven,
> idleness hell and wages the "well done" of the master that
> summons all them that labor, making no distinction between
> the black sweating cotton hands of Georgia and the first
> families of Virginia since all distinction not based on deed

is devilish and not divine.  I believe in liberty for all men, the space to stretch our arms and our souls, the right to breathe, the right to vote, the freedom to choose our friends, to enjoy the sunshine, to ride on the railroad un-cursed by color, thinking, hoping, dreaming, working as we will in a kingdom of God and love.(6)

**NOTES**

1.  Richard Kluger, <u>Simple Justice</u> (New York: Alfred A. Knopf, 1976), 748.

2.  Ibid, 749.

3.  Martin Luther King, Jr., <u>Why We Can't Wait</u> (New York:  Harper and Row, 1964), 83.

4.  Jack H. O'Dell, "On the Transition from Civil Rights to Civil Authority, Part II," <u>Freedomways</u> 18, no. 4 (Winter 1978):  191.

5.  Ibid, 193.

6.  W.E.B. DuBois, <u>The Independent</u>, October 6, 1904, New York.

# 2   A Tribute to
Martin Luther King, Jr.

*David J. Garrow*

I think it is particularly apt to reflect on King's message and the lessons we can draw from his life in light of how the organizers of this
conference have used the "Dream and Reality" title.   There is nothing
that Dr. King himself would want us to appreciate more, after his death,
than the fact that many of the goals that he struggled for, in fact most
of the goals that he talked about following 1965, have not been achieved
and, indeed, in some respects, have not even been advanced.

Reflecting on Dr. King and his legacy, I wish to stress two points.
First, I want to examine briefly Dr. King's emotional evolution and his
own understanding of the role he played during the years between 1955 and
1968 when he devoted his life to the Civil Rights Movement.   Second, I
want to address his political evolution, the increasingly radical evolution in his views and hopes for American society that Dr. King underwent
in the final years of his life.

To grasp Dr. King's understanding of his own life is to appreciate
that King thought of himself as first and foremost a minister, a pastor.
Younger people today, in particular, only see images of King from television news clips that show him as a person giving speeches and leading
marches, which do not highlight his fundamental attachment to the minis-
try and his fundamental roots in the church.   Appreciating the centrality of religion and the church for Dr. King is crucial if we are to make
sense of the very selfless way, the very humble way, he devoted himself
and made himself of service to the movement.

Almost without exception, the people closest to Dr. King always want
to point out to those of us who are younger that he was very self effa-
cing, nonegotistical, and at times even shy.   Dr. King was someone who
had no desire, no need, to be a public figure or a celebrity.   He was not
someone who enjoyed being in the limelight.   Especially when one looks
back at the beginning in Montgomery, the start of the boycott there, and
the very crucial role that women--the black professional women's group in
Montgomery--actually played in getting the boycott under way, one can appreciate even better how King was chosen as the spokesperson, as the
president of the Montgomery Improvement Association, not through any initiative, or desire or self-promoting on his own part; he was very much
drafted for that job and drafted in part because his colleagues recognized, even then, what a very special speaking ability, what a special
ability to articulate the cause of black freedom Dr. King possessed.   We
must keep in mind as well with reference to Montgomery just how young Dr.
King was at that time--he was only twenty-six--when he was drafted for
that position; he was only thirty-nine at the time he was killed.

What one particularly sees in that early part of the Montgomery
boycott is Dr. King somewhat painfully making a commitment of service to

the movement, realizing that this was a calling that he was being asked to take.  This was a commitment and really a self-sacrifice that he was being asked to make, and it was one that he was initially a little bit hesitant about accepting.  Dr. King in later years very often stressed to friends and acquaintances that he would have been quite happy simply to be a pastor; and so when he made that decision early in Montgomery that the movement leadership role to which he was called was something that he was going to accept, he made that decision to go forward out of a fundamentally religious and faith-oriented belief that this is what God and Jesus were asking him to do.  One must appreciate how King understood his acceptance of that role in terms of religious faith and calling if we are really to appreciate the way in which he went forward with his leadership throughout the late 1950s and 1960s.

In terms of that calling and that basic sense of mission that was really at the core of Dr. King's life and being, I think one as well has to underline (and this is a point that Vincent Harding and James Cone have emphasized as much as I believe I have) that we need to see Dr. King as a product of the Black Church.  One sees this, I think, most clearly and most impressively when one has the chance to look at his sermons, both the early sermons in Montgomery and those from the later years, the years after 1960, especially his sermons from his home church, Ebenezer Baptist Church in Atlanta.  When one looks at those sermons rather than at the more public, formal speeches to northern audiences or labor groups, one really comes away realizing that the Bible and the church heritage are the most important sources from which Dr. King spoke.  And although I'll touch on it only very briefly here, when one looks at his earliest statements and speeches during the Montgomery boycott, King is not talking so much about Gandhi or Thoreau or reflecting the influence of what he read in graduate school (which has been the emphasis of much of the academic literature in trying to explain the influences on Dr. King), but rather what one sees as the real sources of his thought and beliefs is the Bible.  He talked about nonviolence and about love from day one in Montgomery, but he talked about them in terms of the teachings of Jesus, and he talked about them in terms of Bible stories.  Both in the context of the roots of King's thought as well as in the context of what motivated, what drove this man, I think we have to stress that centrality of religious roots and faith if we are to appreciate what he was about.

One of the ironies, perhaps one of the most striking of all the ironies of the FBI wire tap transcripts of hundreds of Dr. King's phone conversations with his friends and advisors (preserved for us and now released under the Freedom of Information Act), from the years 1962 and after is that those transcripts give a more immediate, a more powerful sense of how devoted, how tough, how self-critical King was about his own responsibilities and his role, than perhaps any other source we have or could have.  What one sees in those telephone transcripts, and more public statements as well, is a real deepening and strengthening of Dr. King's understanding of his calling to be of service.  We see that even though he very consciously did not want to be on the public stage 365 days a year, he nonetheless increasingly came to an acceptance, at times a somewhat begrudging acceptance, that this was not a commitment of five years or ten years that would at some point end and allow him to go back to a quieter, less public life, but that this was a lifetime commitment, something that would end only with his death.

Where one sees, I think, the greatest strengthening of that commitment on Dr. King's part is right after the Nobel Peace Prize announcement and award in 1964.  That honor, like all the many other public honors that were bestowed upon Dr. King during the 1960s, had for King the most immediate impact of making him redouble his feelings of commitment and, particularly in the wake of the Nobel Prize, encouraged him to adopt an increasingly prophetic understanding that his first responsibility was to speak the truth, preach the truth, regardless of what the personal consequences for himself or the financial consequences for his organization, the Southern Christian Leadership Conference, might be.  If one looks at this carefully and thoughtfully one sees an increasingly courageous King in those years after 1963 and 1964, a man who more and more realizes that he has the responsibility to speak the truth even if it is unpopular.

There is a quality of amnesia now, about which Vincent Harding has written very movingly in several different contexts, wherein we do not fully remember just how much criticism, how much unpopularity Dr. King encountered during those final two or three years of his life.  It is in this regard that I want to discuss King's political evolution across the years towards a much more radical set of goals and understanding of American society after 1965.  Many people today have simply the image of Dr. King from the "I Have a Dream" speech, the speech from the 1963 March on Washington, and that speech gives a very incomplete understanding of what King was about.  When one looks at the Dr. King of the Montgomery boycott of 1955 and 1956, one sees someone who is extremely optimistic about America as a society and about the White South and white southerners' willingness to change.   Even in the first week there in Montgomery, King, Reverend Ralph Abernathy, Mrs. JoAnn Robinson, and the rest of the local leadership had a very naive hope that the boycott would be only a four- or five-day endeavor, that white officials and White Montgomery would recognize the justice of the black community's cause, negotiate, and alter the bus seating practices that had sparked the boycott.   It came as a considerable surprise to King and the other black local leaders that White Montgomery had no interest in meaningful negotiations or making any sort of concessions.  That experience was simply the first step for Dr. King on the road towards an increasingly realistic and, in the end, at times, pessimistic attitude toward American society and particularly toward White America's interest and willingness towards making changes.   One has to underline several times, however, that over the course of twelve years this was a gradual but extremely substantial and significant evolution on Dr. King's part.

In 1960, for example,  with regard to the presidential campaign story that I believe many people know fairly well--about John and Robert Kennedy's phone calls on the occasion of Dr. King's jailing down in Reidsville prison in South Georgia during the 1960 campaign--during that campaign and even after the Kennedy administration took office in 1961, King had a tremendous optimism about what the Kennedy brothers could and would do,  what sort of a difference active presidential leadership on behalf of Civil Rights--in contrast to the Eisenhower years--could make for Black America.  But the period from 1961 through to the early part of 1963 ended up being for King a rather disillusioning experience. He, and other people in the movement, came to realize more and more during those two years that the Kennedy administration was not going to take the initiative, was not going to push for meaningful civil rights change, notwithstanding all of the 1960 campaign promises and rhetoric in that direction.  It was only when the movement took the initiative, the very direct massive initiative, of organizing the demonstrations in Birmingham in May of 1963, that things began to change.   Then the Kennedy brothers came to the realization that civil rights was not going to remain quietly on the back burner, that this was an issue that they were going to have to tackle and going to have to pursue whether they wanted to or not, or whether their sometime southern allies in Congress wanted them to tackle it or not.  Again nowadays many people perhaps have some amnesia in this regard in not fully appreciating how pointedly critical Dr. King was of the Kennedy administration during 1962 and 1963 and how grudging and relatively late the Kennedy brothers' support for or enthusiasm for civil rights actually was during that period.

Now, the peak years, or the "glory years" of the movement, as I think some people would call them, came between 1963 and 1965. Those years were highlighted by the tangible accomplishments of the 1964 Civil Rights Act and 1965 Voting Rights Act. Those accomplishments as of 1965 looked to King and looked to many other people in the movement as perhaps 90 percent of what the movement had been seeking in the early 1960s. I think it is quite fair to say that in that context of 1964 and 1965 there was a tremendous initial sense of accomplishment, of victory. But I think most of us often tend to forget or underappreciate what a really disillusioning period King and other people, particularly people in SNCC, went through in the wake of those legislative victories, when the awareness began to grow more and more strongly that simply that sort of formal, legal anti-segregation, anti-discrimination legislation was not going to have anywhere near as transforming an impact upon the South, upon the conditions of black people's lives in the South, as King and most other people in the movement had presumed or had thought up until that time. I believe that this slowly emerging disillusion lies at the crux of the very significant evolution which Dr. King and others began to undergo in that 1965-1966 period. It was the success of those legislative victories, the abolition of formal segration and legal, statutory discrimination, that allowed King and others to realize that the real roots of black oppression were much more fundamentally economic than segregationist. And what one repeatedly sees time after time, almost day after day, in those final three and a half years of Dr. King's life is his focusing upon economic change and economic issues—jobs, housing, and the quality of urban schooling. Focusing upon those sorts of issues and the class implications of those issues was the next agenda, the much tougher agenda that the movement had to pursue.

I mentioned earlier that if one looks at King simply in the light of the "I Have a Dream" speech of 1963, one gets a very incomplete substantive appreciation of what King was about. More pointedly, one of King's most regular closing lines or perorations in his speeches from 1966 on was that the dream he had had in 1963 had turned into a nightmare. This is essentially an exact quote of something that he used not once or twice but several dozen times. Not only is that specific line something that one rarely, if ever, sees in television newsreel excerpts nowadays, but I think that we also see very little evidence or very few reminders of that very challenging economic agenda that King was talking about in those final three years. What King had in mind by 1967 and 1968 when he was putting together the Poor People's Campaign was a very explicitly redistributive economic agenda for the United States. I think that the degree to which he believed that the country required massive economic change in terms of fighting poverty, in terms of what the society was required to do for what we now term the underclass, required that issues be articulated in class terms if we were to create a truly just and meaningfully equal society. Those sorts of calls and those sorts of demands that Dr. King was articulating in that final year are something about which many people today are not reminded and with which they are not confronted.

By 1967 King's language sometimes was so strong that especially in private, he was describing himself as a socialist, as a democratic socialist, as what interpretively one could most accurately call a Christian Socialist. But what one sees as well in King's statements and sermons from that final year and a half, is someone who is a much more critical, much more pessimistic, judge of American society than the man who started in Montgomery twelve years earlier. Where one sees this most strongly is in King's comments about White America. There is very little of the earlier optimism and hopefulness concerning people's willingness to initiate change, if simply the justice requirements of a situation are spelled out to them. There is little if any of the optimism that one can easily see in the King of 1956-1957.

Now similarly, during those final two or three years, one sees this much more critical attitude of King towards American society in his comments about America's involvement in Vietnam and about America's behavior in the world more generally.    It comes through most clearly in King's willingness to take on the Vietnam issue at a time when opposition to the war was not at all popular, and I think that's a point that really needs underlining because we tend to compact, I think,  and perhaps read back into the context of 1966 or 1967, the relative popularity that opposition to the war had by the Nixon years.    When King first spoke out strongly against the Vietnam war, he was denounced not only by the New York Times, the Washington Post, and other major white media, but he also was criticized by civil rights leaders and civil rights organizations. Of all the contemporaneous editorial comments about King and the war, very few were supportive.  Only two or three upheld both the fairness of King's statements about the war and his right as a civil rights leader to speak out on the issue of the war.

King's strength and willingness to take on the war, to take on an issue that he knew full well would make him distinctly less popular, was a willingness that stemmed quite directly from the prophetic,  almost self-sacrificing understanding of his role that had been growing since the early stages in Montgomery.   It had been strengthened particularly in the international context by the Nobel Prize, for to King the Nobel Prize, even more than his many other awards, could not be accepted simply as praise for what he had done before, but was instead really a renewal of his basic calling, and so it created within King an intensified sense of obligation to continue to live up to that immense responsibility.

In closing, what one sees in the Dr. King of 1968 is a quite mature and fully developed acceptance that he was going to give his life for the movement, a fuller acceptance of what had been a very realistic day-to-day awareness reaching back all the way to 1956 when the pattern of daily death threats had first emerged.   One also sees in the Dr. King of 1968 someone who is setting out very strongly a political agenda for change in America that went far, far beyond what the movement had pursued and had accomplished in the 1964-1965 period.

Finally, what most deserves underlining and conscious appreciation is that what King was talking about in that final year or two in terms of the economic change that our society requires were changes and goals that we have not achieved in the years since his death.   Perhaps even more pointedly, as one can see in the recent work of William  J. Wilson and other people who have been looking at the growing bifurcation that has occurred in Black America over these last twenty years, our record since the time of Dr. King's death has not only been a record of little progress on the issues that he was addressing but has in some respects been a record of retrogression since that time.  Hence in appreciating Dr. King and in appreciating his legacy for us today, we cannot allow ourselves to simply think of Dr. King as a successful reformer for whom the 1964 and 1965 Acts were the major accomplishments, but we must appreciate very forthrightly that Dr. King's agenda and legacy are very much unfulfilled and speak very directly to the issues and challenges that remain before us even today.

# 3 Rediscovering Women Leaders of the Civil Rights Movement

*Rhoda Lois Blumberg*

Scholars and activists agree that the modern Civil Rights Movement was one of the most important forces leading to a resurgence of the Women's Movement.(1) Civil rights and the New Left were crucibles in which women activists were tested for their qualities of judgment, bravery, and commitment under stress. As they learned to fight oppressions, many developed a greater awareness of women as an aggrieved group. Obviously their participation in these movements was significant—but significant to the movements as well as themselves. Yet until recently, the role of women, black and white, in the Civil Rights Movement has been seen mainly in terms of certain dramatic cases. Rosa Parks, a black woman, is known because of her crucial act in precipitating the Montgomery bus boycott; Viola Liuzzo, a white woman, achieved fame when she was assassinated. They are exceptions to a rule—for the historical significance of women both as leaders and as a main source of mass mobilization has been largely overlooked and unexamined.

This paper addresses the issue of African-American and white women's roles in the Civil Rights Movement and suggests some hypotheses about the intersections of gender and race.(2) I maintain that, as is true in other social movements, women had some unusual opportunities to lead, especially in their local communities, but also faced gender-related barriers to their recognition and mobility in leadership roles.

The current reexamination and reconstruction of the Civil Rights Movement has revealed several types of new information and provided analyses that were not possible earlier. For example, the Freedom of Information Act, utilized by a number of researchers, enabled them to confirm suspicions about the role of the FBI, our chief executives, and other officials. Also, the movement itself no longer has to preserve certain secrets or picture itself as spontaneous rather than organized. And now, in dialectical fashion, the Women's Movement is acting back on the Civil Rights Movement, as participants and scholars reexamine the movement from the perspective of gender. Of particular importance are the new autobiographical accounts of such women as Septima Clark, Jo Ann Gibson Robinson, and Mary King. (3) These leading activists are telling their stories of major events as they now perceive and remember them. The movement is called challenging and role-expanding; the women learned skills and contributed ideas but received little national recognition. In the case of Ella Baker, the most influential woman strategist of the movement, recognition as a leader was neither sought nor valued.

Septima Clark's autobiography was told to Cynthia Stokes Brown when Clark was eighty-one years old and is a story "told from a feminist perspective." For, "after the Civil Rights Movement, Mrs. Clark took part in the women's liberation movement and learned to comprehend her own

story, as well as that of women in general, in a framework very different
from that through which she experienced her life as it happened."(4)   In
contrast, Ella Baker was keenly aware of male chauvinism as it occurred.
The analyses of feminists such as Paula Giddings and Angela Davis remind
us of black women's activist history and help put black women civil
rights leaders of the 1960s into context.(5) The work of African-American
women writers, poets, and playwrights are possibly the most revealing and
perhaps for that reason the most controversial in dealing with the cross-
cutting of racial and gender issues in the United States   (e.g. Alice
Walker's The Color Purple).

My own attention to the topic of women in the Civil Rights Movement
came out of my experience as a white activist in the North.   I knew of
black women and white women who had played leadership roles in the integrationist phase of the movement:   they brought civil rights issues to
their own communities, supported southern efforts financially and through
boycotts and demonstrations, and joined national mobilizations such as
the 1963 March on Washington.   Because white women's involvement in the
movement especially in the North received so little notice, and probably
as a key to understanding my own biography, I decided to study a sample
of white activists in the state in which I resided.(6)

Now a growing number of black and white women participants are revealing more fully the actual roles they played in the southern movement,
in some cases prodded on by others to drop their modesty and tell their
stories.   Jo Ann Gibson Robinson's title, The Montgomery Bus Boycott and
the Women Who Started It, turns out to be literally true.   If her account
is to be believed, women did indeed start that famous boycott.   President
of the main branch of an organization called the Women's Political
Council, Robinson and others in her group had periodically protested
about bus conditions to the mayor and city commissioners.   They raised
the possibility of a boycott if improvements were not made.   As she tells
it, Robinson, with the agreement of her organization and the aid of two
trusted students, spent the night of December 1, 1955   (the day Rosa
Parks was arrested for violating segregation statutes) running off leaflets that announced a one-day boycott; this was to be the response of
Montgomery's black women to the arrest.(7)   On the morning of December 2,
1955, the black ministers of Montgomery received these leaflets, which
were also distributed throughout the entire African-American community;
that night the minsters held an organizing meeting for the boycott.
Accounts other than Robinson's leave out her part altogether and credit
local leader E. D. Nixon with initiating the boycott and the leaflet distribution.(8)   Both were part of Montgomery's protest leadership and were
in contact on the issue.

One reason for obfuscating some of the excellent organizing preceding the boycott would appear to be defensive.   Opponents were critical
of "conspiracy," of organized agitation.   It was politically safer to
portray Rosa Parks as a tired worker returning from a job   (not untrue)
than as an NAACP activist (also true).   Morris has tried to correct this
impression by recording Park's long-time involvement in protest efforts;
he has also clarified Ella Baker's importance in getting both the SCLC
and SNCC off the ground.(9)   Although Baker set up SCLC's central
office, as associate director, she came into conflict with the group.
Says Morris:

> Here was a woman, twenty-five years older than most of the
> SCLC's leadership, who possessed a solid organizational
> background, entering an organization controlled by black
> ministers.  During that era men in general, and many black
> ministers in particular, were condescending toward women
> and could not envision them as full-fledged leaders.  This
> stance of the ministers was bound to generate friction with

Baker, who was self-directed and did not feel that women should automatically defer to men. (10)

## THE REPRODUCTION OF RACISM AND SEXISM WITHIN MOVEMENTS

Social movements tend to reproduce the sexism and racism of the larger society, to some extent, even as they fight a particular type of perceived oppression.(11)    Sensitivity to one type of inequality does not necessarily create sensitivity to others, and this appears to be largely true of the Civil Rights Movement.  Further, the very deprivations that bring about the movement may also come into play.  The key article, "Majority Involvement in Minority Movements: Civil Rights, Abolition and Untouchability," by Gary Marx and Michael Useem,(12) has not been surpassed in providing insight into the dilemmas of whites in the Civil Rights Movement.  They were outsiders who were sometimes seen as surrogates for the dominant whites they opposed.  Society's racism was reflected even in the movement that sought to undermine it; society's sexism, an issue much less publicized at that time, surely had its impact.  In fact, the movement's enemies often combined the two "isms" in their attacks.

In the case of subjugated peoples, additional factors affect the relationship of the sexes during periods of struggle.  The powerlessness of black males under slavery was followed by their continuing economic disadvantage.  The manhood theme becomes very prominent among men of a subordinated group, who feel they have been cheated out of their "normal" superordination.  The dominant group model of what manhood means may be unattainable, making it all the more desirable.  The women of the dominated group welcome signs of strength and leadership among their men. These facts help to clarify why men were pushed forward as the formal leaders of the Civil Rights Movement, although other compelling reasons were also involved.  In explaining even greater male chauvinism during the Black Power phase, Giddings maintains, "In periods of black radicalism, which always includes a self-conscious quest for manhood, black men attempt to exercise their male prerogatives more vigorously."(13)

## OPPORTUNITIES FOR WOMEN'S PARTICIPATION

Despite the prevalence of patriarchy, social movements often provide unusual opportunities for women to play important public roles. Now that gender roles in varied social movements are being studied, we can perceive patterns in how women are utilized and how they are permitted to serve.(14)  Movements of social protest, whether reform or revolutionary, are emergent phenomena that have to struggle for existence and hence to utilize whatever scarce resources are available to them.  This helps to explain why women are often important both as part of the mass and as leaders at various stages of movements, as will be discussed later.     Also,   unlike  institutionalized  organizations,  new  social movement organizations are in the process of organizing themselves consciously considering their rationales, ideology, and group processes. There is less initial differentiation, stratification, or credentialism; qualifications develop on the spot, and people with ideas and dedication become leaders.  The need for mass mobilization and unavailability of males may open up leadership positions to women.

In the South, black women had been trained to be strong and tended to take leadership roles because of the presumed greater danger that men would face.  Giddings refers back to the statement of noted black sociologist,  E. Franklin Frazier:  "In the South, the middle-class Negro male is not only prevented from playing a masculine role, but generally he must let Negro women assume leadership in any show of militancy."(15) According to Robinson, males riding the buses in segregated Montgomery generally left at signs of dispute or unrest fearful of the danger should they intervene.  The South's historical and continuing violence against black males could not be taken lightly.(16)  But when it came to assigning credit for successes, that was another story.  Although Rosa Parks had taken the fateful step of refusing to move to the back of the bus, whose picture was flashed across the news media when desegregation came to Montgomery?  It was a picture of male ministers, the Reverends King and Smiley, riding the first integrated bus.  One may wonder whether King had even ridden the buses before, but even then his actions were newsworthy. Reporters had encouraged Mrs. Parks to ride that day as well, and she did, but the King/Smiley picture is the one that can be found in press files.(17)  Despite the role of The Women's Political Council in initiating the boycott, the Montgomery movement was led and dominated by male ministers within a matter of days.

Black ministers throughout the South soon came together, under the leadership of King to form the Southern Christian Leadership Conference. Following the 1960 lunch counter sit-ins, young women and men of the Student Nonviolent Coordinating Committee became a model for their dangerous and daring actions, thus belying Frazier's generalization about an earlier generation of black males.  One must also be cautious not to generalize from SCLC's practices to patterns of male-female relations in other movement organizations.  As in the Montgomery bus boycott, women played key roles in SNCC from its inception.  However that organization's decentralized, consensus-oriented style gave women a more visible presence and role in decision-making.(18)   Nonetheless, men--such as James Forman, Stokely Carmichael, and H. Rap Brown--were chosen for the top formal leadership posts.

SNCC was made up largely of students and former students who were willing to live at a subsistence level.  But generally, women and men's traditionally unequal status in the world of paid work has made women the better candidates for community voluntary group participation and also for social movement membership.  Usually it has been men who refrain from activism for fear of losing their jobs.   Sex role socialization has repeatedly reinforced the notion that women's jobs are not as important as men's or as valuable to the family.  In the Montgomery case the threat of job loss was greater for the women leaders, for many of the members of the Women's Political Council were state employees, professors at traditionally black Alabama State College.  Civil rights activism might well have cost them their jobs or the college been penalized had their leadership been acknowledged.(19)  The male ministers, in contrast, were self-employed professionals, responsible to the black community, and the acknowledged leaders in relationships with whites.  The principle is the same:  in choosing winning strategies, movement decision-makers must take into account people's other roles in the society and utilize women and men to best tactical advantage.  In the process, traditional gender roles are either made to serve the movement or suspended where necessary.

As it turns out, increased political pressure on Alabama State resulted from faculty and student activism; Jo Ann Robinson eventually resigned her teaching post there.(20)   She was not the only victim. Septima Clark, fired from a South Carolina teaching post because of her NAACP membership, went on to create Freedom Schools.(21)   Rosa Parks, dismissed from her department store job in Montgomery, had to move to Detroit to find work since her income was, indeed, needed.(22)   Daisy Bates, the Arkansas NAACP leader who shepherded the nine Little Rock High school students through the tribulations of that desegregation effort, lost the newspaper she and her husband had successfully run for eighteen years.(23)

## BLACK AND WHITE FEMALE PARTICIPANTS:  SIMILARITIES AND DIFFERENCES

Similarities and differences in the role of black and white women have not been carefully examined; the relationships that existed between them have been described stereotypically in terms of sexual jealousies. Little is written of the possibility that common bonds were developed in the struggle.

The literature provides only some hints about certain specialized roles that local African-American women played.  Accounts of SNCC field efforts refer to the bravery of often elderly black women who sheltered civil rights workers.    Their feminine, nurturing role in feeding and providing housing for these activists was, in reality, a dangerous act consistent with their community reputations as fighters. Other extensions of female roles—such as that of teacher or librarian—were utilized in assigning SNCC volunteers.  Yet women and children took part in mass mobilizations, exposing themselves to the dangers of police dogs and fire hoses along with men.   In terms of gender, it seems that women played both traditional and nontraditional roles during the struggle, experiencing a "double-day" such as that of employed women—who contribute both within and outside the home.  Women activists often exposed themselves to danger, beatings and jailings, yet they were expected to prepare the food and sometimes serve the sexual or emotional needs of men.  According to Ladner(24) the responses of black and white women to their varied responsibilities differed.  Southern black women had been reared to assume much responsibility and to function in multiple roles.  They were comfortable with a mix of familial and activist duties.

The dominant racist and patriarchal culture has created barriers between black women and white women by emphasizing differences and underplaying commonalities.  They have been treated differently in the economy and society, and stereotyped as contrast conceptions.  Durr provides a vivid portrait of her training to be a "belle," as a southern white woman growing up in the early half of this century. (25)  The "belle" is supposed to attract men but remain a sexually ignorant virgin.  At the same time she is given to understand that black female servants do something "dirty" with men.

Within the Civil Rights Movement, one group of women were insiders and the others were representatives of the normally privileged dominant group.   The white women were also a traditionally tabooed sexual object for the African-American men with whom they were now associating.(26) Nonetheless, we may expect that the black women and white women who work together in social movements share certain similar experiences as women —such as being expected to perform sex-linked tasks and being the objects of sexual slurs or attacks by the opposition.   More needs to be known about the relationships between black and white female activists. How extensively, for example, was the black woman a role model for the white woman, as suggested by Evans?    To what extent was motherhood a common bond among some, as I found in my studies? (27) Were long-lasting relationships formed?

Information and impressions about women's participation in civil rights suffers distortions due both to the propaganda of opponents and over-generalization from limited studies of a single movement organization or a short time span.  The role of white women as a category seems to have received more notice than that of black women, but most often in negative ways.   Much of the existent research literature consists of limited studies of white female students specifically recruited for summer involvement in southern projects.(28)

Six hundred and fifty northern white women participated in the 1964 and 1965 Freedom Summers.(29)  Inexperienced with the South, some did not know how to handle the overture of black males and did engage in the tabooed interracial sex.   Not only was this dangerous, but it created tensions between African-American men and women.  The behavior of these summer volunteers has been overgeneralized as typical of white woman activists.  Such characterization disregards the key group of young southern women who joined the movement at an earlier stage (such as Jane Stembridge, Casey Hayden,  and Mary King), or the mature southern women who supported the movement (such as Lillian Smith and Virginia Durr), or the northern women who joined CORE chapters or started civil rights projects in their communities.(30)   Mary King, an early member of the SNCC staff explains that she and other whites had to work their way into the movement and gain trust.   They were sensitive to the traditional taboos between black men and white women and did not flout them.   King claims, "In my case, there was no undercurrent of sex affecting my experience in the Civil Rights Movement."(31)

Opponents of the movement accused white female participants, including nuns, of being involved in it for sexual kicks.  Such rumors abounded after the Selma to Montgomery march.  According to one account:

> After everybody cleared out and things began to settle down, the story got around all over Montgomery of the rapes that had taken place in Selma and on the trips from Selma to Montgomery—not only rapes but sexual orgies.  The crazies put out pamphlets saying that nuns weren't nuns and priests weren't priests:  they were just pimps and prostitutes who'd come down here....What was so interesting to me—so terrifying—is that it always got down to sexual relations between a black man and a white woman.(32)

Their opponents' use of society's free-floating sexism to attack activists was not new.  Fighting for any cause, women are the subject of sexual slurs and stereotypes.(33)  By humiliating women and criticizing their participation in the public sphere, opponents divert attention from real issues.  The death of Viola Liuzzo during the 1965 Selma events was minimized by relatives of a woman activist I interviewed, who disapproved of her participation.  They suggested that Liuzzo should have been home with her children.  Male leaders, however opposed by the enemy, tend to be less subject to such derogation on the basis of sex, and their participation in public activities more taken for granted.

Another way of stereotyping white women was to view them as defectors to feminist causes.  More scholarly research has dealt with how the Women's Movement arose out of civil rights than about women's active involvement in civil rights itself.  True, two white veteran SNCC members, Mary King and Casey Hayden, had brought the issue of sexism out into the open in a position paper they developed for that organization.  Their paper was circulated among women activists throughout the country and had a greater impact on them than on the black women in SNCC.(34)  In its later years, white women and men were forced out of SNCC and other formerly interracial organizations.  Still, some white women supported the black cause well into the Black Power period, when there were few interracial organizations left within which to work.  Some of the women I studied attended trials for accused black activists, following the urban disorders of the last half of the 1960s.  They also participated in white support groups for Black Power organizations.(35)  As faculty members and school administrators they aided the Black Student Movement of the late 1960s and early 70s.(36)  For others, the void caused by loss of civil rights roles became filled by activism in allied movements, such as the student left, the Anti-Vietnam War Movement, and the Women's Movement.

During the height of the Civil Rights Movement, white and black women in the North were used strategically as part of testing teams for such groups as CORE and fair housing groups.  One such interracial group of which I was a part served as community watchdog—attending public meetings of the Board of Education and the local governing council.  When eventually this group was strong enough to field a candidate for the Board of Education, it chose the husband of one of our most active mem-

bers.  This leads to a major point--that when a movement becomes successful it tends to select male rather than female leaders.  The women who
have been running organizations may themselves play a part in this
choice.

## FEMALE PARTICIPATION IN DIFFERENT STAGES OF THE MOVEMENT

As in other movements, women are often leaders in the early stages
of a movement and in their local communities.(37)  However, if a movement
attains some success, leadership opportunities for women in sexually
integrated movement organizations decline.  When the cause gains momentum
and greater acceptance, as civil rights did, leadership roles become more
differentiated and prestigious and hence more attractive to men.  More
men will vie for these roles, especially since an increasing division of
labor provides plenty of backup support from women.  The movement roles
become more like esteemed institutionalized roles, and may even lead to
public office.  In addition, real or presumed home and motherhood duties
have tended to limit women's geographic mobility and hence their chance
of becoming national leaders.  There are still few adequate support
systems to facilitate women's involvement in public roles.
Women themselves may search for male leaders, deeming it tactical to
have spokespersons more respected in the general society than they are.
At the time of the Civil Rights Movement, men were considered more
experienced and skillful in dealing with agents of the controlling
society--males headed governmental units, business firms, and law enforcement groups.  The power structures confronting the Civil Rights
Movement were all male, and so it was seen as normal and necessary to
have males play the formal leadership roles.  The momentum of the Civil
Rights Movement emboldened men; the moral legitimacy provided by the
black churches, the male preachers, and the nonviolent doctrine was probably viewed by both male and female strategists as essential to the movement's success.

In northern interracial groups, I also found a preference for male
leaders.  Both black women and white women, who had together created a
strong organization, welcomed a black male as their symbolic head, though
probably for different reasons.  The elevation of the African-American
male as movement leader was not only adaptive to the sexism of the
external society but was congruent with concern for strengthening the
role of the African-American male generally.  In fact, the interweaving
themes of civil rights for all black people and the assertion of a
traditionally conceived manhood role for black men was widely adopted and
accepted by most movement people in the 1960s.  Black women were reject-
ing the black matriarch stereotype, often tired from role overload, when
they pushed their men forward.  Twenty-five years later, some of them are
now critical of the sexism they faced and the lack of recognition that
they received.  Says Septima Clark:

> I was on the Executive staff of SCLC, but the men on it
> didn't listen to me too well.  They liked to send me into
> many places, because I could always make a path in to get
> people to listen to what I had to say.  But those men didn't
> have any faith in women, none whatsoever.  They just thought
> that women were sex symbols and had no contribution to
> make.(38)

White women in the movement were used to male dominance and many
felt comfortable as supporters and followers, especially of black males.
They grew in the belief that blacks needed to lead their own movement and
their relationships with heroic black male leaders may have been more

comfortable than those with less expressive, often racist, dominant white males.(39)

## WOMEN'S ROLE AS MASS PARTICIPANTS

We have only begun to acknowledge the leadership roles of certain key women in the Civil Rights Movement. Many more were known leaders in their local communities. Although some lip service has been given to the participation of women in mass events, the true extent of their contribution has yet to be assessed. The cover illustration of Aldon Morris' book on the origins of the Civil Rights Movement is undoubtedly intended to convey a message. He shows active participants at a mass meeting in Albany, Georgia, "waving papers they have signed saying they will go to jail the next day for marching on city hall to protest segregation." Most of them are women.(40)

## CONCLUSION

This paper has addressed the present and continuing reconstruction of the history of the Civil Rights Movement, in which past omissions or distortions are being corrected. Women's history, as black history, has suffered the fate of being overlooked and downgraded. Since the advent of the modern feminist movement, stimulated as it was by the Civil Rights Movement, new information is coming to light on the role of women leaders at certain crucial phases of the black freedom struggle. Black and white women in the movement welcomed and encouraged black male leadership as it became available--and the men's names were the ones that became known. Regarding mass participation, it is sometimes recognized, but hardly ever emphasized that the mass mobilization of black communities in the South was heavily dependent on women. Hopefully, others will agree that the unveiling of women's roles in the movement is a sign of progress, both for historical accuracy and for the scientific understanding of gender in social movements. I believe we can look forward to the exciting rediscovery of many more forgotten heroines and of women's lost movement history.

## NOTES

I would like to thank Guida West and Helen M. Hacker for their critical comments, and the Douglas Fellows Opportunity Fund of Rutgers University for financial support.

1.    See Sara Evans, Personal Politics (New York:    Alfred Knopf, 1979); and Mary King, Freedom Song:  A Personal Story of the 1960s Civil Rights Movement (New York:   Morrow, 1987).

2.    Some of these ideas were presented in an earlier paper, "The Intersection of Race and Gender in the Civil Rights Movement," at the 55th Annual Meeting of the Eastern Sociological Society, March 16, 1985 in Philadelphia.

3.    Septima Clark, Ready from Within:  Septima Clark and the Civil Rights Movement, edited and with an introduction by Cynthia Stokes Brown (California:  Wild Trees Press, 1986); Jo Ann Gibson Robinson, The Montgomery Bus Boycott and the Women Who Started It, ed. with a foreward by David J. Garrow (Knoxville, TN: University of Tennessee Press, 1987); and Mary King, Freedom Song (New York:  William Morrow & Co., 1987).

4.    Clark, Ready from Within, 19.

5.    Angela Davis, Women, Race and Class (New York:   Random House, 1981); and Paula Giddings, When and Where I Enter... The Impact of Black Women on Race and Sex in America (New York:   Harper and Row, 1984).

6.    Rhoda Lois Blumberg, "Careers of Women Civil Rights Activists," Journal of Sociology and Social Welfare 8 (September 1980):   708-729; and "White Mothers in the American Civil Rights Movement," in Research in the Interweave of Social Roles:   Women and Men, vol. 1, ed. Helena Z. Lopata (Greenwich, CT:   JAI Press, 1980).

7.    Robinson, The Montgomery Bus Boycott, 43-54.

8.    Howell Raines, My Soul Is Rested  (New York:   G. Putnam's Sons, 1977), Viking Penguin, ed. 1983, 37-39, 43-46; Virginia Foster Durr, Outside the Magic Circle, ed. Hollinger F. Barnard (Alabama:   University of Alabama Press, 1985), 279-281. Most versions agree that E. D. Nixon, long-time Montgomery activist leader, was called when Rosa Parks was arrested.   Along with white civil rights lawyer Clifford Durr and his wife Virginia Foster Durr, Nixon went to the jailhouse to make bail for Mrs. Parks.   Once Parks and her family had agreed that she would serve as a test case, Nixon states that he went ahead and organized the boycott.

9.    One source suggests that Baker was also involved in the founding of CORE (King, Freedom Song, 43).

10.    Aldon D. Morris, The Origins of the Civil Rights Movement (New York:   The Free Press, 1984), 103.

11.    Ronald Lawson and Stephen E. Barton, "Sex Roles in Social Movements:   A Case Study of the Tenant Movement in New York City," Signs 6 (Winter 1980):   230-247.

12.    Gary T. Marx and Michael Useem, "Majority Involvement in Minority Movements:   Civil Rights, Abolition and Untouchability," Journal of Social Issues 27, No. 1 (1971):   81-104.

13.    Giddings, When and Where, 60.

14.    Guida West and Rhoda Lois Blumberg, Women and Social Protest (New York:   Oxford University Press, (forthcoming 1991).

15.    Giddings, When and Where, 258.

16.    Robinson, The Montgomery Bus Boycott, 37.   As it happened, women were not immune to the violence of southern whites during the movement.   For instance, Fannie Lou Hamer, the Mississippi grass roots leader, was brutally beaten in jail, sustaining permanent injuries.   Women who were arrested were sometimes subject to rough vaginal searches.

17.    Clark, Ready From Within, 164.

18.    Joyce A. Ladner, "A Sociology of the Civil Rights Movement:   An Insider's Perspective," paper presented at the 83rd Annual Meeting of the American Sociological Association, August 27, 1988, Atlanta, Georgia.

19.    Juan Williams, Eyes on the Prize:   America's Civil Rights Years, 1954-1965 (New York:   Viking, 1987), 69.

20.    Robinson, The Montgomery Bus Boycott, 168.

21.   Clark, Ready from Within, 36, 41-76.

22.   Clark, Ready from Within, 15.

23.   Daisy Bates, The Long Shadow of Little Rock:  A Memoir (New York:  David McKay Co., 1962), 170-178.  See Durr, Outside the Magic Circle, for additional consequences of civil rights activities.

24.   Ladner, "A Sociology of the Civil Rights Movement."

25.   Durr, Outside the Magic Circle, Chapter 2.

26.   Evans, Personal Politics, 51.

27.   Blumberg, "Careers," and "White Mothers."

28.   N. J. Demerath III, Gerald Marwell, and Michael T. Aiken, Dynamics of Idealism (San Francisco:  Jossey-Bass, 1971);  James M. Fendrich, "Keeping the Faith or Pursuing the Good Life:  A Study of Consequences of Participation in the Civil Rights Movement," American Sociological Review 42 (February 1977):  144-157;  Mary Aickin Rothschild, "White Women Volunteers in the Freedom Summers:  Their Life and Work in a Movement for Social Change," Feminist Studies 5, no. 3 (Fall 1979):  466-495.

29.   Rothschild, "White Women Volunteers," 466.

30.   Blumberg, "White Mothers";  Evans, Personal Politics;  and August Meier and Elliott Rudwick, CORE:  A Study in the Civil Rights Movement (Urbana:  University of Illinois Press, 1973).

31.   Mary King, Freedom Song, 465.

32.   Durr, Outside the Magic Circle, 326-327.

33.   Andrea Dworkin, Right-Wing Women:  The Politics of Domesticated Females (London:  The Women's Press, 1983).

34.   King, Freedom Song, and Ladner, "A Sociology of the Civil Rights Movement."

35.   Guida West, "Twin Track Coalitions in the Black Power Movement" in Interracial Bonds, ed. Rhoda Blumberg and Wendell J. Roye, (Bayside, NY:  General Hall, 1979).

36.   Emily Alman, "Desegregation at Rutgers University," in Black Life and Culture in the United States, ed. Rhoda L. Goldstein, (New York:  Thomas Y. Crowell Co., 1971), 210-233.

37.   Lawson and Barton, "Sex Roles in Social Movements."

38.   Clark, Ready from Within, 77; see also Robinson, The Montgomery Bus Boycott.

39.   Blumberg, "Careers" and "White Mothers."

40.   Morris, Origins.

# 4 The Civil Rights Movement: Upheaval and Organization

*Jack Bloom*

Social movements, if they are to succeed, face two problems. First, they must get started and sustain themselves; second, they must pursue a strategy that increases their leverage to win demands. These issues are related; how they get started and sustain themselves will affect their strategy. Scholarly as well as activist writing about these two interrelated issues has tended to fall into two camps--the "spontaneous" upheaval camp and the organizational camp. The upheaval theorists say that the gains of social movements are won by mass upheavals which tend not to be organized; rather these theorists, represented in the past by Robert Michels and more recently by Frances Fox Piven and Richard Cloward, see organizations as inhibiting these upheavals.

Piven and Cloward argued that organizations function to decrease the militancy of the social upheavals of which they are expressions. They contended that this is so because in order to succeed, the organizations must gain concessions from the elite that will aid them in gaining the allegiance of masses of people.(1) The difficulty, however, is that it is not possible to gain concessions from these elites without conditions. The conditions are such as "to facilitate the efforts of elites to channel the insurgent masses into normal politics."(2) It is because of these organizational imperatives, said Piven and Cloward, that organizers, regardless of their intentions,

> fail to do what they can do [which is to] escalate the momentum of the peoples' protests....They typically acted in ways that blunted or curbed the disruptive force which lower class people were sometimes able to mobilize.(3)

So useless are organizers and organizations that, according to Piven and Cloward, "protesters win, if they win at all, what historical circumstances have already made ready to be conceded."(4) They are specific and uncompromising on this point:

> If industrial workers had demanded public ownership of factories, they would probably have still gotten unionism, if they got anything at all, and if impoverished southern blacks had demanded land reform, they would probably have still gotten the vote. (5)

· It is difficult to see how it is possible to argue that the organizations of the Civil Rights Movement did anything but advance that movement--even in Piven and Cloward's own terms. Thus, the Montgomery Improvement Association, a forerunner of the Southern Christian Leadership Conference, did not originally challenge segregated buses in Montgomery, but it did organize the bus boycott that resulted in the end to segregation there.  CORE initiated and, with the aid of SNCC and of the SCLC, continued the Freedom Rides.  SNCC initiated and was joined by the SCLC in the Albany campaign.  The SCLC organized and led the Birmingham campaign that affected not only Birmingham but the whole atmosphere of racial politics in the country.   SNCC and CORE organized the Freedom Summer registration campaign that created the Mississippi Freedom Democratic Party.  And it was a SNCC-organized voter registration program in Selma, later joined by the SCLC, that escalated into a major confrontation and brought about the Voting Rights Act.  All of this is not to mention the struggles in the North in which CORE played a central role.

The organizational camp presents a mirror image to the upheaval theorists. This position says that about the only thing that is important in starting a social movement is organization.  Social movements flow out of social organization because it provides resources, leadership, etc.  These theorists (Anthony Oberschall, Aldon Morris, and the resource mobilization theorists are in this camp) see organization as playing an all-important role in bringing about movement success.

Aldon Morris examined in great detail how the Civil Rights Movement grew out of the already existing organizations of the black community, especially the church, but also the NAACP and black colleges.  The church was the centerpiece of the movement as Morris saw it.  It provided independent leadership for the black community; it sustained the movement as it began, it provided a communications network that helped to spread knowledge of the growing movement and its strategy of nonviolent direct action and even its tactics.  Morris showed that the black church provided organization and financial resources to the growing movement, it educated and often organized the activists.  The church became the instrument through which other organizations were mobilized.  When the NAACP came under sustained attack in the South during the late fifties, the church provided the base for an alternative movement and an alternative organization, the Southern Christian Leadership Conference, which itself became the source of a more militant approach than that of the NAACP.  The church often educated the students who initiated the sit-ins, and played a substantial role in organizing those confrontations.

Morris also explored other organizational sources of the movement, including CORE and what he calls "movement centers":  organizations that helped to shape and direct social movements and to train social activists.  Thus, Morris argued that the original Greensboro sit-ins had been prepared by one of these movement centers, the NAACP Youth Council.  And he contended that the sit-ins were spread and maintained by other movement centers, especially the church:

> To understand the sit-in movement one must abandon the assumption that it was a college phenomenon....The sit-ins grew out of a context of organized movement centers...in many instances it was the leaders of the movement centers who organized the student protesters.  The tie between the students and the centers is crucial because of the atmosphere of intense repression in which the sit-ins spread.  Without the mobilization of the black community by the centers, it is doubtful that the spread of the sit-ins could have been sustained.(6)

Morris traced the Freedom Rides and the Albany and Birmingham campaigns and made the same case:  the movement centers, especially the church-dominated SCLC, organized, created, sustained, and spread the movement.

No evidence of a stirring from below can be discerned in Morris' account.   Indeed, the picture Morris presented appears as though were it not for organizations, there would have been no movement at all.   Morris provided a theoretical basis for this contention.   He rejected the thesis of a "New Negro" which was so widely held in the 1950s and 1960s.   This was a view that argued that blacks were changing their attitudes due to a variety of factors, including urbanization with its consequent creation of a large black community free from the white terrorism which had dominated the rural areas; growing black wealth; black independence and education; the experience of World War II, as well as the weakening of the power structure that had been able to keep blacks in subjection. This thesis saw the "New Negro" as the agency pushing black institutions toward a more activist role.   But Morris saw things differently:

> In some periods members of an oppressed group who appear docile are rapidly transformed into active protesters.... The transformation...remains largely unexplained....The point is that peoples' attitudes are heavily shaped by the institutions with which they are closely affiliated....Therefore, fairly rapid transformation of these attitudes may be accomplished by refocusing the cultural content of the institutions engaged in defining social reality.  Changing attitudes by refocusing the cultural content of institutions can be much more effective than changing the attitudes of separate individuals because institutional refocusing enables organizers to reach large numbers of people simultaneously.(7)

If one is an organizer seeking to effect change, it may make sense, as Morris said, to concentrate on working through institutions.   It is simply a more effective use of one's time than trying to change individuals one by one.   But the input of organizers is not the only way that individuals change.   They can take on new attitudes as a result of new circumstances, a new balance of power and the infectious changes that may alter a community's outlook.   Institutions are not divorced from the community.   They are part of it and partake of its outlook.   If significant change takes place, it may come from the community as well as its institutions.   The changing attitude of black ministers and educators was as much reflective of a larger process of change in the black population as it affected that change.

## MOVEMENT AND ORGANIZATIONS INTERACTING

Both the spontaneous upheaval camp and the organization camp point to real tendencies.   But by exclusively emphasizing those tendencies they distort and misunderstand the dynamics of social movements.   I propose an alternative model that incorporates elements of both approaches.    I demonstrate the value of this approach using evidence from the Civil Rights Movement, which has been the well-spring of much of the new analysis of social movements.

Lewis Killian began a more sophisticated discussion of these issues in a careful reexamination of the Civil Rights Movements in Tallahassee, Florida.    Killian demonstrated that in some times and in some places spontaneous activity is more important;  and in other times and places organization plays a more central role.   He was more specific: "spontaneity is especially likely to be important in the early stages of a social movement and during periods of transition from one type of action to another."(8)

I agree with Killian's conclusions, and I wish to amplify them: I do not believe merely that at some times and places spontaneity or organization are more likely to occur and be useful in developing social movements.   Rather, the two build upon and complement one another.   Broader

social changes open up new opportunities for social action and help to
change the vistas of potential participants in social movements.  They
act, often spontaneously (and often partly because of the previous
efforts of organizations).  Their actions change the situation, requiring
organization to extend and give focus to their efforts. They may create
new organizations (as with the Southern Christian Leadership Conference
and the Student Nonviolent Coordinating Committee)  or transform old ones
(as with the Congress of Racial Equality). The organizations can, then,
plan new activities which, if successful, mobilize more people with a
greater sense of efficacy.  They provide something for people to join, to
be active in. These newly-mobilized people, in their turn, by expanding
the movement, make possible new, bolder activity on the part of organizations.    They also often require more militancy with respect both to
demands and tactics, thus putting new pressures on the organizations.
This process proceeds in a kind of spiral that escalates the movement, at
least so long as its efforts are successful.  Each aspect, upheaval and
organization, complements the other.

## THE CIVIL RIGHTS MOVEMENT

Profound alterations among blacks began, in fact, to take place as a
result of the wrenching changes of the Depression, the New Deal, and
World War II.   Clearly, there were important demographic changes as
blacks moved from the South to the North and from rural areas to southern
cities.   These changes freed blacks from the terrorism that rural
isolation permitted.  Blacks became less dependent on local whites for
income and were in a position to act collectively.(9) Those who moved to
the North were able to vote and to aid their southern brethren through
political action.(10)  Blacks in the armed forces who wore uniforms, who
were armed, who saw military action, and who were treated differently
abroad than they had been at home became emboldened to challenge racial
practices. Some examples:

*President Roosevelt established a school at the Tuskeegee
Institute in Alabama to train blacks as pilots.  In 1942 a
black soldier at the school was arrested in town for public
drunkenness.  A black MP witnessed the arrest, drew his gun,
and took custody of the soldier from the white policeman.
The policeman soon got reinforcements who confronted the MP
and others who had joined him, seriously beating one of the
black MPs.  In response, a group of airmen armed themselves
and set out to free the soldier.  They were intercepted by an
officer and the confrontation was averted, but it illustrated
what could happen.(11)

*Right after the war black veterans marched on the Birming-
ham, Alabama, courthouse, demanding the right to vote.

*A. Philip Randolph demanded an end to segregation in the
United States Armed Forces and threatened to lead a movement
for draft resistance.  He picketed the Democratic Convention
in 1948, and his efforts succeeded in prodding President
Truman to issue an executive order that year desegregating
the Armed Forces.

*In Columbia, Tennessee, a black veteran struck a white man
when the latter slapped the veteran's mother.  That night a
lynch mob was stopped by an armed black population which
included veterans and members of the left-wing Mine, Mill,
and Smelter Workers' Union.(12)

*A number of observers of the time reported growing racial consciousness, self-assertiveness, and racial pride.(13)

*The Brown v. The Board of Education Supreme Court Ruling of 1954 intensified these feelings and created new hopes and demands.  In Greensboro, North Carolina, for example, black parents' visits to the school board meetings were "more frequent... and more assertive, but less patient.  They wanted it done boom, boom, boom."(14)

*In the summer of 1955 a young black boy named Emmett Till was visiting his grandparents from Mississippi.  He allegedly talked "fresh" to a white woman.  That night he was kidnapped and murdered.  His case became a cause célebre among blacks. What was remarkable about this instance was that his grandfather, at great personal risk, testified in court against the whites who had taken his grandson from his home.  That act illustrated once again that blacks were willing to take risks that they previously would have avoided.

These examples, part of a broader trend, help to provide the context for the Montgomery bus boycott and for the Little Rock High School desegregation confrontation in the fifties.  The boycott was organized from the churches.  It brought Martin Luther King, Jr., to national prominence and from it emerged the Southern Christian Leadership Conference.  But the Montgomery upheaval cannot be understood outside of the vast changes that had already taken place among the black population. Nor was the boycott simply a product of the church.  It is true that it was organized through the churches, that it was led by King and by other ministers.  It is also true that Rosa Parks was a long-time militant who had been active for years in the NAACP and had been at training sessions at the Highlander Folk School:  these were other organizational bases for this movement.  But in the year before Mrs. Parks refused to give up her seat to a white man, the act which precipitated the boycott, five black women and two black children had been arrested for the same act as Parks. Parks' act was one of a series that indicated that blacks were no longer willing to tolerate the treatment they had previously accepted.  Obviously, the whole situation was changing and black consciousness with it.  In this case it is clear that neither King nor other leaders had to change the attitudes of the black population.  They had already changed a great deal—and were still in the process of changing.

At the same time organizations, including the church, played an important role in pushing the struggle forward.  The boycott did not emerge merely out of amorphous changed attitudes or spontaneous upheavals.  It was planned by E. D. Nixon, a unionist in the Brotherhood of Sleeping Car Porters and long-time president of the local chapter of the NAACP, in conjunction with a black women's political organization, and it was organized through the churches and the new, church-based Montgomery Improvement Association.  Its ability to last for an entire year was a result of the organizational backbone.

In Little Rock, the nine black students who were supposed to enter the white high school stood their ground, with the support of their parents and the guidance of Daisy Bates, in the face of white mobs and the Arkansas National Guard.  Bates, active in the NAACP and publisher of the Little Rock black newspaper, demanded that President Eisenhower protect the students.  She and the students prevailed and in so doing encouraged others to struggle.

All of this is to say that there was a general movement on the part of blacks toward greater militancy, a greater sense of power, an increasing reluctance to allow whites to decide what blacks must do.  This movement affected black institutions and organizations and helped to change their direction. The Montgomery bus boycott, as well as other boycotts and confrontations, were both a manifestation of change that had already taken place, and a help to hasten, broaden and extend the changing attitudes.

Moreover, blacks did not all move at the same pace; some black leaders opposed the move. There was a struggle for leadership within the black community over these issues. Those who were willing to press forward had to do so in the face of white repression. But even here the struggle for black leadership did not take place simply among the leaders. It was the black population who intervened in the struggle and chose their own leaders and in doing so chose the type of leadership they wished. Observers found this to be true in New Orleans,(15) in Durham, North Carolina,(16) and in Little Rock, Arkansas. By the end of the decade of the fifties a study in Little Rock found in reference to a black leader who remained openly pro-segregationist:

> He used to do a lot of...speaking in the streets supporting segregation; but it is now too dangerous to do this for there have been threats of physical injury. Even the kids will stone his house or automobile when they pass going to school. A Negro leader who advocates segregation immediately draws the ire and dislike from Negroes generally. (17)

Even in Montgomery, King and other leaders were often surprised by the activity from below; it was not all organized. Thus, when King was arrested and denied bail, a huge gathering of blacks outside the jailhouse brought his quick release by the police.

But, while unorganized activity was clearly important, at the same time, the organized boycott in Montgomery gave blacks the opportunity to act militantly in concert, to practice skills the broader society had not until then permitted. Their ability to stand together against white pressure and the victories they won helped to engender and deepen black pride and black militancy. The same thing happened in Birmingham, in Tallahassee, in Little Rock and elsewhere where blacks became involved in struggles. Even in black communities where these confrontations did not take place, blacks felt stronger simply by virtue of the example of Montgomery and elsewhere. Thus, it was evident that neither the Montomery Improvement Association nor the other local organizations created by blacks to press their struggles served to retard the movement. Rather they helped to push it forward by increasing black self-consciousness and militancy. In the context of the boycott, on several occasions blacks acted in ways that surprised their white opponents in Montgomery and, perhaps, even themselves. The whites' efforts to intimidate them frequently forced them to respond with courage. So, when the city escorted the buses with police to intimidate the black population, blacks held steadfast in their refusal to board. When black taxi drivers were harassed for providing rides at low rates, middle-class blacks formed a car pool to ferry people to work. This act, forcing blacks to transcend class lines, created a unified black population.(18)

At one point in the boycott, a bomb exploded in King's home. A crowd gathered outside and when one man was told by the police to move, he responded angrily, "You white folks is always pushin' us around. Now you got your .38, and I got mine, so let's battle it out." This man, who was challenging the white police, the symbol of oppression to blacks in the South, was giving voice to what many must have felt. That he could utter the words indicated how much many blacks had changed.(19) The self-deprecation was being put aside. King noted increased self-respect and respect for others. The old tendency to deprecate other blacks was disappearing. A janitor told King: "We got our head up now, and we won't ever bow down again--no sir--except before God."(20)    In Montgomery the New Negro had taken a big step forward, and this had taken place within the context of the organized boycott movement.

The effects of the boycott rippled out far beyond the city of Montgomery. The action of Montgomery blacks were noted in many cities, and their example inspired others:

> That was when we began to understand things don't have to be the way they are. We learned in school there was a new law that segregation in commercial transportation was illegal. So Jesse [Jackson] and I got on the bus and stayed in front. It was our first challenge. But nothing happened. Everybody was real nice to us.(21)

Direct action to desegregate buses spread to Tallahassee, Birmingham, Mobile, and Atlanta. Blacks in New Orleans decided to boycott the Mardi Gras carnival there to support the efforts in Montgomery and Tallahassee. "It is immoral for Negroes in New Orleans to dance while Negroes in Montgomery walk," they said. In Durham, blacks began an effort to desegregate the schools, and in Greensboro they became more persistent over the same issue.(22) By no means were all of the ripples the result of organizations. There was genuine movement from below here resulting from the organized boycott.

This _movement_ created a new _organization,_ the Southern Christian Leadership Conference. The mere fact that the SCLC was constituted as a new organization that gave expression to the political sentiments of a new breed of ministers suggests that the more conservative elements within the black church resisted change and had to be prodded into acton. The SCLC was created in the fifties by King and other movement leaders most of whom were church-affiliated. It was built upon the new black movement that emerged in the mid-fifties based upon the open confrontations in several southern cities. The new organizations had a leadership that was different from any the Black South had known. King and his collaborators were young men who had attained their stature through open confrontations with the white power structure. They brought together a group of leaders who had been similarly proved, or who intended to proceed by their example. The SCLC thus became the organization expression of the "New Negro." Its aim was to extend the new militancy and to make room for the new kind of leadership that King and his collaborators represented. (23) It was further based on the perception that there was an emerging stratum of young men who had been affected by the changes in the black community and inspired by the recent black struggles. Sociologist Elaine Burgess found at the time that a new "radical" leadership was emerging in Durham, North Carolina:

> Many are young ministers just out of divinity school--Martin Luther King is their ideal. They want an end to segregation in all areas of life immediately. They are angry young men who prefer boycott and mass demonstration to the slower procedures of arbitration and litigation.(24)

The purpose of forming the organization was the need to broaden and extend the Civil Rights Movement. Thus, according to Bayard Rustin (who worked closely with King in this period): "The movement needed a sustaining mechanism that could translate what we had learned into a broad strategy for protest in the South."(25) The SCLC's formation came at a time when the movement had yet to "take off" as it did in 1960. Nonetheless, it was able to create a skeleton which could be fleshed out and put to the service of the movement as it emerged.

The experiences of the fifties inspired young people of that time.

In that way, they created the basis for a new wave of confrontations. Though Morris makes much of the organizational connections of the Greensboro four and of the sit-in participants, it is clear that the youth who burst on the scene in the sixties had watched and been profoundly influenced by the struggles of the fifties. Youth were not all churchgoers, but many sympathized with the movement and its leadership:

*John Lewis, who was a leader of SNCC recalled the impact that the Montgomery bus boycott had on him:

> Montgomery was only fifty miles away....Seeing Martin Luther King Jr., and the black people of Montgomery organize themselves in such a way that fifty thousand people, for more than a year, walked rather than rode segregated buses had a tremendous impact on me....I think that particular event probably changed the direction of my life more than anything else.(26)

*Joseph Washington of New Orleans had been eleven years old when the events of Little Rock unfolded. He told psychiatrist Robert Coles he would "never forget if I live to be one hundred. I was walking every inch with those kids." In 1960, when New Orleans began desegregation and experienced serious rioting by whites, Joseph worried about his seven year-old sister: "I kept on picturing her going through it, and I figured if she did, I'd walk beside her, and just let anyone try anything." When Coles witnessed the treatment endured by Washington, one of the first to desegregate the high school in New Orleans, he frankly wondered, "I don't know how you can take that sort of treatment; I really don't." Coles recorded Washington's response:

> You don't know how I can take it because you haven't ever had to take it. You see.... I had to learn to expect that kind of treatment.... Well, now I'm getting it again, but it's sweet pain this time, because whatever they may say to me or however they try to hurt me, I know that just by sticking it out I'm going to help end the whole system of segregation; and that can make you go through anything.(27)

*Cleveland Sellers, a SNCC leader:

> I spent many hours thinking about "the problem." My thoughts always culminated with the same vow: I've gotta help do something about this shit!... When reporters asked them [the Greensboro Four] "How long have you been planning this?" they replied, "All our lives!" I knew exactly what they meant.... My identification with the demonstrating students was immediately personal.(28)

When four black college students sat down at a lunch counter in Greensboro and demanded service, their action caught the imagination of their peers, and the movement rapidly spread. In Greensboro, according to one of the four:

> We actually got to the point where we had people going down in shifts....I think at the height of the sit-in movement in Greensboro, we must have had at least, oh, ten or fifteen thousand people downtown who wanted to sit-in, but obviously there weren't that many chairs in downtown Greensboro for people to sit-in....It spread to places like the shopping centers, the drugstores in the shopping centers, the drive-

ins.(29)

The movement soon spread way beyond Greensboro among a body of students who were ready to act and looking for some means to be effective.

> Some of these people were active in their high school NAACP, and when they got to college they were almost in place holding, and they probably didn't know they were waiting, but they were poised and ready to jump in. When the Greenboro sit-ins happened in early 1960, that was it. It wasn't that much of a conscious decision of what to do. Greensboro became the model, almost a blueprint.(30)

So we have seen so far a complicated pattern of interaction: a changing black consciousness helped to transform black leadership and black institutions. That same new consciousness was manifested, for example, in Rosa Parks' refusal to abandon her seat. From there, organization helped to cohere and focus black activity, to create a victory which inspired others to struggle. This victory and others like it became the basis for a new organization, the SCLC. These struggles also inspired black youth who, in the sixties, expanded the struggle. They also created a new organization, the Student Nonviolent Coordinating Committee, to extend their struggle.

SNCC was established when the Black Student Movement was clearly a dynamic force, and it sought to strengthen an action-oriented movement. SNCC searched for people in local areas who they felt were natural leaders and then cultivated them. The SNCC people used their organization to strengthen the power, abilities, and sense of confidence of those down below:

> There are some towns you go into and you find a man who has none of the characteristics of leadership as we identify them. He is the leader...and has been and is unquestioned, and mess with him wrong—forget it....We learned over and over again how to find potential leadership, how to groom it, and the most painful lesson for some of us was how to let it go, once you've set it into motion.(31)

The SNCC cadre often acted as a leavening agent, coaxing out others and imparting confidence to them, encouraging them to take some risks. The combination of the brave example set by SNCC and the evidence of the gains blacks were winning helped to bring more people into the movement. In one case a young man went to a meeting after the murder of a civil rights worker.(32)  He signed up:

> How it got to me...was hearing a colored boy my age speaking better than any white man I ever heard. I told myself that's no boy, he's a man, and since he's about your age, you can be just like him, which after a while I did become.(33)

Together with CORE, SNCC worked on the Freedom Rides, supported by the SCLC. The Freedom Rides, together with the violence they encountered and the lack of protection provided by the federal government for the Freedom Riders, angered and radicalized the SNCC youth and many others who watched. Thus, SNCC, like the SCLC helped to spread the movement.

So did several other acts including some not the products of organization like James Meredith's private decision to carry out his war against segregation by attending the University of Mississippi. Mobs of whites came out to try to stop him. There were other provocative attacks by whites on blacks who were breaking the color line. All of these functioned to pull more people into activity.

With more blacks (and whites) prepared to participate in the struggle there were both new opportunities for and new pressures on the civil
rights organizations. The possibilities that emerged under these circumstances were first made manifest by SNCC in Albany, Georgia. SNCC tried
to mobilize the whole black community of Albany for an assault on segregation in that city in its many manifestations. SNCC, with the aid of
King, succeeded in bringing out a large portion of the black population
to demonstrate and even to get arrested. The movement was defeated in
Albany but even in defeat it had shown the potential of mobilizing the
black population for more intensive confrontations than had been previously possible.

The pressures emerged from the increasing numbers of blacks who had
been mobilized by the successes of the Civil Rights Movement. Greater
numbers of people were willing to participate in civil rights activity,
to take the risks that were involved. More people felt both a sense of
anger, and perhaps despair. Increasingly, King's strategy of nonviolent
direct action came under assault. The successes of the organized struggles for civil rights engendered new demands and forced the civil rights
organizations to up the ante in terms both of goals and tactics.

This situation led King to undertake the Birmingham campaign. His
aim was to carry out an offensive that would dramatically demonstrate the
validity of his strategy and gain it new adherents. The way to attain
this victory was through massive disruption of commerce. The Albany
demonstrations had made apparent the possibility of moving beyond
previous efforts that had relied on either a cadre of trained and
committed volunteers for active participation, as in the sit-ins and
Freedom Rides, or the less confrontational involvement of the whole black
population, as in the Montgomery bus boycott. In Albany large numbers of
blacks had engaged in mass marches and submitted to arrests. A similar
strategy could be employed in Birmingham, whose purpose was to disrupt
downtown commerce; this act could force political and economic leaders to
act to accommodate black demands. Moreover, if unjustifiable brutality
were used against the demonstrators, northern middle-class public opinion
would be mobilized in favor of federal governmental action. These
outside forces would pressure the Birmingham power structure and, through
civil rights legislation, bring about much broader gains for blacks
throughout the South.

The strategy worked. As the demonstrations reached their height,
over three thousand blacks were in jail; four thousand more were still
demonstrating; blacks were closing Birmingham down. Ed Gardner, a local
activist, described what happened:

> We had 4500 folks in jail, and we had about ten or twenty
> thousand wanted to get in, and "Bull" Connor had filled up
> the Bessemer jail, had filled up the Fair Park. He run out
> of space and when he run out of space he got the firemen and
> turned the water on, but the more water he would pour, the
> more they would come.(34)

The businessmen, who were meeting to consider what to do during this
massive demonstration, were shocked, and they capitulated. Northern
public opinion was terribly inflamed by the sight of brutality employed
against children, women, and others who were harming no one. President
Kennedy was moved by the spectacle, and by its impact on public opinion,
to propose the Civil Rights Bill that was enacted into law after his
assassination.

Clearly, King had won a great victory. His calculation of the
centrality of Birmingham was proved correct. Yet ironically, the victory
in Birmingham, which simply would not have taken place without organiza-

tion, began to change radically the character of the Black Movement. Once again the dynamic we have been observing unfolded. The victory in Birmingham appears to have significantly extended the sense of power (efficacy) among the black population. This change is manifested in several ways:   many more blacks became involved in civil rights activity across the country; the scope of their demands grew significantly;  the boldness of their projects grew (Birmingham preceded by a year the Mississippi Freedom Summer Project);  opinion polls showed that blacks were more willing to take risks, more willing to subject themselves to arrest; pressures grew on the Black Muslims who had talked tough, but did not participate in the movement.  It was not long before Malcolm X split from the Muslims over just this issue.  Birmingham made a qualitative difference in the Black Movement and gave new strength to political currents in the Black Movement that King bitterly opposed.(35)

At the same time, white brutality grew.  It embittered blacks at the very time that they were developing a greater sense of efficacy.  White violence did not stop once blacks had won their victory.  Bombs were planted at the home of King's brother and at the motel where the movement had been headquartered.  The black population of Birmingham responded with the first of the urban riots, in 1963.  They threw stones and bricks and bottles at police and drew their knives in anger; they set fires and looted stores.  This response and a general melee that King's lieutenants could neither control nor abate prefigured what was yet to come in the nation's black ghettos.  No one was yet aware that black riots would become the most widespread form of political expression.  The layers of people that King had tapped in Birmingham--that he had _had_ to tap--went beyond his methods.  These people, and those like them, would face a revision of black goals as they began to make their social weight felt.

## CONCLUSION

This quick review illustrates something of the rich tapestry created by the intersection of movements and organizations.  It is evident that organizations were crucial to advancing the Civil Rights Movement.  It is also evident that the organizations that emerged were, at least in part, a response to upheavals that were not simply organizationally controlled but that emerged from a changing black consciousness and a new sense of efficacy. The best way to understand this movement is to see the contributions both of spontaneity and of organization, each playing a role which the other augmented.  Emphasis on only one of these moments of a process distorts our understanding of the development of a social movement by missing the point precisely that it _is_ a process.

Changing black consciousness and political power brought about acts which challenged white supremacy.  These acts led to the creation of ad hoc organizations in several cities (like the Montgomery Improvement Association).  The victories of these organizations broadened the base of the movement and made it possible to contemplate another organization, the Southern Christian Leadership Conference, to further extend the reach of the movement; they further changed mass consciousness.  The struggles of the fifties, as well as organizational connections, helped to stimulate the youth movement of the sixties.  The movement crafted its own organization, the Student Nonviolent Coordinating Committee.  These organizations in their turn pressed forward the movement which in its turn put renewed pressure on and created new opportunities for the civil rights organizations.

The Birmingham demonstrations best illustrate this dynamic.  In part, they were a response to the defeat in Albany.  They were also mindful of growing black impatience with southern intransigence.  The hammering of Malcolm X against nonviolent direct action in general and Dr. King in particular may also have increased the pressure on King.  In

any case, to be successful, the Birmingham demonstrations needed to in-
volve masses of blacks.  But with that involvement, and the brutality
with which "Bull" Connor responded, black anger could not be controlled.
It is an often ignored but indubitable truth that the first urban riot
was in Birmingham.  The atmosphere among blacks within the nation was
profoundly altered by the Birmingham demonstration.    Blacks everywhere
were more militant and more angry.  The next summer saw the first wave of
the recognized black riots before, during, and after the democratic
convention.  Soon, black nationalism, black power, and black rioting were
widespread.    All of these emerged organically from the Civils Rights
Movement.    No effort to understand them can ignore either the popular
upheavals or the efforts of black organizations to guide, and in some
cases to create, those upheavals.

**NOTES**

1.    Frances Fox Piven and Richard Cloward, Poor People's Movements
(New York:  Pantheon, 1977), xx.

2.    Ibid., xxi.

3.    Ibid., xxi-xxii.

4.    Ibid., 36.

5.    Ibid., 33.

6.    Aldon Morris, The Origins of the Civils Rights Movement (New
York:  The Free Press, 1984), 197, 200.

7.    Ibid., 96.

8.    Lewis Killian, "Organization, Rationality and Spontaneity in
the Civil Rights Movement," American Sociological Review 49 (December
1984), 780.

9.    Jack Bloom, Class, Race and the Civil Rights Movement
(Bloomington:  Indiana University Press, 1987), 59-73.

10.    Ibid., 74-86.

11.    Robert Norrell, Reaping the Whirlwind  (New York:  Vintage,
1986), 49.

12.    Carl Rowan,  South of Freedom (New York:  Alfred A. Knopf,
1952), 28-49.

13.    See Morton Rubin, Plantation Country (Chapel Hill:  University
of North Carolina Press, 1951), 97; Bob Smith, They Closed Their Schools
(Chapel Hill:  University of North Carolina Press, 1965), 169-173; Floyd
Hunter, Community Power Structure  (Garden City, NY:  Anchor Books,
1963), 138-139; William Chafe, Civilities and Civil Rights  (New York:
Oxford University Press, 1980), 320-339;  Harry Halloway, The Politics
of the Southern Negro (New York:  Random House, 1969), 240-242; Hylan
Lewis, Blackways of Kent (Chapel Hill:  University of North Carolina
Press, 1955), 298-299, 186, 257; David Thompson, The Negro Leadership
Class  (Englewood Cliffs, NJ:  Prentice-Hall, 1963), 86, 167-168; Edgar
French, "Beginnings of a New Age," in The Angry Black South, ed. Glenford
E. Mitchell and William H. Peace III (New York:  Cornith Books, 1962), 32.

14.    Chafe, 83-84.

15.    Thompson, 79.

16.    Elaine Burgess, <u>Negro Leadership in a Southern Town</u> (New Haven: College and University Press, 1976), 136.

17.    Tilman C. Cothran and William Phillips, Jr. "Negro Leadership in a Crisis Situation," <u>Phylon</u> 22, no. 2 (1961):  112.

18.    Martin Luther King, Jr., "Our Struggle," <u>Liberation</u> (April 1956):  5.

19.    David L. Lewis, <u>King:  A Critical Biography</u> (New York: Praeger, 1970), 70.

20.    Martin Luther King, Jr., <u>Stride Toward Freedom</u>  (New York: Harper and Row, 1964), 164.

21.    Joyce Purnick and Michael Oreskes, "Jesse Jackson Aims for the Mainsteam," <u>The New York Times Magazine</u>, November 29, 1987,  34.

22.    Thompson, 104; and Burgess,  125.

23.    Bloom, 149.

24.    Burgess, 185.

25.    Bayard Rustin, <u>Strategies for Freedom</u> (New York:  Columbia University Press, 1976), 26.

26.    William R. Beardslee, <u>The Way Out Must Lead In</u> (Atlanta: Center for Research in Social Change, Emory University, 1977), 4.

27.    Robert Coles, <u>Children of Crisis, Vol. 1</u> (Boston:  Little Brown & Co., 1967), 107-117.

28.    Cleveland Sellers, <u>River of No Return</u> (New York:  William Morrow and Co., 1973), 16-18.

29.    Howell Raines, <u>My Soul is Rested</u> (New York:  Bantam Books, 1978), 81.

30.    Julian Bond, "The Movement Then and Now," <u>Southern Exposure</u> (1976): 7.

31.    Raines, 31.

32.    Bloom, 164.

33.    Coles, 209

34.    Raines, 156.

35.    Bloom, 176-177.

# 5 Blacks and the New South: Civil Rights in the Eighties

*Robert D. Bullard*

## INTRODUCTION

The South during the fifties and sixties was the center of the Black Civil Rights Movement. The 1970s and early eighties catapulted the region into the national limelight again, but for different reasons. The South during this period was undergoing a number of dramatic demographic and economic changes. It was now a major population and economic growth center. Growth in the region during the 1970s was stimulated by a number of factors. They included: a climate pleasant enough to attract workers from other regions and the "underemployed" workforce already in the region; weak labor unions and strong right-to-work laws; cheap labor and cheap land; attractive area for new industries, i.e., electronics, federal defense, and aerospace contracting; and aggressive self-promotion or booster campaigns.(1) The South beginning in the mid-seventies was transformed from a "net exporter of people to a powerful human magnet."(2)

The theme of this essay centers on the extent to which blacks shared in the South's new growth. Several questions are explored. Did the boom of the seventies pass over the region's black community? Did black population gains translate into comparable economic and political gains? What impact did the economic recessions, or "bust" period of the early 1980s, have on black progress in the South?

## THE RISE OF THE NEW SOUTH

The South in the 1970s desperately attempted to rid itself of the image of a socially and economically "backward" region. The region was vigorously promoted as the "New South." However, many of its old problems remained despite the growth. For example, both in-migrants and incumbent residents who had marginal skills generally found themsevles in the growing unemployment lines.(3)    Individuals who did not have the requisite education often became part of the emerging underclass. The new prosperity in the South heightened the status differences in the region. Poverty coexisted amid affluence. Poverty in the South represented a source of "cheap labor." The large pool of nonunionized labor was also part of the so-called "good business climate."(4)

Many household heads whose jobs only paid the minimum wage had to work an extra job just to pull themselves above the poverty level. Uneven development within the region's central cities and suburbs, and companies' systematic avoidance of areas that had large concentrations of blacks heightened the social and economic inequalities between blacks and whites. Morever, white racism permeated nearly every institution in the region. This persistent problem caused many writers to challenge the existence of a New South.  Chet Fuller, a black journalist, traveled across the South in the late seventies and discovered that "the much touted progress of some southern cities is more illusion than reality."(5)    The New South was portrayed as booming with industrial growth and expanding employment opportunities that were once closed to the black masses.    The New South was marketed as a changed land where blacks could now share in the American Dream.    Fuller argues that "power has not changed hands in the South, not from white hands to black hands" and that "economics is money is power is still white."(6)

The boundaries of the South have been defined in different ways by a host of journalists, social scientists, and government bureaucrats.    For example, the U.S. Bureau of the Census has defined the South as a statistical entity comprised of sixteen states and the District of Columbia. However, the South is more than a statistical entity because of its distinct history, culture, and development pattern.    Because this study is about changes that have occurred in the Old South, a broad belt which stretched from Virignia to Texas, it seems logical to define the New South on the basis of state boundaries.    The South, in this paper, includes twelve states:  Virginia, North Carolina, South Carolina, Georgia, Florida, Kentucky, Tennessee, Alabama, Mississippi, Arkansas, Louisiana, and Texas.

## DEMOGRAPHIC SHIFT SOUTHWARD

The South has the largest population of any region in the country. More than 64.9 million inhabitants, nearly one-third of the nation's population, lived in the South in 1980.    All of the southern states experienced a net in-migration during the seventies.    The South, during the 1971-1980 period, also grew at a faster rate than the nation as a whole.    The nation's population expanded by 21.9 percent during the seventies.

The southern region has the largest concentration of blacks.    In 1980, there were more than 12.2 million blacks living in the South. Blacks were nearly one-fifth (18.9 percent) of the South's population. The 1970-1980 period saw the region's black population increase by nearly 18 percent.    Six of the southern states had black populations which exceeded 20 percent (i.e., Mississippi, South Carolina, Louisiana, Georgia, Alabama, and North Carolina).

The South has always been home for a significant share of the black population.    More than ninety percent of Black Americans lived in the southern states at the turn of the century.    A little more than one-half (fifty-three percent) of all blacks were living in the South in 1980—the same percentage as in 1970.(7)    In an effort to improve their life situation, millions of rural blacks migrated from the South to other regions of the nation.    From the mid-forties to the late sixties, nearly 4.5 million more blacks left the South than migrated to it.    Beginning in the mid-seventies, however, the number of blacks moving into the South exceeded the number departing for other regions of the country.    For the period 1975-1980, more than 415,000 blacks moved into the South, while only 220,000 left the region (or a net in-migration of 195,000 blacks) thereby reversing the longstanding black exodus.    More than 411,000 blacks migrated to the South during the 1980-1985 period while 324,000 moved out of the region, a net in-migration of 87,000 blacks.(8)

This reverse migration stream appears to be an indication of the changing social, political, and economic structure of the South.    As industry and jobs relocated to the region, job seekers were soon to follow.  The movement of blacks to the southern United States is expected to continue as more nonagricultural jobs are added to the region's economy.  More than 17 million new jobs were added in the South between 1960 and 1985, compared to 11 million jobs added in the West, and a combined total of 13 million jobs added in the Midwest and Northeast.(9)

The six largest Standard Metropolitan Statistical Areas (SMSAs) in the South are Dallas-Fort Worth, Houston, Atlanta, Miami, Tampa-St. Petersburg, and New Orleans. These ranked 8, 9, 16, 21, 24, and 33 in population among all the nation's SMSAs in 1980. Blacks make up a significant share of the region's metropolitan and central city population. Blacks comprised one-third of the population in the Memphis, Jackson, and New Orleans metropolitan and central city population. Blacks make up one-fourth of the Birmingham, Richmond, and Atlanta SMSAs. The Miami and Atlanta SMSAs registered the largest percentage increase in the number of blacks between 1970 and 1980. The black population in metropolitan Miami grew by 47.8 percent in the seventies, while blacks in the Atlanta SMSA increased their numbers by 43.5 percent during the same period. On the other hand, the Birmingham metropolitan area experienced the smallest increase in its black population in the 1970s. Birmingham's black population grew by only 8.2 percent between 1970 and 1980. Blacks were the majority of the central city population in Atlanta, Birmingham, New Orleans, and Richmond in 1980. The black population in Memphis and Jackson approached the fifty percent mark in 1980.

The challenges that southern cities must face rest with how their resources, i.e., housing, jobs, public services, political representatives, etc., are shared with blacks and other ethnic minorities who historically have not gotten their fair share of the region's economic advances. The major reason for this has been the location preferences of industry. Industry that relocates to the South tends to "build new factories where it can find surplus white labor and has avoided places with a high ratio of poor and unskilled blacks."(10)

Many communities with large black populations were passed over during the height of the economic push southward. Economic growth patterns in the Deep South generally occurred along racial and geographic lines. This meant that millions of rural and urban blacks in the South were racially and economically segregated from the expanding job centers in the region. The plight of black southerners has been exacerbated by the combination of economic recession (and depression-like conditions in many black communities), federal budget cuts, growing tension among individuals competing for limited jobs and other scarce resources, and the federal retreat on enforcement of civil rights and anti-discrimination laws.(11)

## SHARING THE ECONOMIC PIE

The "Go South" and "Stay South" themes became potent messages in black communities across the nation. Blacks again were searching for the promised land in the New South, a region that was prominently displayed in booster campaigns of emerging southern cities. The region attracted both the skilled and unskilled, educated and uneducated, as well as low-income and middle-income blacks who sought to make their fortune in the city.

The economic picture of black workers in the South has been one of persistent and chronic unemployment. The unemployment rate for blacks remained more than two times that of whites in the region since the late sixties. Morever, the 1970s ended with double-digit black unemployment rates in eight of the twelve southern states. By 1980, a double-digit black unemployment rate was the established trend through the mid-eighties in all twelve southern states. The recessions of the early 1980s exacted an especially heavy economic toll on the black work force. The 1983 annual average black unemployment rate, for example, was a high of 26.5 percent in Alabama, 24.0 percent in Mississippi, 23.9 percent in Arkansas, and 23.1 percent in Tennessee. There was very little for black communities in these economically depressed states to cheer about since

nearly a quarter of their work force was unemployed. The evidence of a
New South was not compelling when one considers the fact that blacks in
Arkansas, Mississippi, and Tennessee were three times more likely to be
unemployed when compared with their white counterparts.

Economic conditions by the mid-eighties saw some improvement in the
region as exhibited by declining unemployment. Black unemployment
figures (which had shown a downward trend) continued to be significantly
higher than that of whites. Economic recession in the oil industry
locked many Texas and Louisiana residents out of the job market and
caused revenue shortfalls in state financing. Texas, which had long been
thought to be "recession proof," struggled with ways to balance its
budget. Louisiana, another oil-producing state, was nearly bankrupt.
The 1985 black unemployment rate averaged more than 14.2 percent in Texas
and 19.9 percent in Louisiana. The gap between black and white unemployment actually widened over the years. Revenue losses from the oil-rela-
ted industries spelled doom for many black workers, businesses, and home
owners. Moreover, this depression-like condition had a destabilizing effect on many middle-income black neighborhoods and exacerbated existing
social problems of crime, physical decline, abandonment, disinvestment,
and school closures in many low-income black neighborhoods.

The national unemployment rate in 1985 was 6.2 percent for whites
and 15.7 percent of blacks. The black unemployment rate in the South
census region averaged 14.0 percent compared with 12.0 percent in the
Northeast, 22.2 percent in the Midwest, and 13.0 percent in the West.
Youth unemployment (16 to 19 year-olds) continued to be a national
problem. This problem was more acute in the black community. More than
40.6 percent of black teenagers and 15.7 percent of white teenagers were
unemployed in 1985. Employment prospects for black youths during the
mid-eighties were slightly better in the South than in the Midwest or
West and about the same in the Northeast. Still, more than 37.8 percent
of the black youths in the South were unemployed in 1985.

The city's role as an economic "launching pad" for upwardly mobile
blacks was diminished by the disinvestment process taking place in
central cities and the relocation of new industries to distant suburbs.
The social climate of the South was drastically changed by the Civil
Rights Movement, a movement concentrated mainly in southern cities. The
region's major cities became the center of economic and political change
and rising black expectations. Blacks were drawn to the region's large
central cities. From Atlanta to Memphis, blacks were struggling to get a
piece of the American Dream and reap some of the benefits of the emerging
New South. The struggle of blacks in Birmingham, a city tagged the
"Johannesburg of the South" in the sixties, is legendary.(12) The
expectations of black citizens were similar in Houston, Tampa, as well as
in Memphis. Blacks, in city after city wanted and expected what all
Americans wanted and expected, an opportunity to fulfill their dreams.
High black unemployment rate in southern cities is a reflection of the
changing job market in postindustrial America that is characterized by "a
capital-intensive restructuring of the industrial and manufacturing
sector and a phenomenal growth of the service industry."(13) It is also
a reflection of central city-suburban housing and business location
patterns. The post industrial job market in urban areas often calls for
levels of education and skills beyond that of many innercity blacks.(14)
A growing black underclass is trapped in declining central cities where
few opportunities are available to reach job centers located in the
suburbs. Public transit is often inadequate or nonexistent. This
dilemma is probably epitomized in metropolitan Atlanta where MARTA, the
city's modern bus-rail system, is cut off from job-rich suburban
Gwinnette and Cobb counties, the area's "Golden Crescent."(15) The
decision by the mostly white suburban counties not to become a partner in
MARTA and the decisions by industries to locate in these counties have

contributed to whites gaining a greater share of the Atlanta metropolitan area work force.  The economic renaissance that has fueled the Atlanta success story has benefited the mostly white suburban counties that surround the mostly black city of Atlanta.(16)

Double-digit unemployment ravaged many black communities in the mideighties.  In 1986, for example, black unemployment was 19.3 percent in Memphis, 19.2 in Houston, 16.8 in New Orleans, and 11.6 percent in Tampa-St. Petersburg. The same year, whites had a 4.9 percent unemployment rate in Memphis, an 8.9 percent rate in Houston, an 8.5 percent rate in New Orleans, and a 5.0 percent unemployment rate in Tampa-St. Petersburg. Rising unemployment and poverty undermined the stability of black family and community life.  Extreme poverty existed amid the palm trees in Tampa and New Orleans and in the shadow of the steel and glass high-rise office towers in Atlanta and Houston.  More than one-third of black families in New Orleans, Tampa-St. Petersburg, and Memphis, for example, fell below the poverty line in 1980;  more than one-fourth of the blacks in Atlanta and Birmingham were below the government poverty threshold in 1980; and one-fifth of all black Houstonians lived in poverty in 1980.  Black poverty coexisted with the rising New South.  The New South for many residents translated into heightened status differences and a widened economic gap between the skilled and unskilled.

The black-white income gap was part of the Old South and persisted in the New South.  Houston and Atlanta had one of the most affluent black communities in 1980.  Still, black families in metropolitan Houston earned just sixty-one percent of the income earned by whites in the area. Black families in metropolitan Atlanta, on the other hand, earned fifty-nine percent of the income earned by white families.  The income gap will likely continue as long as blacks are concentrated in low-wage service occupations.  Blacks in large southern cities are still two and one-half times more likely to be employed in service occupations than their white counterparts.  Black workers are also more highly concentrated in blue collar jobs than are whites.  Conversely, blacks are less likely to be found in white collar occupations.  The largest concentration of blacks in white collar occupations is found in the Atlanta and Houston metropolitan areas.  A little over two-fifths (43.5 percent) of metropolitan Atlanta's blacks and two-thirds (65.2 percent) of whites held white collar occupations in 1980.  Two-fifths (41.7 percent) of the blacks in metropolitan Houston and nearly two-thirds (65.2 percent) of the whites worked in white collar jobs.

## BLACK BUSINESS DEVELOPMENT

Economic recessions of the early eighties pushed many low-income black neighborhoods further down the economic pecking order while destabilizing middle-class black neighborhoods and businesses.  Hard times in the oil patch in Texas and Louisiana, for example, left a trail of business foreclosures and for sale signs in once stable black communities along the Gulf coast from Houston to New Orleans.  Many black-owned businesses in the Urban South grew despite the recurring recessions.  The majority of black-owned businesses is located in the southern United States where the majority of the nation's black population is also found. The South in 1982 accounted for more than fifty percent of the nation's black-owned business enterprises and forty-five percent of their business receipts.(17)  Black-owned businesses in the South grossed nearly $5.6 billion in 1982, the most recent year for which government figures are available.

Black business operations continue to be concentrated in southern cities that have large black populations.  Houston had by far the largest number of black-owned business enterprises with 10,019 firms in 1982. Houston's black-owned businesses grossed $283.7 million in 1982.  Atlanta's 3,493 black-owned business enterprises' gross receipts totaled $283.5 million in 1982. Atlanta's black business community, though much smaller in number, is one of the most widely known and firmly established in the nation. There were six Atlanta area firms listed on <u>Black Enterprise's</u> "Top 100" in 1986.(18)    Chicago was the only other city that could match that statistic in 1986.

A substantial share of the resources within the black community is still owned by outsiders. Black business owners, however, play an important role in the economic stability of the black community. Black-owned financial institutions contribute to the building of a solid economic base within areas that have been systematically redlined by white institutions. Black-owned banks, savings and loans, mortgage companies, and insurance firms enable the black community to expand its home and business ownership base. Atlanta, for example, is home of the nation's second largest black-owned bank (Citizen Trust) and second largest black-owned insurance company (Atlanta Life). Other southern cities also have an array of black-owned financial institutions.

As the nation experiences an era of scarcities, everyone has had to learn to live with less. Many cities have had to grapple with ways of coping with dwindling local revenue and federal financial support, and rising municipal service costs. Close monitoring by citizen watchgroups needs to be undertaken to evaluate how the dwindling public monies are spent. Special efforts need to be undertaken by black elected officials to see that funds designated for urban "poverty pockets" and blighted inner-city areas are not diverted away from these areas and channeled into affluent "downtown" projects, convention centers, and "yuppie playgrounds." The problem of indequate housing, declining neighborhoods, underrepresentation of blacks in the business area, and the absence of a coherent economic "master plan" for the black community are major obstacles to black economic independence and political empowerment.

## BLACK POLITICAL EMPOWERMENT

Blacks made substantial gains toward political empowerment with the passage of the Voting Rights Act in 1965. There were 1,469 black elected officials in 1970, 4,912 in 1980, and 5,654 in 1984.(19)   The number of black officeholders increased to 6,681 in 1987. There were 23 blacks in the U.S. Congress in 1987. This number represented only 5.3 percent of the 435 members of the U.S. House of Representatives. Blacks made up 12 percent of the nation's population and 20 percent of the South's population in 1980. However, only 4 blacks from the Deep South were serving in Congress (Harold Ford of Memphis, Mickey Leland of Houston, John Lewis of Atlanta, and Michael Espy of Yazoo City, Mississippi) in 1987. Espy in 1986 became the first black elected to the U.S. Congress from Mississippi since Reconstruction. Reapportionment plans that were developed from the 1980 census have meant more black political representation in municipal, country, state and federal elective offices.(20)   A little more than one-half, or 53 percent of the nation's blacks live in the South. However, nearly 62 percent of the black elected officials were found in the South. The North Central Region has 20 percent, the Northeast 12.2 percent, and the West 5.9 percent of the black elected officials.

The 1980s have seen the southern states emerge as a political battleground for the black vote. A number of large southern cities had black mayors in 1987 including Atlanta, New Orleans, Charlotte, Richmond, Birmingham, and Little Rock. After repeated attempts, Memphis has failed to elect a black mayor in a city that is one-half black. Memphis continues to be racially polarized and its black community severely fragmented. Overall, voter education and registration drives along with intensified "get out the vote" campaigns have been a boon to black political office seekers in large cities and urban areas that have substantial black

voting age populations.  In 1984 Atlanta led all southern cities with 43
black elected officials followed by Houston with 29 black officeholders.
(21)  There were 26 black elected officials in Memphis, New Orleans had
20, Birmingham had 18, and Tampa had 4 black elected officals in 1984.
Despite the efforts at the local level, blacks remain underrepresented as
political officeholders.(22)

There are clear indications that the "sleeping giant," the black
electorate in the South, is awakening.  Blacks are also gradually moving
into decision-making offices on local school boards and in superintendent
positions that have the potential of shaping future educational policies.
For example, Atlanta, New Orleans, Memphis, and Birmingham all had black
school superintendents in 1987.  The struggle to control large urban
school districts in the South has become the new civil rights bone of
contention in the eighties.  Battles often revolve around issues such as
the underrepresentation of blacks in administrative positions, minority
teacher hiring, teacher experience in poor and affluent schools, and the
quality of educational programs in inner-city schools.  Urban school
boards have become polarized along racial and class lines.  A number of
factors have contributed to this polarization: teacher discontent,
teacher assignment, teacher hiring and termination, school closing, pupil
transfers, and pupil assignment to magnet programs, and special education
classes.

A new form of school segregation appears to be emerging in large
urban school districts.  A disproportionately large share of lower-income
black students attend schools apart from whites but also apart from their
middle-income black counterparts.  The conflict over magnet schools and
the limited slots in the talented and gifted programs most often is
between middle-income blacks and their white counterparts who have
remained in the public school system.  Lower-income black youth more
often than not end up in overcrowded, poorly equipped, and inadequately
staffed inner-city schools.

## CONCLUSION

The expanding economy of the South during the seventies heightened
status dilemmas and social inequities between blacks and whites.
Economic recessions in the eighties eroded many of the gains made in the
seventies.  A large segment of the Black South, many rural and central
city blacks, received few, if any, benefits from the rise of the New
South.  Social, economic and political progress passed over thousands of
black households.  Moreover, the favorable business climate that was so
often cited for the southern region's popularity in the 1970s often
translated into low wages, poverty, and powerless black workers.  To many
blacks, the New South was nothing but an extension of the Old South with
only minor modifications.

Resistance to black economic and political parity with the larger
society has not disappeared.  Black southerners still encounter obstacles
registering to vote and in actually voting.  Black voters still must face
at-large elections, distant polling places, gerrymandered districts,
annexations, acts and threats of intimidation, economic blackmail, and
similar practices designed to dilute their voting stength.  The issues
surrounding school desegregation have not all been resolved.  Black
workers continue to be denied jobs and promotions because of their race.
Discrimination has taken on a more sophisticated face which makes it easy
to practice but difficult to prove.

Living conditions for many black southerners were unaffected by the
boom of the seventies.  The eighties, on the other hand, saw the region's
black urban underclass expand along with other problems which often ac-
company fiscally strained cities.  Included in these problems were a
dwindling tax base, inadequate public services, loss of low-and-moderate

income housing stock, jobs shifting to the suburbs, strained employment markets, rising crime and drug trafficking, business closures and disinvestment in poor and minority neighborhoods, and a host of other problems. Until blacks, a group that makes up one-fourth of the region's population, share more fully in the resources of the South, there will not be a New South.

## NOTES

1.    U.S. Department of Housing and Urban Develoment, Report of the President's Commission for a National Agenda for the Eighties (Washington, D.C.: U.S. Government Printing Office, 1980), 165-69; John D. Kasarda, "The Implications of Contemporary Distribution Trends for National Urban Policy," Social Science Quarterly 61 (December 1980): 373-400.

2.    John D. Kasarda, Michael D. Irvin, and Holly L. Hughes, "The South Is Still Rising," American Demographics 8 (June 1986): 34.

3.    Robert D. Bullard, "Blacks in the New South: Problems and Prospects," paper presented at the Mid-South Sociological Association Meeting, Memphis (October 1987): 1.

4.    David C. Perry and Alfred J. Watkins, The Rise of the Sunbelt Cities (Beverly Hills, CA: Sage, 1977): 77.

5.    Chet Fuller, "I Hear Them Call It the New South," Black Enterprise 12 (November 1981): 41.

6.    Ibid., 41-44.

7.    William C. Matney and Dwight L. Johnson, America's Black Population: A Statistical View 1970-1982 (Washington, D.C.: U.S. Government Printing Office, 1983), 1.

8.    Ibid., 2; Isaac Robinson, "Blacks Move Back to the South," American Demographics 9 (June 1986) 40-43.

9.    Kasarda et al., "The South Is Still Rising," 32.

10.    Gurney Breckenfeld, "Refilling the Metropolitan Doughnut," in The Rise of the Sunbelt Cities, ed. David C. Perry and Alfred J. Watkins, (Beverly Hills, CA: Sage, 1977), 238.

11.    See Robert D. Bullard, Invisible Houston: The Black Experience in Boom and Bust (College Station, TX: Texas A&M University, 1987), Chapter 1.

12.    See Virginia Van der Veer Hamilton, Alabama: A Bicentennial History (New York: W.W. Norton, 1977), 139.

13.    William J. Wilson, The Truly Disadvantaged: The Inner City, The Underclass, and Public Policy (Chicago: University of Chicago Press, 1987), 180-81.

14.    John D. Kasarda, "Caught in the Web of Change," Society 21 (1983): 41-47; also William J. Wilson, "The Black Underclass," Wilson Quarterly (Spring 1984): 88-89.

15.    David Beers and Diana Hembree, "The New Atlanta:  A Tale of Two Cities," The Nation 244 (March 1987):  347, 357-60;  Margaret Edds, Free at Last:  What Really Happened When Civil Rights Came to Southern Politics (Bethesda:  Adler and Adler, 1987), 51-76.

16.    See Bradley R. Rice.  "Atlanta:  If Dixie Were Atlanta,"  in Richard M. Bernard and Bradley R. Rice, eds. Sunbelt Cities:  Politics and Growth Since World War II (Austin:  University of Texas Press, 1984), 31-57; Art Harris, "Too Busy to Hate," Esquire 103 (June 1985):  129-33; Charles Jaret, "Black Migration and Socioeconomic Inequality in Atlanta and the Urban South," Humboldt Journal of Social Relations  14 (Summer 1987):  62-105; Nathan McCall, "Atlanta:  City of the Next Generation," Black Enterprise 17 (May 1987):  56-58.

17.    U.S. Bureau of the Census,  1982 Survey of Minority Owned Business Enterprises (Washington, D.C.:  U.S. Government Printing Office, 1982), 16.

18.    Black Enterprise, "Top 100 Black Businesses," Black Enterprise 16 (June 1986):  105-113.

19.    Joint Center for Political Studies, Black Elected Officials:  A National Roster (New York:  UNIPUB, 1984), 61.

20.    Michael Preston, Lenneal J. Henderson, and Paul Puryear, eds., The New Black Politics:  The Search for Political Power  (New York: Lingman, 1987), vii.

21.    Joint Center for Political Studies, Black Elected Officials, 349.

22.    See Chandler Davidson, ed. Minority Vote Dilution (Washington, D.C.:  Howard University Press, 1984).

# 6 Improving the Plight of Black, Inner-City Youths: Whose Responsibility?

*Ronald L. Taylor*

Despite genuine improvements in the general socioeconomic status of Black Americans over the past two decades, conditions among the nation's black youths have deteriorated. Indeed, compared to the mid-1960s, more black youths today are unemployed, living in poverty, undereducated, involved in crime and drug abuse, and are having babies out of wedlock. These problems are particularly severe among inner-city youths, where an estimated eighty-one percent are living in poverty, four out of ten are unemployed, nearly a third drop out of high school, more than a quarter are involved in crime and delinquent activities, and where the percentage of unwed births to black teens has approached unity.(1) As a result, an increasing number of inner-city youths are joining the ranks of the so-called black "underclass," i.e., that entrapped population of poor persons in urban areas who are largely isolated from the mainstream of American life.

These data are now all too familiar and present a grim and disturbing portrait of the plight of black youths in contemporary American society. The important questions are _why_, during a period of unprecedented black progress, have the problems of black youths grown worse and become so widespread, and _what_, if anything, is to be done, and by _whom_. The literature in this area has far more to say on the first of these questions than on the others.

## TWO EXPLANATIONS

Some observers identify the locus of black youth problems in perverse demographic trends, deteriorating local economies, and the functional transformation in urban structures during the past two decades which have converged to exacerbate the problems of inner cities and predicament of black youths. In fact, the number and percentage of black youths in central cities across the country increased dramatically during the past two decades. Black youths, ages 16-19, increased by 72 percent in central cities between 1960 and 1970, while young black adults, ages 20-24, increased by 66 percent during the same period. By 1980, 56 percent of blacks under 25 years of age resided in central cities, more than twice the percentage for whites in these age groups.(2) As William Wilson observes: "On the basis of these demographic changes alone, one would expect blacks...to account disproportionately for the increasing social problems of the central city."(3)

Concomitant with the sudden increase in the youth component of central city black populations has been the precipitous decline in the number of jobs available in primary and secondary labor markets resulting from industrial relocations from the urban core to other areas of the city and suburbs, together with shifts in economic activities from goods-producing to higher order service-providing industries.  These shifts, as Kasarda has shown, in combination with the continuing outflow of middle-income families and resources from the city to the suburbs, have contributed to a number of social and economic problems for inner-city residents,

> including a widening gap between urban job opportunity struc-
> tures and the skill levels of disadvantaged residents (with
> correspondingly high rates of structural unemployment), spa-
> tial isolation of low income minorities, and intractably high
> levels of urban poverty.  Accompanying these problems have
> been a plethora of social and institutional ills further ag-
> gravating the predicament of people and places in distress:
> rising crime, poor public schools, and the decay of once vi-
> brant residential and commercial subareas.(4)

While acknowledging the major contribution of structural changes to urban social problems, an alternative perspective emphasizes the spread of self-destructive values and behaviors among inner-city residents as both cause and effect of the multiple problems besetting black youths. Commenting upon the current crisis within the inner cities, and echoing a theme advanced more than two decades ago by Kenneth Clark in his book, Dark Ghetto, Eleanor Holmes Norton, former chairman of the Equal Employ-ment Opportunity Commission, writes:  "At the heart of the crisis lies the self-perpetuating culture of the ghetto."(5)  In her view, the spread of this predatory subculture, characterized by crime, violence, drug addiction, illegitimacy, and welfare dependency, has grown powerful and "ruthless in its demands for conformity."  Mired in a malignant way of life, and without adequate education or marketable skills, a growing number of black youths seem unwilling or incapable of escaping the de-structiveness of inner-city life.  In his analysis of the roots of the urban black underclass, Nicholas Lemann reaches much the same conclusion, noting that the growth in influence of the ghetto subculture, made possible in large part by the rapid exodus of the black middle-class, and the continuing influx of rural southern blacks to the inner cities, now stand as the single greatest obstacle to further improvements in the condition of the black underclass.  Like Norton, Lemann believes that the best strategy for improving the plight of inner-city youths and the underclass is one which "attacks their culture as well as their economic problems."(6)

While structural explanations of inner-city social problems are generally favored by policymakers and liberal social scientists in their treatment of the topic, an emphasis on the subcultural values and norms of inner-city youths and adults as impediments to material improvements in their condition has gained ascendancy in recent years, as an increas-ing number of writers, both black and white, call for more attention to the attitudes and values of the black underclass in concert with the exercise of greater moral leadership in addressing their problems.  Thus Glenn Loury, the Harvard economist, has argued that the breakdown of values, norms, and moral behavior of a growing segment of inner-city blacks, part cause and part effect of economic deprivation, requires the sort of attention and moral leadership that only blacks are in a position to provide:

> When faced with the ravages of black crime against blacks,
> the depressing nature of social life in many low-income black
> communities, the alarming incidence of pregnancy and unwed
> black teenagers, or the growing dependency of blacks on
> transfer from an increasingly hostile polity, it is simply

insufficient to respond by saying "This is the fault of racist America. These problems will be solved when America finally does right by its black folk." Such a response dodges the issue of responsibility, both at the level of individual behavior (the criminal perpetrator being responsible for his act), and at the level of the group (the black community being responsible for the values embraced by its people).(7)

This view, it should be noted, is by no means limited to so-called neoconservatives but finds wide acceptance among writers of all political persuasion. Anthony Downs, for instance, is critical of big city minority communities for failing to exercise more effective leadership in solving the problems of the black underclass, contending that "elements of any solution must come from within minority communities themselves, just as happened with other ethnic groups in the past."(8) Likewise, a recent statement issued by thirty prominent black leaders and intellectuals on the array of social problems confronting the black community, acknowledges the crisis of norms, values, and behavior among impoverished segments of the community and the moral imperative this development imposes on black leadership when it observes that "the leadership of the black community must more forcefully articulate, reaffirm, and reinforce the black value heritage...," a legacy which has sustained the black community in difficult times but has been subjected to enormous and diverse social changes in recent decades. (9) Thus the black community, through its various religious, civic, and social organizations, is urged to "take the lead in defining the new and continuing problems it faces, in communicating the urgency of these problems, and in both prescribing and initiating solutions."(10)

## CONFUSING CATEGORIES AND IGNORING CONTRADICTIONS

It is indubitable that considerably more leadership and active involvement by members of the black middle-class are critical in prescribing and initiating solutions to the problems of black youth and the underclass. Yet it must also be recognized that sole reliance on black initiatives and leadership in solving these problems is fraught with a number of unrecognized and unresolved difficulties and is likely to meet with limited results unless such difficulties are adequately addressed.

If, as Loury and others maintain, the problems of inner-city youths consist mainly of a crisis in norms, values, and behavioral codes, then the immediate prospects for correcting such maladaptive subcultural patterns are bleak indeed, if only because there exists little consensus or knowledge as to how one proceeds to effect such changes. As Daniel P. Moynihan reminds us, "Social science is at its weakest, at its worst, when it offers theories of individual or collective behavior, which raises the possiblity...of bringing about mass behavioral change. No such knowledge now exists."(11) While youth counseling and associated services could be employed as remedial or short-term measures, it is difficult to see how advising black youths to adopt more constructive attitudes and values would substantially enhance their prospects for employment and quality education, or alter the array of social conditions which shape the larger context within which attitudes and values are formed.

In addition to these difficulties are other problems associated with programs or strategies designed to bring about changes in attitudes and behavior. One of the lessons of the 1960s, as Murray has noted, is that programs designed to facilitate change in attitudes and behavior are often forced to offer inducements or rewards that unavoidably add to the attraction of or reduce the penalties for engaging in the behavior or holding the values in question. "Theoretically," he writes, "any program that mounts an intervention with sufficient rewards to sustain participation and effective results, will generate so much of the unwanted behavior (in order to become eligible for the program's rewards) that the net effect will be to increase the incidence of the unwanted behavior."(12) The lesson is not that social programs designed to induce behavioral change do no good at all but that such efforts must be carefully conceived in order to bring about the desired results.

Perhaps the greatest difficulty the leadership of the black community faces in attempting to assume greater responsibility for improving the general conditions of the black underclass is bridging the physical and economic distance which now divides the community. The success of civil rights legislation in reducing the barriers to education, employment, and housing during the past two decades, contributed not only to greater socioeconomic diversity within black communities but also increased the level of socioeconomic segregation, as more and more middle- and working-class black families abandoned the inner cities for other communities within the metropolitan area and the suburbs. These developments, their implications for the structure and functioning of inner-city neighborhoods, and the capacity of black leadership to exercise its traditional influence and authority in this new context, have yet to be fully assessed, and are likely to impose major limitations on efforts to improve the plight of the black underclass as these processes continue unabated.

## THE BLACK MIDDLE CLASS AND THE PARADOX OF CHANGE

The impact of rapidly increasing structural integration of the black middle class on the institutional life of the inner city was forecast with remarkable prescience by St. Clair Drake more than twenty years ago in his analysis of the social and economic status of Black Americans. Drake took note of new forms of black victimization arising from the unintended consequences of social actions designed to eliminate caste victimization. He observed that the advent and rapid acceleration of residential desegregation, in concert with the integration and dispersal of the black elite, though advantageous to the latter, would in all likelihood be deleterious to the interests of the larger black community, contributing "to a new kind of victimization of the Negro masses which would be permanent unless the conditions of life for the lower classes were drastically changed."(13)   Drake, of course, was writing in the context of a black community structure fairly well integrated by social class and a network of civic, religious, and social organizations dominated by a black middle- and working-class element whose physical presence exerted a powerful influence on the quality of social life in black communities. But even as he wrote, the processes he identified were well underway and advancing at an accelerating pace.

Although historically a significant force in the social and political life of black communities, the black middle class has never represented more than a small fraction of the black population. In fact, as recently as 1950, fewer than 10 percent of black workers held middle-class jobs or had family incomes above the median for whites. The proportion of black workers in occupations usually identified with white collar status (including craftsmen and kindred workers), increased to just under 20 percent in 1960, and climbed to 32 percent by 1970.(14) While much of the increase in white collar jobs during the period 1950-1970 occurred among black clerical, sales, and kindred workers, significant gains were also made in the professional category.   For example, the number of black lawyers and judges increased by 180 percent during this period, while the number of physicians and surgeons rose by more than 50 percent.   In addition, the number of black engineers and architects increased tenfold during the same period, as did the number of natural scientists.(15)  In short, as a result of a complex of interrelated developments occurring over the previous two decades, including a general rise in demands for black labor (especially in the government sector), and the erosion of restrictive barriers to equal opportunity which resulted in increases in the level of human capital skills among black workers, the 1970s was the decade in which a significant proportion of the black population reached middle-class status.  Indeed, by the end of the decade, some 30 percent of black households had incomes at or above the median for white households.(16)

Beginning in the 1970s, with better jobs and higher incomes, a growing number of black families were poised to take advantage of new opportunities for better housing outside the neighborhoods of the inner city and increasingly in the suburbs.  This was made possible through the decline in housing discrimination and a falling white demand for housing in the "inner" suburbs of metropolitan areas.  Indeed, the increase in black suburbanization during the 1970s was dramatic, signaling a new and quantitatively significant trend.(17)  Over the decade, the black suburban population increased by nearly 40 percent, compared to a 10 percent rise for suburban whites, and a 4 percent increase for blacks in central cities.  As Robert Lake has shown, the increase in the black suburban population during the seven-year period 1970-1977 was considerably greater, in both absolute and relative terms, than black suburban increases registered for the entire decade of the 1960s.  In 1977, 4.6 million blacks, or 19 percent of the national black population, lived in the noncentral city suburban portions of metropolitan areas.  By the end of the decade, fully 25 percent of the black population in metropolitan areas resided in the suburbs.  While this was far below the corresponding white suburban percentage of 63 percent, blacks increased their share of the suburban population from 4.8 percent in 1970 to 6.1 percent in 1980.(18)

Like the upwardly mobile of other ethnic groups, middle-income blacks are leaving the central cities for the suburbs in record numbers in order to maximize the benefits associated with their new economic position and to secure a constellation of values.  For many, the once vibrant and familiar environment of the inner city has given way to fear and estrangement in the face of intractable social problems and the unmanageable consequences of living in close proximity to an underclass whose life-styles and values threaten their security and imperil their ability to maintain a middle-class milieu for themselves and their children.  They complain of the frightening rise in crime and public incivility, of widespread physical deterioration and inadequate services, of low-quality education and dangerous public schools, and the ordeal of maintaining discipline and control over their children.  The pervasiveness of these conditions has contributed to the value of suburbanization.

It was perhaps inevitable that the departure in large numbers of the more capable, affluent, and stable elements from the inner cities would serve to exacerbate the predicament of the black underlcass by depriving it of effective leadership and the network of social organizations which had for generations been the sources of black survival and progress.  Yet it is hard to see how these developments could have been avoided since spatial mobility has historically accompanied economic mobility in this country.

Nor is it clear why the black middle class should be expected to bear a special burden for the problems of the black underclass it did little to create.  Martin Katzman puts the matter succinctly:

To ask blacks who have a most tenuous hold on their status to sacrifice the well-being of their families for some dubious benefit for those left behind is to impose a higher standard

of morality upon the black middle class than upon their white
counterparts.  Middle class members of white ethnic groups
have never been seriously called upon to make a similar
sacrifice.(19)

While it may be supposed that members of the black middle class have a
proprietary interest in improving the general welfare of the black
underclass (if only because many of its members have relatives who still
reside in the neighborhoods of the inner city and are daily exposed to
its physical and psychological assaults), they currently possess neither
the power nor the resources sufficient to eradicate the worst of these
conditions which operate to produce and reproduce the urban underclass.
    It is easy to overestimate the power and resources of the black
middle class in the glow of its recent achievements.  Despite its greater
affluence and political empowerment, the black middle class is far from
the economic and political equal of its white counterpart.  The economic
fragility of this class is highlighted not only by the recency of its
origin but by the nature and sources of its wealth.  With few exceptions,
the current generation of middle-income black wage earners are first
generation claimants of middle-class status and, on average, have fewer
assets (and are more indebted) than whites of similar status.(20)    In a
recent assessment of the capital assets and other resources of the black
and white middle class, George Sternlieb observed that the "principal gap
between the black and white middle class may thus be the absence of
multi-generational asset formation passed down through inheritance and—
particularly in recent years—generated and enhanced through successful
home investment."(21)    Homeownership, he notes, has been the principal
source of capital accumulation—through home equity—for most White
Americans.   But given the recency of their arrival and patterns of
settlement, black suburbanites have yet to replicate the experience of
suburban whites.
    The largely segregated employment function of the black middle class
offers additional evidence of the economic fragility of this class.    A
major source of occupational mobility and income for blacks during the
past two decades has been government employment, particularly at the
federal level.    Freeman analyzed the employment data for the decade
1960-1970 and concluded that a much larger proportion of blacks than
whites became government employees during this period.   The proportion of
blacks in government service increased from 15 to 27 percent between 1960
and 1976, compared to a 13 to 16 percent rise for whites.(22)    In all,
more than half (55 percent) of the net employment gains for blacks since
1960 occurred in the public sector, compared to one-quarter for whites.
The majority of these jobs are concentrated in social services oriented
toward or disproportionately used by the black underclass, and heavily
dependent upon federal revenue for their continued existence.(23)    The
economic and political implications of this development are noted by
Brown and Erie in their analysis of social programs of the Great Society.
One of the principal economic legacies of such programs for the black
community, they argue, "has been the creation of a large-scale social
welfare economy of publicly funded middle class service providers, and
low-income service and cash transfer recipients,"(24) the effect of which
has been to "foster a form of welfare colonialism," whereby the black
middle class has functioned to legitimize and subsidize black underclass
dependency, and alter the "economic relationship between the black middle
class and the poor, by generating incentives to maintain the new class
relationship."(25)
    In sum, the social welfare economy created by the Great Society
transformed the economic and political relationship between middle-class
blacks and the underclass, and contributed not only to a relationship of
growing tension between those who dispensed and those who received

government services but to an increasing divergence in economic and political interests. Thus, what Kilson has termed the "community of race interests,"(26) presumably shared by all blacks by virtue of their common experiences, has been eroded under the weight of these recent developments. Viewed from the perspective of other ethnic groups whose members experience upward mobility, the divergence in interest of the haves and have-nots in the black community is perfectly normal, if not inevitable. Whether further deterioration in the community of race interests can be halted or reversed remains to be seen, but it is clear that deepening ghettoization and isolation of the black underclass represent major challenges to the leadership of the black community in its efforts to exercise greater moral and political influence.

## BLACK YOUTHS AND THE PATHOLOGIES OF POST-INDUSTRIAL SOCIETY

If the increasing structural integration and economic segregation of the black middle class impose new constraints on its ability to exercise moral leadership and influence among black youths and the underclass, the failure of social policy to reverse the growth and spread of the ghetto subculture and its accompanying problems, is a source of continuing confusion and controversy among scholars and policymakers. From one perspective, however, the crisis among black youths and the underclass may be seen as a result not of the failure but of the success of social policy, a phenomenological outcome aptly referred to by Moynihan as the "pathology of post-industrial society." As he puts it: "Because it is entirely possible that many of the processes that are producing prosperity are also producing much of our poverty, it may be that both sets of problems are in fact part of a single phenomenon: the pathology of post-industrial society."(27) Thus it may be argued that the same forces creating opportunities for upward mobility among some segments of the black community are condemning others to life in the underclass.

Such an argument has been most forcefully advanced by William Wilson who cites structural shifts in the economy (e.g., the shift from manufacturing to service industries) and social changes in black communities (e.g. the dramatic rise in female-headed households and the black youth population explosion in the central cities) as major causes of deteriorating conditions among black youths and the underclass.(28) In Wilson's view, "everything from growing unemployment to the growth of female-headed families can be traced to economic dislocations" in the inner cities.(29) He rejects the argument advanced by some that increasing rates of unemployment, school failures, out-of-wedlock births, and other problems among youths in the inner city can be traced to the spread of attitudes and values associated with the "culture of poverty," contending instead that cultural values are not determinants of behavior or success: "Rather, cultural values grow out of specific circumstances and life chances, and reflect one's position in the class structure."(30) Thus Wilson regards the subcultural patterns and norms of behavior of the black underclass as adaptive responses to restricted opportunities which are subject to change when new social and economic opportunities arise.

But if subcultural norms and behavior of the black underclass are largely adaptive responses to restricted life chances or opportunities, it must also be acknowledged that the manner in which some segments of the underclass adapt to their desperate situation may exacerbate the effects of adverse structural conditions to which their behavior and norms are a response. Indeed, it is a sociological commonplace to observe that micro-level forces often determine macro-level outcomes. No better illustration of this point can be found than that provided by Lee Rainwater twenty years ago in his poignant analysis of ghetto families and the process by which they sought to adapt to the realities of ghetto life. He observed that while the creation of subcultural patterns and

norms among these families enabled their members to cope with the problems of the ghetto world, such "strategies of survival" often diminished
their capacity to function in any other world.  Those who succumbed to
the more destructive aspects of this world, he noted, had "the greatest
difficulty responding to the few self-improvement resources that [made]
their way into the ghetto."(31)    In short, the underclass may be the
victims of their subcultural values and norms as well as the victims of
larger structural forces.

Indeed, for a large and growing number of inner-city youths, their
ability to adjust to recent transformations in the economy and in the
black community has been overwhelmed by the magnitude and intensity of
such changes.  Fed by a disappearing local economy and disintegrating
community institutions, by social isolation and spatial concentration, an
apparent subculture of disengagement from the wider society has surfaced
among some segments of inner-city youths, reflected in the dramatic rise
in teenage gangs and violent behavior, in drug use and abuse, in an
accelerating rate of out-of-wedlock births, and in the shunning of school
and work for less constructive (and often more criminal) pursuits.
Recent research reported by Freeman and Holzer indicates that neither
poverty nor unemployment alone are sufficient to explain these
developments, nor is continuing racial discrimination or segregation
adequate to explicate these trends, though all are important pieces of
the puzzle.(32)  Yet none is nearly as important as the aggregate changes
that have occurred in the black community and the wider society during
the past two decades.

The upward spiral of social alienation and self-destructive behavior
among inner-city youths is unlikely to be reversed in the face of an
apparent triage approach to urban social problems favored by some social
analysts, which tends to accentuate the very conditions it seeks to
alleviate.  Citing fiscal constraints and an inability to cope with the
intractable problems of the inner city, some city administrations have
proceeded to eliminate municipal social services and reduce expenditures
in poor inner-city neighborhoods in an effort to conserve resources for
the benefit of more viable communities.  Such actions have often served
to accelerate the cycle of economic disinvestment in and abandonment of
inner-city neighborhoods, contributing to the erosion of city tax bases,
and diminishing the capacity of institutions left behind to effectively
respond to the growing problems of inner-city youths.  Indeed, as Wilson
has observed, in many inner-city neighborhoods, the church is all that
remains of social organization to provide a minimum of social structure
for those trapped in these areas.(33)    In the absence of social
institutions which have traditionally functioned as feeder systems to the
larger society, black youths in growing numbers are being groomed for a
marginal existence in a tripartite economy of welfare, low wages, and
criminal activities.

To be sure, the human casualties produced by criminal involvement,
school failures, and pregnancies among unwed black youths in the inner
cities exact a considerable cost from the rest of society.  Though
surprisingly little systematic research is available on the subject, some
indication of the economic impact of soaring inner-city crime, welfare
dependency, and school failures on state and local budgets is suggested
by data reported for the city of Chicago and the State of Illinois.
According to the Chicago Tribune the city of Chicago spent more than
$40,000 a day in 1986 policing the high crime area of Northlawndale, a
largely black inner-city community on Chicago's West Side, and expended
an additional $247,000 a day on government assistance to residents in
this area, an amount four times the statewide per capita average.  Moreover, a 1985 study assessing the statewide economic impact of unwed
teenage pregnancies revealed that the cost of such pregnancies in
Illinois was $835 million a year, or an average of $200 per taxpayer

household.(34)    And,  in  the  city  of  Chicago, where nearly half of all
high school students drop out before graduation, and where the dropout
rate exceeds two-thirds in some low-income minority schools, the city's
Panel on Public School Finances studied the economic impact on the city
of high school dropouts and disclosed that of the 29,815 members of the
class of 1982 in the Chicago public high schools, 12,616, or 42 percent,
dropped out before graduation:

> The annual costs to society of these 12,616 dropouts alone
> were $7.3 million in lost taxes, $50.5 million in welfare
> payments and $1.6 million in crime costs....Over the course
> of their lifetimes, these dropouts would be expected to cost
> society nearly $2.7 billion in welfare payments, crime costs,
> and lost taxes, while earning $1.8 billion less than
> graduates.(35)

In addition to economic costs are the potential sociopolitical consequences to society resulting from the persistence of these problems.
Though increasingly skeptical of government's role and effectiveness in
solving social problems, both conservatives and liberals, now disenchant-
ed by the failure of social interventions to alleviate these problems,
acknowledge the potential threat to the health and stability of the
social system posed by the growth and isolation of a large underclass in
our cities.  Even so severe a critic of government intervention in urban
affairs as Edward Banfield could acknowledge that the existence of huge
enclaves of blacks and Hispanics in large cities constitutes a genuine
crisis in the body politic:

> Whatever may be the effect of this on the welfare of individ-
> uals—and it may possibly be trivial—it is clear that the
> existence of a large enclave of persons who perceive
> themselves and are perceived by others as having a separate
> identity, not sharing, or not sharing fully, the attachment
> that others 'feel for the city,' constitutes a potential
> hazard not only to present peace and order, but—what is more
> important—to the well being of the society over the
> long-run.(36)

Nearly twenty years later, the crisis to which Banfield referred per-
sists.  A crisis of more than a decade and a half must surely be considered a castastrophe.

## THE CARROT AND THE STICK

It has often been observed that how one thinks about a problem
affects one's resolve.  In the case of black youth and the underclass,
there is little consensus on what to do about their problems.  For some,
the choice is between public policies and programs which encourage more
self-reliance and independence among the poor through education, job
training, employment opportunities, and a "get tough" approach to
inner-city crime and welfare dependency which, while not addressing the
causes of these problems, serves to keep them in check.
Those who believe that government programs designed to eradicate
poverty and improve the conditions of the poor during the past two
decades have succeeded only in making matters worse for their would-be
beneficiaries, have found their voice in Charles Murray's Losing Ground:
American Social Policy, 1950-1980.  Murray contends that increases in
unemployment, crime, illegitimacy, and welfare dependency during the past
twenty years are a direct result of changes that social policy made in
the incentive structure (i.e., the rewards and penalties) that govern

human behavior. The effect of such policy changes was to reward failure and punish success: "Once it was assumed that the system is to blame when a person is chronically out of work and that the system is even to blame when a person neglects spouse and families, then moral distinctions were eroded."(37) Such a shift in social policy direction, he argues, was especially disastrous for black youths, whose values are more plastic than those of their elders, and who tend to respond more quickly to changes in the incentive structure. Under the new rules, black youths found it easier to drop out of school and participate in crime than to remain in school and prepare for work, easier to have babies without the benefit of marriage, and easier to avoid the consequences of their actions with the aid of public assistance. If such self-destructive behaviors are to be extinguished, Murray contends, then the current imbalance between rewards and penalties which inspired them must be redressed. "There is this truth," he writes:

> The tangible incentives that any society can realistically hold out to the poor youth of average abilities and average industriousness are mostly penalties, mostly disincentives: 'Do not study, we will throw you out; commit crimes, and we will put you in jail; do not work and we will make sure that your existence is so uncomfortable that any job will be preferable to it.' To promise much more is fraud.(38)

Perhaps. But black youths and the underclass are a diverse lot, only a small proportion of whom (by some estimates) may be incapable, given a combination of behavioral, attitudinal, and environmental factors, of responding to the more positive incentives encompassed by well-conceived social programs designed to increase their level of competence and self-sufficiency through training and legitimate employment opportunities. Indeed, as the results from the national experiments conducted by the Manpower Demonstration Research Corporation (MDRC) have shown, even among that segment of the underclass hardest to reach, viz., long-term welfare recipients, ex-convicts, school dropouts, and delinquent youths, the carrot of opportunity is apparently more productive of positive results than the stick of deprivation.(39)

But the MDRC experiments also reveal the structural and behavioral complexities of the problem which neither liberal nor conservative scholars adequately address. Based upon his first-hand experience with participants in the MDRC experiments, and assessing the successes and the failures of this project, Auletta concludes:

> Pushing aside the pieties, charts and stereotypes [of the poor], one sees that a segment of the poor are sometimes victims of their own bad attitudes, sometimes victims of social and economic forces. Neither the right's desire to blame individuals, nor the left's to blame the system, addresses the stubborn reality of the underclass. Somewhere between the stale shibboleths, the MDRC experience suggests, lies the truth.(40)

## BREAKING THE CYCLE

The problems of black youth and the underclass are immensely complex and are unlikely to yield to remedial solutions predicated on the assumption that such problems are the principal outcomes of dysfunctional values, behavioral disorders, or the consequences of structural forces. On the contrary, what seems indicated is a synergistic relationship between structural forces and subcultural norms, each reinforcing and exacerbating the effects of the other. Thus it is unlikely that a focus solely on correcting the maladaptive attitudes and behavior of black youths will effectively reduce the magnitude of their problems, or that the provision of training and jobs alone will materially alter the debilitating aspects of the ghettos. What is required is a judicious mix of both public and private interventions which, as Lemann and others have suggested, simultaneously attacks the maladaptive subcultural norms of the poor, as well as their socioeconomic problems.(41)   And given the complexity and intractability of these problems, solutions must be long-term ones, sustained over generations, not abandoned with changes in the national administration.

In devising new and more effective solutions to the problems of black youths and the underclass, the MDRC experiments conducted during the late 1970s and early 1980s, provide valuable lessons regarding what works and what does not for the diverse populations included in the nation's underclass.  For instance, the MDRC's Supported Work program, involving 10,000 participants, was clearly more beneficial to long-term welfare recipients anxious to work, than to ex-addicts burdened with a host of other problems, and only marginally beneficial to ex-offenders, accustomed to a life of criminal activities, and practically of no value to delinquent youths who dropped out of school.(42)  However, under its Youth Incentive Entitlement Pilot Project, which guaranteed jobs to youth between the ages of 16-19 in return for staying in or returning to school, the MDRC produced more encouraging results. Based on a sample of 80,000 youths across the country who participated in the project, the MDRC reported that its Entitlement program had a large effect on the level of youth unemployment: Nearly half of all eligible disadvantaged youths at its various demonstration sites were employed by the project, in contrast to an estimated twenty-five percent of the control group youths who would have been employed in the absence of the project. Despite its effectiveness in increasing participants' employment and earnings during the period of program participation, the Youth Entitle-ment program was less successful in increasing school completion or retention of disadvantaged youths.(43)  Nonetheless, in its final report, based on the evidence from its eighteen months' experience, the MDRC declared that, "Youth Entitlement is a strategy with promise."(44)

Given its strong research orientation, its targeted approach, the high quality and diversity in programs it developed, the MDRC's experi-ments were unique among antipoverty programs.   According to a recent report by the National Research Council, the Youth Incentive Entitlement Pilot Project, as well as most of the other programs established under the Youth Employment and Demonstration Projects Act of 1977, provided large numbers of disadvantaged youths with jobs that were more than "make work," and "demonstrated the capacity of the employment and training system to mount and run large-scale jobs programs for young people."(45) But like many of its predecessors, the MDRC experiments encountered serious difficulties in the production of more positive outcomes in the attitudes and behavior of many of its participants, whose expectation of failure, low self-esteem, and "exaggerated sense of vicitimization," diminished their efforts and undermined their progress toward self-sufficiency.  Such debilitating attitudes and insecurities were difficult to overcome in an environment which fed and sustained them, and in the context of an apparent public indifference grown callous in its disregard.

Despite their modest success in reducing unemployment and enhancing the human capital of black youths, the Youth Entitlement Project and other employment and training programs (e.g., Job Corps), offer important insights for further action, and belie the myth that "nothing works." Indeed, as Schorr's careful review of highly successful programs in health, family support, and education for children and youth makes clear, we now know a great deal more about what works and what does not, and how to break the cycle of disadvantage for youths at risk than we knew two decades ago. Although much of this knowledge remains segregated by academic, professional, and bureaucratic boundaries, there is a remarkable convergence in the literature on the nature of successful interventions. Programs and services for disadvantaged youths and their families (whether in education, employment, health care, or family support services) are far more effective than conventional programs in producing long-term positive outcomes when they are intensive, comprehensive, flexible, "and include aggressive outreach and attention to a broad range of need."(46) Moreover, such programs recognize and treat the problems of youths in the context of their social milieu rather than in a vacuum. As Schorr observes, to harness and disseminate the large body of knowledge now available on effective interventions for disadvantaged children and youth will require not only leadership at the national level but also a well-coordinated and supported multidisciplinary effort.

As critical as national leadership and resources may be in any solution to the problems of black youths and the underclass, there is no substitute for a diversity of state and local efforts to end the enormous waste of human potential which the inner-city ghettos now represent. The "Boston compact" is one example of what can be achieved when local business, governmental, and educational leaders join forces to create an education, training, and employment system that works for impoverished inner-city youths. Likewise, the work of David and Sister Falaka Fattah in reducing crime and violence among black youth gangs in Philadelphia, the success of Marva Collins in raising the level of academic performance of poor children in Chicago, and the decisive impact of Eugene Lang on the lives of black and Hispanic youths at one school in Harlem, are all valuable illustrations of the difference individuals can make in altering the prospects of inner-city youths mired in the crippling web of poverty, violence, and welfare dependency.

As to the role of the black middle class in addressing the problems of black youths and the underclass, its major responsibilities are succinctly set forth in the statement issued by the Committee on Policy for Racial Justice which exhorts the leadership of black communities to take the lead in devising solutions to these problems and includes the following directive:

> To assume a new command of its problems and facilitate more rapid advancement, the black community must strengthen its institutions, help them adjust to new circumstances and new challenges, increase its financial and participatory support, and encourage more purposeful communication and collaboration ....Organizations at all levels, particularly locally-based community organizations, need to address more vigorously the appropriate role and implementation of collaboration across class lines between blacks who enjoy some of the advantages of the society and those who do not.(47)

To be sure, these are formidable challenges but moral imperatives, certain to tax the ingenuity and resources of black communities.

More than two decades of experience with social programs should convince us that there are no inexpensive solutions to the problems of black youths and the underclass; no magic bullet that will produce a cure. No doubt optimists will insist that only more government spending and compassionate involvement will remedy these problems, while pessimists will assert that no amount of compassion or federal intervention will produce the desired results. One thing appears certain, however: should we fail in our effort to meet the challenge of inner-city social problems, the predicament of black youths will grow worse and threaten the capacity of a new generation to assume responsibility for its own fate.  Such an outcome, to cite the Chicago Tribune, would be "inconceiv-able for a nation this moral, [and] unbelievably stupid for a nation this smart."(48)  In truth, finding solutions to the problems of black youths and the underclass is a moral imperative for all of society, not just the black middle class, and is no less compelling for the improvidence, indolence, or other alleged deficits of the poor.

## NOTES

The  helpful  comments of Michael Gordon, Herbert Hunter and Earl Smith on an earlier draft are gratefully acknowledged.

1.    On youth poverty, see Bureau of the Census, Current Population Reports, "Characteristics  of  the  Population  below  the  Poverty  Level: 1982," Series P-60 (Washington, D.C.:  Government Printing Office, 1982); on unemployment, see Department of Labor, Employment and Training Report of  the  President  (Washington,  D.C.:    Government  Printing  Office,  1982), and Richard Freeman and Harry Holzer, eds., The Black Youth Employment Crisis  (Chicago:   University of Chicago Press, 1986); on school dropouts, see Bureau of the Census, Current Population Reports, "School Enrollment: Social and Economic Characteristics of Students,"  Series P-20 (Washing-ton, D.C.:  Government Printing Office, 1986); on youth crime and delin-quency, see Department of Justice, Uniform Crime Reports for the United States (Washington, D.C.:  Government Printing Office, 1986); on unwed teenage pregnancies, see National Center for Health Statistics, Vital Statistics of the U.S.  (various editions).

2.    U.S. Bureau of the Census, 1982.

3.    William J. Wilson, "Inner-City Dislocations," Society 21 (Nov/ Dec. 1983):  83.

4.    John D. Kasarda,"Caught in the Web of Change," Society 21 (Nov/ Dec. 1983):  41.

5.    Eleanor Holmes Norton,"Restoring the Traditional Black Family," New York Times Magazine,   June 2, 1985, 43.

6.    Nicholas Lemann, "The Origins of the Underclass," The Atlantic Monthly 257 (June/July 1986):  31-55.

7.    Glen C. Loury, "The Moral Quandary of the Black Community," Public Interest 79 (Spring 1985):  11.

8.    Anthony Downs, "The Future of Industrial Cities," in The New Urban Reality, ed. Paul Peterson (Washington, D.C.:  Brookings Institu-tion, 1985),  292.

9.    Committee on Policy for Racial Justice, Black Initiative and Government Responsibility (Washington, D.C.:  Joint Center for Political Studies, 1987), 5-6.

10.    Ibid., 10.

11.    Daniel P. Moynihan, Maximum Feasible Misunderstanding (New York:  Free Press, 1970):  198.

12.    Charles Murray, Losing Ground: American Social Policy 1951-1980 (New York:  Basic Books, 1984), 217.

13.    St. Clair Drake, "The Social and Economic Status of the Negro in the United States," Daedalus 94 (Fall 1965): 808-809.

14.    U.S. Bureau of the Census, "The Social and Economic Status of the Black Population in the United States," Current Population Reports, ser. P-23, no. 38 (Washington, D.C.: Government Printing Office, 1971).

15.    G. Franklin Edwards, "Occupational Trends and New Lifestyles," in Dilemmas of the New Black Middle Class, ed. Joseph R. Washington, Jr. (Philadelphia, PA:    University of Pennsylvania [Afro-American Studies Program], 1980),  15-25.

16.    Bart Landry, "The New Black Middle Class" (Berkeley, CA: University of California Press, 1987).

17.    Kathryn P. Nelson, Recent Suburbanization of Blacks:  How Much, Who, and Where (Washington, D.C.:  U.S. Department of Housing and Urban Development, 1979).

18.    Robert W. Lake, The New Suburbanites:  Race and Housing in the Suburbs (New Brunswick, NJ:  Rutgers University Press, 1981).

19.    Martin T. Katzman, "The Flight of Blacks From Central City Schools," Urban Education 18 (October 1983):  278.

20.    Landry, The New Black Middle Class.

21.    George Sternlieb, "Foreword," in Robert Lake, The New Suburbanites:  Race and Housing in the Suburbs (New Brunswick, NJ:  Rutgers University Press, 1981), xiii.

22.    Richard B. Freeman, The Black Elite: The New Market for Educated Black Americans (New York:  McGraw-Hill, 1976).

23.    Sharon M. Collins, "The Making of the Black Middle Class," Social Problems 30 (April 1983):  369-382.

24.    Michael Brown and Steven Erie, "Blacks and the Legacy of the Great Society:    The Economic and Political Impact of Federal Social Policy." Public Policy 29 (Summer 1981):  311.

25.    Ibid., 328.

26.    Martin Kilson, "The New Black Political Class," in Dilemmas of the New Black Middle Class, ed. Joseph R. Washington, Jr. (Philadelphia, PA:  University of Pennsylvania [Afro-American Studies Program], 1980), 81-100.

27.    Daniel P. Moynihan, "A Family Policy for the Nation," America 113 (September 1965):  280.

28.    William J. Wilson, The Truly Disadvantaged: The Inner City, the Underclass, and Public Policy (Chicago: University of Chicago Press, 1987).

29.    William J. Wilson, "Race-Oriented Programs and the Black Underclass," in Race, Poverty, and the Urban Underclass, ed. Clement Cottington (Lexington, MA:  Lexington Books, 1982), 127.

30.    Wilson, "Inner City Dislocations," 86.

31.    Lee Rainwater, "Crucible of Identity:    The Negro Lower-Class Family," Daedalus 95 (Winter 1966):    173.

32.    Richard Freeman and Harry J. Holzer, eds., The Black Youth Employment Crisis (Chicago:    University of Chicago Press, 1986).

33.    Wilson, "Inner City Dislocations."

34.    Chicago Tribune, The American Millstone:    An Examination of the Nation's Permanent Underclass (Chicago:    Contemporary Books, 1986).

35.    Ibid., 47.

36.    Edward Banfield, The Unheavenly City Revisited, (Boston, MA: Little Brown, 1968), 12.

37.    Murray, Losing Ground, 180.

38.    Ibid., 177.

39.    Manpower Demonstration Research Corporation, Findings on Youth Employment: Lessons from MDRC Research (New York:    Manpower Demonstration Research Corporation, 1983).

40.    Ken Auletta, The Underclass   (New York: Random House, 1982), 319.

41.    Lemann, "Origins."

42.    Robinson G. Hollister, Peter Kemper, and Rececca A. Maynard, eds., The National Supported Work Demonstration (Madison, Wis.:    University of Wisconsin Press, 1984).

43.    The National Research Council, Youth Employment and Training Programs:    The YEDPA Years (Washington, D.C. National Academy Press, 1985).

44.    Auletta, The Underclass, 238.

45.    National Research Council, Youth Employment.

46.    Lisbeth B. Schorr, Within Our Reach: Breaking the Cycle of Disadvantage (New York: Doubleday, 1988), 202.

47.    Committee on Policy for Racial Justice, Black Initiative, 9.

48.    Chicago Tribune, The American Millstone, 294.

# 7 Racial Attitudes of Black and White Adolescents Before and After Desegregation

*George E. Dickinson*

Studies on the effects of desegregation in public schools are inconclusive. Schofield and Sagar state that although numerous studies suggest
that school desegregation can have a positive impact on intergroup
attitudes and behavior a greater number reveal no effect or even a
negative effect.(1) Webster found that desegregation reduced prejudice
for blacks toward whites,(2) while Sheehan reports a "modest improvement"
in students' attitudes after desegregation in the Dallas school
system.(3)

Pettigrew noted that most research on the effects of school desegregation has been in schools not meeting Gordon Allport's criteria for promoting positive interracial attitudes and behavior: equal status within
the contact situation, shared goals, cooperative dependence in reaching
these goals, and the support of authorities, law, and custom.(4) There
is support for Allport's contention that mere desegregation (simply
mixing of students) does not necessarily result in more positive intergroup attitudes.(5)

Simpson and Yinger state that prejudice is sometimes explained as a
result of the lack of contact with members of a minority group and sometimes as a result of the presence of such contact.(6) Unpleasant
contacts probably increase the strength of prejudice, while certain kinds
of contacts are effective in reducing the strength of a tradition of
prejudice.

There is evidence that stereotype-breaking contacts reduce prejudice. Deutsch and Collins found that in integrated housing projects in
which blacks and whites were scattered indiscriminately, agreeable
relations between whites and blacks were much more common than in two
segregated projects.(7) Another survey by the United States War Department concluded that two months after desegregating soldiers in U.S. army
platoons in 1945 in Europe over seventy-five percent of white officers
and noncommissioned officers expressed more favorable feelings toward
blacks.(8)

With inconclusive evidence regarding the results of desegregation in
public schools, further research is needed. The present study involves
two follow-ups (after desegregation in 1970) of an earlier investigation
in 1964 of a racially segregated high school system in a Northeast Texas
community (population of 4000 in 1960 and 6000 in 1980) with a racial
composition of two-thirds white and one-third black.

Although desegregation occurred in 1970, racial segregation remains
throughout the community in churches, residential areas, government, and
jobs. While mixing of the races tends to be largely limited to school-
related activities, Dickinson reported in a 1974 follow-up of the 1964
study that changes for black adolescents' behavior over time are evident

and in the direction of whites' behavior.(9)   The changes reveal more homogeneous patterns for black and white adolescents after desegregation. It was suggested that through social participation the perspectives shared in a group are internalized.  Blacks tended to be using whites as their reference group.

Since black and white adolescents are in the same social milieu of the desegregated school, sit in the same classroom, eat in the same cafeteria, have lockers next to each other, play on the same athletic teams, participate in the same musical groups, serve on school committees together, and are members of the same voluntary organizations, it is assumed that interaction between racial groups will have increased over previous levels during segregation.   With more equal status contact situations between the races since desegregation in 1970, it is hypothesized that more favorable interracial attitudes will have evolved.

## METHODOLOGY

A questionnaire was administered during the school day by the author in all English classes of the tenth, eleventh, and twelfth grades in the segregated schools in 1964 and the desegregated school in 1979 and 1984. Fifty-six questions were asked in 1964; fewer were asked in the later surveys (only a portion of the questions related to the subject of this study).   The number participating in 1964 was 367 (260 whites and 107 blacks), 459 adolescents (296 whites and 163 blacks) responded in 1979, and 372 (263 whites and 109 blacks) completed questionnaires in 1984.

Students in all three studies constituted over eighty percent of the high school enrollment.   Less than one percent present on the days of questionnaire-administering refused to complete the survey.   Others were absent on these days.  No effort was made to follow up the absentees.

The Chi-square test of significance was used in data analysis.   A content analysis of open-minded responses of attitudes toward desegregation was made.

## FINDINGS

In the 1964 questionnaire students were asked "Would you object to attending school with a person of a different race?"   In 1979 and 1984 they were asked "Do you object to attending school with a person of a different race?"   Students were then instructed to explain their answers.

A statistically significant difference over time was found for white males' and white females' opinions on attending school with another race, as is shown in Table 1.   In 1964, prior to desegregation, over 75 percent of whites objected to attending school with a person of a different race. Nine years after desegregation in 1970, however, less than 15 percent of whites objected; in 1984 only 8 percent of whites objected.  No statistically significant difference was found over time for black males' and black females' opinion on attending school with another race, as they remained fairly consistent in their attitudes over the twenty-year period.   Less than 10 percent of blacks in 1964, 1979, and 1984 objected to attending school with a person of a different race.   Thus as interactions increased, more favorable attitudes by whites toward attending school with blacks have emerged.

Results of the open-ended question asking the students to explain their answers are shown in Table 2.

The most frequently cited objections by whites to attending school with the opposite race in 1964 were:  God separated us and meant for us to stay separated, each has good schools--should go to them, it will not work--too much difference, and violently opposed.  Reasons most cited by blacks favoring school attendance with one of a different race in 1964 were:   all are equal if they desire to learn and could become better

TABLE 1

Attitude Toward School Integration by Year, Race, and Sex

| | N | Object % | Not Object % | Chi Square | P |
|---|---|---|---|---|---|
| **White Males** | | | | | |
| 1964 | 138 | 77 | 23 | | |
| 1979 | 136 | 16 | 84 | 98.75 | .0000 |
| 1984 | 143 | 10 | 90 | 1.49 | NS |
| **White Females** | | | | | |
| 1964 | 109 | 76 | 24 | | |
| 1979 | 155 | 11 | 89 | 112.78 | .0000 |
| 1984 | 120 | 5 | 95 | 2.41 | NS |
| **Black Males** | | | | | |
| 1964 | 50 | 6 | 94 | | |
| 1979 | 65 | 12 | 88 | .673 | NS |
| 1984 | 50 | 6 | 94 | .673 | NS |
| **Black Females** | | | | | |
| 1964 | 55 | 7 | 93 | | |
| 1979 | 97 | 2 | 98 | 1.33 | NS |
| 1984 | 59 | 3 | 97 | .0001 | NS |

Note:   Question: Would you (1964) Do you (1979, 1984) object to attending school with a person of a different race?  In all cases df=1.

TABLE 2

Reasons for Objecting/Not Objecting to School Integration by Year and Sex

| Reasons for Objecting | | | | | | |
|---|---|---|---|---|---|---|
| | 1964 | | 1979 | | 1984 | |
| | Whites | Blacks | Whites | Blacks | Whites | Blacks |
| Prejudiced (1) | 107 | 0 | 16 | 0 | 6 | 0 |
| Produces Conflict | 0 | 0 | 19 | 0 | 2 | 0 |
| God's Will | 35 | 0 | 0 | 0 | 0 | 0 |
| Intermarriage | 8 | 0 | 0 | 0 | 0 | 0 |
| Reasons for Not Objecting | | | | | | |
| Equality (2) | 15 | 44 | 95 | 55 | 105 | 35 |
| Conditional (3) | 20 | 15 | 24 | 4 | 9 | 0 |
| Cooperation (4) | 6 | 13 | 23 | 15 | 13 | 2 |
| Why Not (5) | 3 | 0 | 29 | 15 | 26 | 13 |
| Educational (6) | 0 | 0 | 13 | 8 | 5 | 3 |

(1) Responses such as: I'm prejudiced; we're not too different; social-ly unfit; strongly opposed; good separate schools--use them.

(2) Responses such as: All are equal; equal rights to education; God made us the same; skin color is no judge.

(3) Responses such as: If all cooperate; if they don't act superior; if they don't cause trouble; if they stay to themselves; if they stay in their place, if they desire to learn.

(4) Responses such as: Should get along with all; good friends in other race; could become better friends; get along fine with other race.

(5) Responses such as: Doesn't matter to me; no choice; I'm not preju-diced; have been doing it all my life; have to learn to live with them sometime.

(6) Responses such as: Good to know other races and helps to adjust to society.

friends. Whites in 1964 cited all are equal and if they stay in their place as major reasons for not objecting to desegregation.

The few reasons stated in 1979 and 1984 by whites for being opposed to desegregation were: I'm very prejudiced and simply do not like the opposite race, too much difference produces a strain, and conflict results. Whites and blacks unopposed to attending school with one from a different race in 1979 and 1984 most often cited the following explanations: everyone is equal no matter the color, should have equal right to an education, good friends in opposite race, it is good to get to know different kinds of people, doesn't matter, God created us all, and we should cooperate with everyone.

## CONCLUSIONS

These findings run counter to many desegregation studies cited earlier. White attitudes toward attending school with blacks in this community have definitely improved over time. Fourteen years after de-segregation, over ninety-two percent of these white and black adolescents do not object to attending school with another race. In explaining their feelings, they stress equality of the races, equal opportunity, becoming better friends, cooperation, why not?, and the importance of hetero-geneous relationships. The few who are opposed admit being prejudiced and feel the differences are too great, resulting in stress and conflict. In 1964 the "deemed by God" explanation supported segregation, while in 1979 and 1984, it tended to support desegregation. One student in 1984 noted, "If parents wouldn't teach their kids to be against one another, everyone would get along fine." Kowalski suggests that the success of desegregation may depend on the effort taken to educate both the parent and the student about the relatedness of desegregation to the goals of the school system.(10) For those few students still objecting to deseg-regation, parental influence may play a vital role.

As was true of students, the majority (seventy-nine percent) of teachers and administrators in this school system like being in a desegregated system.(11) Color of skin was not as important to many teachers as was the opportunity to teach in a "more realistic environment."

In explaining the relatively smooth desegregation process in this school system, one administrator cited the rural location. Since busing of students had occurred for years in this rural setting, most students were accustomed to being bused. With desegregation, it simply meant more of the same--possibly going to a different location. Being a small com-munity, differences in school locations would not vary significantly. The fairly large size of the minority group (33 percent) possibly contributes to a more equal status racial situtation. Coleman notes that both whites and blacks improve most where schools are 51-75 percent white.(12)

Another administrator in this school district noted that racially integrated activities outside of school contributed to a positive environment within the school. He cited such activities as little league baseball, sandlot basketball, softball for girls, and scouting as examples of organized and unorganized programs outside of school. A good relationship outside of school should carry over into the school milieu. Yet another administrator commented that band activities seemed to be a positive force in helping desegregation work.

The author observed in 1979 and 1984 a voluntary random seating of students in the classrooms. This integrated seating arrangement was typical throughout the school system. A random arrangement of students should contribute to a positive outcome in such an integrated setting.

When this school system desegregated in 1970, the whole system from elementary through high school was involved. Rather than piecemeal desegregation (for example, a partial 9-12 or K-6), a comprehensive plan such as this might be more conducive to a successful mixing of racial groups.

During early integration efforts, workshops were held for teachers to prepare them for the upcoming merger. These sessions may have made an impact that contributed to good relations between the racial groups.

In explaining how school desegregation might work, Miller presents a "cognitive sophistication interpretation" as suggested by Glock.(13) This view emphasizes the role of cognitive complexity, sophistication, and cynicism in curtailing the development of prejudice and builds upon stereotypes which emphasize their substantial basis in truth.  In addition to representing an explanantion of group difference by way of completion of self-fulfilling prophecies, prejudice more fundamentally rests on the perception that true group differences do exist.  Miller says that cognitive sophistication promotes immunity to prejudice by enabling one to deal more effectively with the truth component of stereo-types.  It allows one to discriminate between relative versus absolute differences, to reduce these overgeneralizations, and by increasing one's understanding of how differences arise to resist prejudicial responses to them.

Maybe Miller's explanation applies in this school system after four-teen years of contact between the races.  The stereotypes of blacks expressed by whites in 1964 as being too different and socially unfit subsided in 1979 and 1984, and were replaced with more favorable descrip-tions of blacks.  Allport's equal status within the contact situation, shared goals, and cooperative dependence in reaching their goals may be operating here toward improved racial attitudes.

The findings of Deutsch and Collins in integrated housing units and the soldier study in 1945 which concluded that stereotype-breaking contacts reduce prejudice seem to be supported by these data.  Stephan and Rosenfeld suggest if desegregation has positive effects, it is prob-ably that "more than a year or two" is required for them to evolve.(14) More than a "year or two" has passed—more than "mere desegregation" seems to be occurring in this high school.

## NOTES

1.  Janet W. Schofield and H. Andrew Sagar, "Peer Interaction Patterns in an Integrated Middle School," Sociometry 40 (June 1977): 130-138.  See Martha W. Carithers, "School Desegregation and Racial Cleavage, 1954-1970:  A Review of the Literature," Journal of Social Issues 26, no. 4 (Autumn 1970):  25-47; Nancy St. John, School Desegregation Outcomes for Children (New York:  John Wiley, 1975); Elizabeth G. Cohen, "The Effects of Desegregation on Race Relations," Law and Contemporary Problems 39 (Spring 1975):  271-299; David Gottleib and Warren D. TenHouten, "Racial Composition and the Social Systems of Three High Schools," Journal of Marriage and the Family 27 (May 1965): 204-212;  D.J. Amor, "The Evidence on Busing," The Public Interest 28 (Summer 1972):  90-126; John A. Green and Harold B. Gerald, "School Desegregation and Ethnic Attitudes," in Integrating the Organization, ed. H. Franklin and John J. Sherwood (New York:  Free Press, 1974); E. L. Horowitz, "Development of Attitudes Toward Negroes," in Readings in Social Psychology, ed. Theodore M. Newcomb and Eugene L. Hartley (New York:  Holt, 1952); Irwin Silverman and Marvin E. Shaw  "The Effects of Sudden Mass School Desegregation on Interracial Interaction and Attitudes on One Southern City," Journal of Social Issues 29, no. 4 (1973):  133-142; John E. Williams, Deborah L. Best, and D. A. Boswell in  "The Measurement of Children's Racial Attitudes in the Early School Years," Child Development 46 (June 1975): 494-500.

2.   Staten W. Webster, "The Influence of Interracial Contact on Social Acceptance in a Newly Integrated School," Journal of Educational Psychology 52 (December 1961):   242-296.

3.   Daniel S. Sheehan, "A Study of Attitude Change in Desegregated Intermediate Schools," Sociology of Education (January 1980):   51-59.

4. Thomas F. Pettigrew, "Social Evolution Theory:   Convergences and Applications," Nebraska Symposium on Motivating Vol. 15, ed. Daniel Levine (Lincoln, Nebraska:   University of Nebraska Press, 1967); and Thomas F. Pettigrew, Marshall Smith, Elizabeth Useem, and Clarence Normand, "Busing:   A Review of the Evidence," Public Interest 30 (Winter 1973):   88-118.   See also Gordon W. Allport, The Nature of Prejudice (Cambridge:   Addison-Wesley, 1954).

5. Yehuda Amir, "Contact Hypothesis in Ethnic Relations," Psychological Bulletin 71 (May 1969):   319-342.

6. George E. Simpson, and J. Milton Yinger, Racial and Cultural Minorities, 3rd Edition (New York:   Harper and Row, 1965).

7. Morton Deutsch and Mary E. Collins, Interracial Housing:   A Psychological Evaluation of Social Environment (Minneapolis:   University of Minnesota Press, 1951).

8. United States War Department, Information and Education Division, "Opinions About Negro Infantry Platoons in White Companies of Seven Divisions," in Readings in Social Psychology, ed. Theodore M. Newcomb and Eugene L. Hartley (New York:   Holt, Rinehart, and Winston, 1947).

9. George E. Dickinson, "Dating Behavior of Black and White Adolescents Before and After Desegregation," Journal of Marriage and the Family 37 (August 1975):   602-608.

10. Bruce W. Kowalski, "Voluntary Desegregation:   Objective Accomplishments and Racial Group Perceptions," Journal of Negro Education 50 (Spring 1981):   134-155.

11.   George E. Dickinson and Kent Freeland, "Student, Teacher, and Administrator Attitudes Toward School Desegregation 1964-1981," Integrateducation 19 (May/Dec. 1982):   40-43.

12.   James J. Coleman, et al., Equality of Educational Opportunity (Washington, D.C.:   U.S. Government Printing Office, 1966).

13.   Charles Y. Glock, Robert Wuthnow, Jane A. Pilliavin, and Metta Spencer, Adolescent Prejudice (New York: Harper and Row, 1975) and Norman Miller, "Making School Desegregation Work," in School Desegregation: Past, Present, and Future, ed. Walter G. Stephen and Joe. R. Feagin (New York:   Plenum Press, 1980).

14.   Walter G. Stephan and David Rosenfield, "Effects of Desegregation on Race Relations and Self-Esteem," Journal of Educational Psychology 70 (October 1978):   670-679.

# 8 The Ills of Integration: A Black Perspective

*Gerald Anthony Foster*

## INTRODUCTION

More than twenty-five years after the historic March on Washington there is little disagreement regarding the widespread progress blacks have made in this country in terms of narrowing the gap between themselves and their white counterparts in social, economic, and political arenas. Yet we hasten to make two points: (1) a clear distinction must be made between progress and parity; there has in fact been much forward movement that suggests an improvement of a previous condition; however, if we speak of parity between blacks and whites which is more akin to the civil rights goal of equality of resources and results, then one is compelled to be far less optimistic; (2) one of the most important questions that must be asked by black people of black people is "at what price has this progress been achieved?"

When the landmark 1954 Brown Supreme Court decision was handed down, it indeed ushered in a new era of race relations in America. Many people, black and white, at that time naively thought that widespread social and systemic change would occur because of the revolutionary nature of the decision rendered by the pinnacle of American jurisprudence, the U.S. Supreme Court.

The position advanced in this essay is that the cost of desegregation and integration was much too high in that it has drained the black community's vitality that historically sustained its black families in the worst of times. Central to that vitality was a sense of black pride and black patronage, both of which seem absent today. In the great push for integration and assimilation blacks have all but lost that which was so important to the race for hundreds of years, a positive sense of self in relationship to the external environment.

Instead of strengthening the black community, racial desegregation and integration have caused blacks to venture into a hostile white world that from the outset had no intention of truly pursuing and supporting racial integration.

Therefore instead of becoming a means of achieving more equal treatment in education, employment, housing, and the like, integration has tended to build false hopes of open acceptance of blacks by whites when in reality the racism that existed in 1954 still exists in large part today, and blacks as a people are less prepared to cope with it because the community and intraracial supports that existed 25-30 years ago do not exist today. Integration in large part has proven to be the bane of black life in America today.

## HISTORICAL OVERVIEW

The original intent of the Brown Supreme Court decision and civil rights challenges prior to Brown were primarily predicated on a call for equal education resources and facilities for blacks on a par with those provided to whites. Anthony Lewis writes:

> In 1950, the NAACP won important victories in the Sweatt and McLaurin cases on the grounds that Negro educational facilities were inferior to those offered whites, and, therefore, violated the 'separate but equal' yardstick. Southern states sensed the changing judicial temper, and in the early fifties, they began a massive effort to physically upgrade the Negro school systems. It was their hope that if Negro schools were substantially improved, school integration would be thwarted. It was at this point that the NAACP made a crucial tactical decision. It would gamble on a new approach, arguing that racial segregation, without regard to equality of facilities, damaged Negro children.(1)

This so-called damage that was being visited upon black children was identified as psychological and therefore supposedly engendered feelings of inferiority. It is important to note that there is no question that the marked disparity in fiscal resources allotted for blacks and whites in the decades preceding the Brown decision were deplorable. For example, in 1915 South Carolina spent an average of $23.76 on the education of a white child and a mere $2.91 for a black child. Similarly, in 1931 southern states such as Alabama, Georgia, North and South Carolina spent less than one-third as much per black public school student as they did on a white public school student.(2) This gross inequity also existed in monies expended for other public services such as hospitals and public works. A favorite plan of southern states to avoid racial desegregation was the establishment of what the white power structure identified as "comparable" facilities. For example, in 1950 the U.S. Supreme Court ruled that a hastily conceived "law school" for blacks did not constitute separate but equal law school facilities by any stretch of the imagination. Chief Justice Fred M. Vinson identified clear and measurable inequalities in areas such as reputation of faculty and quality and experience of administration and alumni influence as being but a few of the criteria that negated any vestige of equality.

In hindsight, had the court cases dealt exclusively with issues of equality of faciliIties and resources rather than calling for an artificial mixing of the races, perhaps different and better results would have been realized for the black community.

There is no attempt here to detract from the benefits blacks have received as a result of the Brown decision. However, Brown needs to be seen for what it is rather than a treatise on how to achieve black educational excellence.

Jennifer Hochschild states that two former general counsels for the NAACP, Nathaniel Jones and Thomas Adkins put the Brown decision in better perspective when they asserted that:

> Brown is not a case dealing with education, but rather a case dealing with race in which the setting happened to be schools ....Thus, U.S. District Court Judge Robert Carter, an attorney in Brown and former NAACP general counsel, argues that, in 1954, Plaintiffs and Supreme Court alike agreed that 'equal education and integrated education...were synonymous'; but that view may have been mistaken. Desegregation does not in many cases eliminate racism, poor education, and white

dominance, which are the real evils of segregated schooling. Perhaps equal education, regardless of the racial composition of classrooms, will render better results. Judge Carter is not sure, but he warns against 'allowing ourselves to become the prisoners of dogma' and insisting on desegregation regardless of its consequences.(3)

## WHAT IS INTEGRATION?

How ironic it is that two of the leading social science supporters of Kenneth Clark's Supreme Court social science brief had at that time or shortly thereafter developed some rather rigid but accurate behavioral and attitudinal guidelines for true integration to occur. Talcott Parsons' Theory of Racial Assimilation and Gordon Allport's Theory of Social Contact are widely known in the field as appropriate prescriptions for racial integration through rejection of prejudice. However, nowhere in the literature being advanced at that time (early 1950s) do we hear of these rather precise guidelines being presented as necessary prerequisites for integration. Consequently, the conventional wisdom then was largely predicated on integration being achieved artificially through legally imposed mandates. This approach is directly antithetical to the theories of Parsons and Allport.

In commenting on Parsons' assimilation theory, Herman George, Jr., states:

> Talcott Parsons maintains that 'the process of inclusion' is similar to the supply and demand process of economics. The inclusion (this is Parsons' word for assimilation) process acts hierarchically and temporally through three levels: the civil or legal as lowest; the political as intermediate; and the social as highest. The speed of the ethnic group in gaining each level is determined by the demands of inclusion, both from within and outside of the group, and by the supply of positions. Moreover, 'Assimilation, so conceived, is fundamentally dependent on the command of resources, financial, political, and social. And, it is not accidental that those who occupy the commanding heights of the American resources structure are most concerned to define assimilation in their own interests. These interests most often coincide with the social philosophy which enshrines gradualism and an ethical viewpoint based on liberal individualism.'(4)

Similarly, Allport states:

> Prejudice (unless deeply rooted in the character structure of the individual) may be reduced by equal status contact between majority and minority groups in the pursuit of common goals. The effect is greatly enhanced if this contact is sanctioned by institutional supports (i.e., by law, custom or local atmosphere), and if it is of a sort that leads to the perception of common interests and common humanity between members of the two groups.(5)

Accordingly, in this paper integration is defined as harmoniously evolved bi-racial situations predicated on mutual respect and mutual acceptance, a manifestation of which is expressed behaviorally and attitudinally.

Though integration and desegregation are often erroneously used interchangeably it is important to note critical distinctions between the terms.

Desegregation in its simplest form is the removal of legal restrictions on bi-racial mixing that results in two races being able to utilize common resources.  In other words, desegregation is the absence of legally imposed segregation.

Another classical social science theory that seemingly is ignored in this thirty year desegregation-integration struggle is Franklin Giddens' "Consciousness of Kind" which advances the notion that, sociologically, people are most comfortable with those who are most like themselves.

This is of particular importance when looking at how re-segregation though not legally imposed, often occurs within legally desegregated schools.

Absent the racial element, more often than not in social situations people tend to interact with others who share some commonality, be it a profession, a school, a geographic locale, ethnicity or gender. Similarly if one observes school children in relatively unrestricted spontaneous activities, i.e., lunch time and recreation, you will most often find them mixing with those most like themselves.

The point being advanced here is that laws and Supreme Court decisions,  be they ever so momentous, will not automatically change people's attitudes that have been held for many generations.

Moreover, the question must be asked why many of Clark's learned and respected social science colleagues did not take a stronger prescriptive stance in terms of how and under what conditions true integration could be achieved.  At this point one can only speculate that Clark was satisfied to simply make the distinction between the legal and the social issues associated with the abolition of segregation without too much thought being given to what to do once it was rendered unconstitutional. Thirty years later Clark appears to have come to somewhat the same conclusion in terms of how slow the process of integration has been.  In a 1985 newspaper interview conducted by Walter Goodman of the New York Times News Service, Goodman reports:

> He (Clark) recalled the words of Thurgood Marshall, who represented the civil rights forces in the Brown case before he was named a justice of the Supreme Court:  'Kenneth, there is only so much lawyers can do.  After we get the law clear, the hard job begins.'(6)

## THE INTENT AND THE REALITY OF BROWN

Dr. Kenneth Clark has been a leading proponent of racial integration for over forty years and is the architect of the social science brief filed in conjunction with the 1954 Brown case material.  He recently reported to the 1987 conference of the American Psychological Association that forty years after his original research (commonly referred to as the "Dolls Study") low self-esteem still lingers in black youths.

The same study undertaken in the 1940s by Dr. Clark was conducted again in 1986 in the United States and Trinidad.  The New York Times reported hat:

> The findings duplicate those from a series of studies performed by the Clark studies in the 1940s, which used the identical procedure, and found that about two-thirds of black children preferred white dolls. The Clark studies were highly influential; in 1954 the Supreme Court, in its school desegregation decision, cited the studies as evidence that segregation was harmful to blacks.(7)

In all probability Clark as well as the other thirty-two social scientists who endorsed the document entitled, The Effects of Segregation

and the Consequences of Desegregation: A Social Science Statement, truly
believed that a real psychological benefit would be derived from the
Supreme Court calling for the dissolution of the 'separate but equal'
doctrine.  Certainly the majority of blacks in 1954 could only be
heartened by the words of Chief Justice Earl Warren when he suggested
that not only was it legally wrong to continue segregation of the races
but it was morally wrong because of the injury it inflicted on the hearts
and minds of black children.

Thus, the intent of Brown was clearly to go beyond simply rendering
segregation unconstitutional.  It appears that a social science position
was included in this particular Supreme Court decision as it chose to
confront over 300 years of entrenched racism because it was assumed that
this case alone would mark the beginning of full equality for blacks.
Most blacks and some liberal-minded whites wanted to believe that Brown
could in fact achieve this idealistic goal.  Perhaps the late black
author Louis Lomax best summed up the prevailing attitudes in the black
and white communities in 1954 when he quoted black Congressman Adam
Clayton Powell:

This is a great day for the Negro.  This is democracy's
finest hour.(8)

On the other side, Mississippi's white Senator James Eastland said:

The people of the South will never accept this monstrous
decision.  I predict this decision will bring a century of
litigation.(9)

In many ways there were vestiges of truth in each gentleman's statement.
The Brown decision is truly one of the most significant Supreme Court
civil rights decisions in this century.  Yet the expectations of the
decision have clearly exceeded the positive outcomes in terms of
widespread equality and justice of Black Americans.

For example, the 1954 Brown decision had been pending on remand for
thirty-three years.  On April 9, 1987, the original case for all intents
and purposes ended when U.S. District Court Judge Richard D. Rogers
handed down a lengthy opinion indicating that the court could find no
evidence of intentionally contrived segregation or segregationist
policies in the Topeka, Kansas, public schools.

Similarly, in December 1986, U.S. District Judge R. Allan Edgar
dismissed a twenty-six year-old school desegregation suit in Chattanooga,
Tennessee, stating that the court could find no evidence of unlawful
segregation in the public schools of Chattanooga, Tennessee.

Perhaps the greatest flaw in Brown was the assumption that the
American social order could be drastically altered by identifying the
public schools as its primary battleground.  Former Department of Health,
Education, and Welfare Secretary Elliot L. Richardson in testimony before
the Senate Education Sub-Committee on March 24, 1972, presented a comment
made by former President Richard M. Nixon that aptly captures this
notion.  He stated:

One of the mistakes of past policy has been to demand too
much of our schools:  they have been expected not only to
educate, but also to accomplish a social transformation.
Children, in many instances, have not been served, but used--
in what all too often has proven a tragically futile effort
to achieve in the schools the kind of multiracial society
which the adult community has failed to achieve for itself.
If we are to be realists, we must recognize that in a free
society there are limits to the amount of government coercion

that can be reasonably used: that in achieving desegregation, we must proceed with the least possible disruption to the education of the nation's children and recognize that our children are highly sensitive to conflict and highly vulnerable to lasting psychic injury.(10)

Thus, the reality of Brown reveals a society that thirty years later still confronts issues of racial inequality and racism; a society black and white that on the one hand fully acknowledges the landmark Brown decision, yet on the other hand also knows that integration in many ways, in the words of civil rights activist James Meredith, has proven to be the "nemesis of Black Americans."

The reality of Brown is ably presented in an analysis prepared by Jennifer Hochschild.  The essence of the current and future problems associated with integration is captured in the following statistics:

Across the United States the proportion of blacks in predominantly minority (more than 50 percent) schools dropped from 77 percent in 1968 to 63 percent in 1980.  The proportion of blacks in racially isolated schools (90-100 percent minority) declined from two-thirds in 1968 to one-third in 1980.

On the other hand:

Almost one-half of all northern black students now attend all-minority schools compared to one-quarter of southern blacks.

Looking further at the Hochschild data we find some rather revealing facts under the heading of "Resegregation within Desegregated Schools."

Black students in the South are being placed in classes for the educable mentally retarded at a rate 300 to 500 percent higher than their white counterparts.  About half of all black students are in low-achievement reading groups compared to one-fifth of whites.  Post-desegregation segregation also occurs through disproportionate suspension, punishment and expulsion of black students.  In 1973 between 35 percent and 85 percent of southern school districts (depending on the state) punished blacks more than twice as often as whites.(11)

These findings, though reflective of conditions ten years ago, remain consistent today.  A study conducted in 1985 by Gerald Foster and Maurice Taylor reveals that in a fairly representative southeastern urban school district where blacks comprise forty-four percent of the total student body, they represented sixty-five percent of those suspended during the 1983-84 academic years.(12)

M. Marable in his article "The Paradox of Desegregation" states:

Perhaps the greatest challenge facing the black community today is the 'Paradox of Desegregation.'  Neither Martin Luther King, Jr., nor his contemporaries inside the civil rights leadership a generation ago anticipated the political and social problems which would be generated by the very successes of their social movement for equality.(13)

Marable notes the sad demise of blacks supporting and patronizing blacks in black communities.  Prior to desegregation black professionals and black entrepreneurs had little choice but to open offices in the black community where blacks were clearly more inclined to patronize black professionals primarily because whites refused to serve them. Though in no way extolling the virtues of legal segregation, blacks have lost this sense of community under desegregated living patterns.

Perhaps the most devastating effect of attempts at integration is captured in a work written by Nancy Levi Arnez entitled The Struggle for Equality of Educational Opportunity. She states:

> An NEA Task Force III survey conducted in 75 school districts in Louisiana and Mississippi during January and February of 1970 revealed that disproportionately large numbers of black principals had been demoted to administrative assistants, assisting visiting teachers or classroom teachers. Others were discharged on trumped up charges or told they lacked sufficient knowledge of teaching, despite the fact that the majority of black principals had superior academic qualifications to their white counterparts.(14)

The positions created for blacks had little or no authority and essentially they were locked out of the school policymaking process. The same fate prevailed for black teachers in newly "integrated" school settings. Arnez concludes by saying:

> It should be obvious to any reader of the NEA report, School Desegregation: Louisiana and Mississippi, that public education in the South deteriorated, in many instances, to non-education for black students. Laws that were designed ostensibly to correct inequities were twisted to perpetuate racist behavior on the part of the controlling white interests. White resistance to desegregation had a particularly damaging effect on the black community. Blacks lost at least 31,000 teaching and administration jobs in the South, through dismissals, demotions, or displacement, and it is estimated that approximately $200 million was lost to black communities as a result.(15)

## BLACK POWER REVISITED

Today it is neither fashionable nor politically savvy to espouse the virtues of black power although a mere 15-20 years ago it was the watchword on the lips of most of the acclaimed and self-proclaimed black leaders. Far too many blacks embraced the rhetoric of the Civil Rights Movement without embracing the attendant responsibilities and risks. For the most part the call for institutional and systemic change has gone unheeded. Though blacks enjoyed unprecedented gains and progress individually, collectively blacks are still struggling with the same tentacles of racism and discrimination that Martin King and others forcefully attacked in the 1950s and 1960s.

A notion currently being advanced that is far from a minority opinion is that integration attempts on an overall basis have failed. It may be true that blacks now work, live, and recreate in places which heretofore have been closed to them; however, it is patently clear that these blacks do not significantly participate in the decision-making and policy-oriented deliberations that affect mainsteam America.

An admonition given by black educator Benjamin Mays some twenty years ago in a Centennial Commencement Address at Howard University rings true today. He states:

> Finally, let me warn you that we must not be swept off our feet by the glamour of a desegregated society. By all means,

> enjoy the swankiest hotels, eat in the finest restaurants,
> live on the boulevard, ride anywhere, worship anyplace, work
> anywhere, get high-paying jobs, send more men to Congress,
> get more judgeships—but remember that we can do all these
> things and not be a part of the policy-making bodies that
> shape education, industry, and government. We can do all
> these things and still be grossly discriminated against when
> there is no sign of segregation in sight. This kind of dis-
> crimination which we will meet in the interim between deseg-
> regation and integration will be subtle and will be adminis-
> tered not by the Maddoxes, the Wallaces, and the Barnetts,
> but by our liberal friends in Congress, in education, and in
> industry. If we aren't careful, we will live another century
> dangling between desegregation and integration, with all the
> discrimination inherent therein.(16)

In the same year (1967) that Dr. Mays delivered his prophetic address, a
black militant and a black scholar collaborated to write a book, Black
Power: The Politics of Liberation in America. Although it never enjoyed
the distinction of being on mainstream America's best seller lists, its
crisp analysis and recommendations hold as true today as they did two
decades ago.

Carmichael and Hamilton state:

> The adoption of the concept of Black Power is one of the most
> legitimate and healthy developments in American politics and
> race relations in our time. The concept of Black Power
> speaks to all the needs mentioned in this chapter. It is a
> call for black people in this country to unite, to recognize
> their heritage, to build a sense of community. It is a call
> for black people to begin to define their own goals, to lead
> their own organizations. It is a call to reject the racist
> institutions and values of this society. The concept of
> Black Power rests on a fundamental premise: Before a group
> can enter the open society, it must first close ranks.(17)

The painful lessons blacks learned in futile attempts at integration
demand a new mindset which clearly states that black children need not
attend predominantly white schools to learn; blacks need not live in
white communities to be comfortable and safe; and blacks need not patronize white entrepreneurs exclusively to receive quality products and
services. All blacks, but black children particularly, need to learn
that all of the so-called good things in life are not attained only in
the white community.

In the language of the 1954 Brown decision, constantly being told
that one can only attain the best that life has to offer outside of one's
home and community environment is injurious to the minds and hearts of
Black Americans.

## NOTES

1. Anthony Lewis, "The School Segregation Cases," in Black
History: A Reappraisal, ed. Melvin Drimmer (Garden City, NY: Anchor
Books, Doubleday, 1969), 423.

2. Ibid., 429.

3. Jennifer L. Hochschild, Thirty Years After Brown (Washington,
D.C.: Joint Center for Political Studies, 1985), 19, 20.

4.   Herman George, Jr., American Race Relations Theory:  A Review of Four Models (New York:  University Press of America, 1984),  2.

5.   Gordon Allport, The Nature of Prejudice   (Garden City, NY: Anchor Books, Doubleday, 1958), 267.

6.   Walter Goodman, "Civil Rights Progress Comes too Slow for Educator," Virginia Pilot and The Ledger-Star, January 6, 1985, 7.

7.   Daniel Goldman, "Data Shows Low Self Esteem Lingers in Black Youth," The New York Times,  August 31, 1987, 5.

8.   Louis Lomax, The Negro Revolt (New York:  Signet Books, 1963), 85.

9.   Ibid.

10.   Elliot L. Richardson, "Statement to the Senate Education Committee," in The Great School Bus Controversy, ed. Nicholaus Mills (New York:  Teachers College Press, 1970), 174.

11.   Hochschild, 5.

12.   Gerald A. Foster and Maurice C. Taylor, "Bad Boys and School Suspension:  Public Policy Implications for Black Males," Sociological Inquiry 56, no. 4, (1986):  498-506.

13.   Manning Marable, "The Paradox of Desegregation" in The Hampton Script,  October 7, 1986.

14.   Nancy L. Arnez, The Struggle for Equality of Educational Opportunity (New York:  The National Urban League, 1975), 19.

15.   Ibid., 20.

16.   Benjamin E. Mays, "Higher Education and the American Negro," in What Black Educators are Saying, ed. Nathan Wright (New York:   Hawthorne Books, 1970), 111.

17.   Stokely Carmichael and Charles V. Hamilton, Black Power:  The Politics of Liberation in America (New York:  Vintage Books, 1967), 44.

# 9 A Dream Deferred for Quality Education: Civil Rights Legislation and *De Facto* Segregation in the Cincinnati Schools, 1954-1986

*Michael H. Washington*

The failure of the civil rights legislation to adequately address de facto educational segregation in the North permitted northern urban school districts to continue operating their dual school systems. Beginning with a synopsis of the weaknesses of the civil rights legislation in the 1950s and 1960s, the purpose of this essay is to demonstrate that despite blacks' struggle for quality education, the educational policy makers in Cincinnati were able to take advantage of the weak federal legislation and refine de facto segregation in the schools.

The first week of December of 1955 marked the official beginning of the Civil Rights Movement. The December 1 arrest of Mrs. Rosa Parks for violating the Montgomery, Alabama, city segregation code after refusing to relinquish her bus seat to a white man, and the subsequent success of the boycott which began on December 5, led the Supreme Court to uphold the decision that Alabama's state and local bus segregation laws were unconstitutional. Moreover, the victory in Montgomery led to numerous struggles throughout the South to bring an end to the odious Jim Crow laws. It also led to demonstrations throughout the North and the West against de facto segregation.

The heroic struggles in Birmingham, Alabama; Atlanta and Albany, Georgia; Greensboro, North Carolina; St. Augustine, Florida and the sit-ins and demonstrations in New York, Philadelphia, Boston, Chicago, Englewood, New Jersey, Los Angeles, and San Francisco led to the "March on Washington for Jobs and Freedom" on August 28, 1963. Over 200,000 blacks and whites from all over the United States converged upon Washington, D.C., and thus staged the largest demonstration in the history of the nation's capital. The "I Have a Dream" speech delivered by Dr. Martin Luther King became a classic in American oratory. Yet some activists and critics such as Malcolm X considered the march itself to be the "farce on Washington," an almost festive affair used to promote the Kennedy Civil Rights Bill then pending before Congress.(1)

The historical origins of Kennedy's Civil Rights Bill were rooted in the struggle against Jim Crow and the demand of Black Americans for the enforcement of the Brown decision. In addressing the issue of segregation and discrimination, the Kennedy bill proposed to end segregation at lunch counters and public facilities and to create a permanent committee on Equal Employment Opportunity. In regard to education, the bill proposed to enforce the Brown decision by giving the attorney general the authority to initiate court cases against local school districts and institutions of high learning. The final proposal was one which in its final form would have the greatest effect on American education. Kennedy argued that programs and institutions receiving federal assistance should be required to end all discriminatory practices. Unfortunately though, even the march on Washington failed to provide enough leverage for action and Kennedy's program was trapped in Congressional committees and made very little headway through Congress. To make matters worse, Kennedy's assassination on November 22, 1963, ended the possibility of his ushering the program through Congress.

These events occurred in the wake of the previous administration's feeble attempts to address the issues of civil rights and school desegregation. Although during the Brown proceedings in 1954, the court approved the findings that "segregation of white and colored children in public schools has a detrimental effect upon the colored children,"(2) the Eisenhower administration continued to walk the thin line between not denying civil rights and not antagonizing the white southern voter. So that, while Eisenhower's Civil Rights Act of 1957 was historically important because it was the first civil rights legislation since 1885 and marked the beginning of the Second Reconstruction, it provided no meaningful way to hasten the speed of school desegregation. Similarly, his Civil Rights Act of 1960 contained no provisions for involvement of the attorney general in the area of school desegregation nor aid in getting school desegregation suits into the courts. In fact the legislation was so worthless in addressing the issue of civil rights that the leading lawyer in the NAACP school desegregation cases, Thurgood Marshall, stated that the Civil Rights Act of 1960, "isn't worth the paper it's written on."(3) Recognizing the half-hearted efforts of Eisenhower and continuing to support the legislative efforts of Kennedy, Lyndon B. Johnson appeared before Congress five days after Kennedy's assassination and declared: "No memorial oration or eulogy could more eloquently honor President Kennedy's memory than the earliest possible passage of the Civil Rights Bill for which he fought for [sic] so long." Johnson then relied on his mastery of congressional strategy to move the legislation through Congress and on June 19, 1964, after passing the House on February 10, and a debate which lasted 74 days in the Senate, the bill passed by 73 to 27.(4)

The Civil Rights Act of 1964 was one of the most significant pieces of social legislation in the United States in the twentieth century. Under eleven different titles the power of the federal regulation was extended in the areas of voting rights, public accommodations, education, and employment. Titles IV and VI were directed toward ending school segregation by providing authority for implementing the Brown decision. Title VI was the most important section because it established the precedent for using disbursal of government money as a means of controlling educational policy. It stated that no persons, because of race, color, or national origin, could be excluded from or denied the benefits of any program receiving federal financial assistance. It required all federal agencies to establish guidelines to implement this policy. Refusal by institutions or projects to follow these guidelines was to result in the "termination of or refusal to grant or to continue assistance under such program or activity." The result was that the fate of desegregation was more rapid after passage of the 1964 Civil Rights Act than before, but by the end of the 1960s an abundance of evidence showed that segregated education continued in the South. In other words, compared to the ideal of total integration the actual results were mere token.(5)

Moreover, because the civil rights legislation had been passed in reaction to legalized segregation in the South, it proved ineffective in addressing the issue of de facto segregation outside of the southern states. The failure of Title VI to be applied effectively in the North occurred at a time when segregation was actually increasing in northern metropolitan areas. The United States Commission on Civil Rights reported in 1967 that the level of racial separation in the city schools was increasing. It found that seventy-five percent of black elementary students in cities attended schools that were nearly all black, while eighty-three percent of the white students attended all-white schools. This situation was increasing as the white population moved from the city into suburban areas. Hence, the Civil Rights legislation in general and Title VI specifically had been the result of the hopes of civil rights leaders for full implementation of the Brown decision, but because Title VI had little effect outside the South and provided only token integration within the South, the dream of quality public education for black youth was a dream which would be long deferred. In fact, in 1977, ten years after the Commission on Civil Rights reported the increase in racial separation in schools, only 26 percent of blacks in the 18 to 21 age group were enrolled in college while 34 percent of whites in the same age group were enrolled. These low college enrollment statistics occurred at a time when blacks were severely underrepresented in law, medicine, dentistry, pharmacology, engineering, and the sciences. Consequently, when the Supreme Court ruled in the Bakke case in 1978 that universities could, but need not, consider race as one factor in determining admissions policy in order to diversify student bodies and to redress past discrimination, the deferred dream of pursuing higher and professional education had become for black youths a veritable nightmare. Moreover, the educational aspirations of many black youths throughout the North and South were seriously circumscribed by segregated inferior education in the public schools which created a legacy of dimmed hopes and shattered dreams of ever gaining a foothold in mainstream America.

Since the Civil Rights Movement was not designed to end northern de facto segregation, blacks in urban centers throughout the North waged relentless struggles to desegregate the public schools in efforts to assure quality education for their youths. These efforts, though, were met with resistance from local school boards. In fact, to a considerable extent, the refinement of de facto segregation in education in northern school systems during the post-Brown era was the result of the resistance of reluctant school boards to desegregate the schools. The situation in Cincinnati, Ohio, provides an excellent case in point.

## THE BLACK STRUGGLE IN CINCINNATI AND THE REFINEMENT OF DE FACTO SEGREGATION

In 1954 when the Supreme Court outlawed racial segregation in the schools, the Cincinnati Board of Education continued to abide by policies which resulted in the perpetuation of racial segregation. Such policies consisted in (a) the refusal to dismantle the dual school system, (b) discriminatory faculty, administrative, and other personnel assignments and (c) the utilization of segregated facilities.(6)    The refusal to abide by the desegregation mandate was consistent with the past practices of the Cincinnati School Board. In fact, by the time the Brown decision was rendered, the Cincinnati School Board had been practicing de facto segregation by maintaining a dual school system for sixty-seven years in violation of the 1887 state desegregation mandate, the Arnett Law of Ohio.(7)  By the mid-twentieth century, the board's method of maintaining de facto segregation by blatantly maintaining separate colored schools shifted to using the segregated housing patterns which had developed during the early part of the century to construct its school attendance policy.(8)   Hence, the neighborhood school policy became the official policy of the Cincinnati School Board and became rigidly enforced despite blacks' efforts to desegregate the schools. For instance, throughout the 1950s and early 60s the Cincinnati chapters of the NAACP and later, CORE, had led in the struggle to desegregate the schools.(9)  Nevertheless, in 1963 the School Board, by way of the Court of Appeals for the First Appellate District of Ohio, in the Ashcraft case, legitimized the Neighborhood School Policy making it a rigid mandate of state law.(10)  When forty-five black children sued the School Board on November 6, 1963, in the Tina Deal case charging that they and black teachers were confined to segregated black schools and alleging that twenty-one public schools were "attended predominantly, if not exclusively, by Negro students,"(11) the Board responded on July 26, 1965 with an adverse decision which in effect legally enforced de facto segregation.(12)    Hence, despite blacks' efforts to desegregate the schools, by 1965 both the Ashcraft and Deal cases combined to give defacto school segregation the legitimacy of law.

As fate would have it, by the early 1970s the black struggle for quality education had been transformed from a mere protest movement to the seizure of ideological control of the School Board.    On December 10, 1973, the two black board members and the two white liberals who comprised the majority on the School Board passed a resolution to redraw the boundary lines and completely desegregate the system by race and class so that when schools would open the following September there would be roughly a forty-nine percent black and fifty-one percent white student population in the district.(13)    When the newly elected conservative board took office in January of 1974, they rescinded the desegregation resolution and replaced it with the Alternative or Magnet school plan to bring about a racial balance in the schools.    Being enraged by what they considered to be "unconstitutional" action on the part of the conservative School Board, the NAACP filed the Bronson Law Suit on May 29, 1974, in an effort to get the U.S. District Court to order the Cincinnati Board of Education to racially and economically integrate the schools.(14)

Being content with the possibility for a long-term settlement, the conservative board proceeded to implement their alternative school plan. In doing so there was left a legacy of school closings, black student displacements, and low achievement in the neighborhood schools.(15)    Despite the negative effect of the conservatives' alternative school plan on the educational conditions of black youths, on February 16, 1984, the NAACP acquiesced to an out-of-court settlement with the School Board. Criticized by one of the black conservative School Board members as "...a compromise made in light of the present administration in Washington, D.C., which is taking the country to a more conservative mood," the settlement essentially was an agreement to expand the alternative school program in an effort to achieve a racial balance by 1991.    The board member's criticism of the settlement was based on the fact that "some schools will remain racially isolated...."(16)    He was indeed correct. The schools that suffered the most from racial isolation happened to be in black neighborhoods and attended by black students.    Two years later in 1986 it was observed by the Cincinnati Federation of Teachers that "20 of the 21 lowest achieving schools are predominantly black."(17)    It was also observed that, "Cincinnati high schools with the highest percentage of black students offered the fewest college-oriented courses...."(18)

Hence, despite the struggle among black Cincinnatians to desegregate the Cincinnati Public Schools during the post-Brown era, the School Board has effectively curtailed the educational achievement of the majority of black youths by refining its system of de facto segregation.    The evolution of the neighborhood schoolpolicy into the alternative school plan was in response to the victories of the vigilant black community.    And while the educational hopes of most black students are systematically crushed by the inferior education of the black neighborhood schools, the black community continues its vigilance and concern.    For example, the School Board elections of 1985 and 1987 resulted in a progressive white and two black elected members.    As a result of the 1987 elections, there became, for the first time in Cincinnati's 200-year history, a black majority on the School Board.    In addition, even before the black majority was elected to the board, in 1986 a black woman was appointed superintendent of schools after the untimely death of the white superintendent having achieved the position of occupying the highest level of formal educational decision making in the system.    Blacks are in a strategic position to bring fruition to the educational dreams of Cincinnati's black youths which have been long deferred.  Only time and struggle will tell.

## NOTES

1.    Manning Marable, "Jobs, Peace, Freedom: A Political Assessment of the August 27 March on Washington," The Black Scholar 14, no. 6 (November/December 1983): 2.

2.    Betsy Levin and Philip Moise, "School Desegregation Litigation in the Seventies and the Use of Social Science Evidence:  An Annotated Guide," Law and Contemporary Problems XXXIX, no. 1 (Winter 1975): 56-57.

3.    Joel Spring, The Sorting Machine  (New York: David McKay Co., 1976), 169-170.

4.    Ibid., 175-176.

5.    Ibid., 182.

6.    Thomas I. Atkins, Theresa Demchak, Solvita A. McMillan, Leonard D. Slutz, William E. Caldwell, G. Phillip Arnold, Elizabeth McKana and John Guthrie, Plaintiffs Supplemental and Final Answer to the Cincinnati Board's Fifth Interrogatories, In the United States District Court For the Southern District of Ohio Western Division, Civil Action No. C-1-74-205, Mona Bronson, et al., Plaintiffs vs. Board of Education of the City School District of the City of Cincinnati, et al. 127-182.

7.    David Gerber, Black Ohio and The Color Line 1860-1915 (Urbana: University of Illinois Press, 1976), 244.

8.    Gene D. Lewis, "Cincinnati Neighborhood Schools:    Past, Present, and Future," The Cincinnati Historical Society Bulletin 38, no. 2 (Summer 1980):  30.

9.    Michael Washington, The Black Struggle for Desegregated Quality Education: Cincinnati, Ohio 1954-1974, unpublished doctoral dissertation, University of Cincinnati, 1984, 144-154.

10.    Robert Manley, "The Neighborhood School:  A Legal Perspective," The Cincinnati Historical Society Bulletin 38, no. 2 (Summer 1980): 137.

11.    Michael Washington, The Black Struggle, 150-151.

12.    Ibid., 153.

13.    Ibid., 254-257.

14.    Cincinnati Post and Time Stars, March 29, 1974.

15.    Michael Washington, The Black Struggle, 325-327.

16.    Cincinnati Herald, February 25, 1984.

17.    Cincinnati Federation of Teachers Newsletters, March 27, 1986.

18.    Cincinnati Enquirer, October 2, 1986.

# 10 The Housing Conditions of Black Americans: 1960s-1980s

*Wilhelmina A. Leigh**

Since the 1963 march on Washington for jobs and freedom, both legislation and judicial decisions have shaped housing opportunities for blacks in this nation. The major pieces of legislation were the 1964 Civil Rights Act and the 1968 Civil Rights Act, whose Title VIII is known as the Fair Housing Act. One of the more important court cases was Jones v. Alfred H. Mayer Co. (1968) in which the Supreme Court found that the 1966 Civil Rights Act precludes all discrimination on the basis of race in the sale or rental of real property, however private the transaction.

Given this legislative and judicial support for an environment in which blacks could have a greater array of housing opportunities, how would one define the "dream" for the housing circumstances of Black Americans? What has been the "reality" of housing circumstances for blacks since 1963?

The dream for housing equality of blacks in America could be defined in many ways. This paper considers three possible definitions and assesses the reality corresponding to each. The final section presents conclusions from the analysis.

The three dream definitions considered are as follows:

1.    Equal percentages of blacks and whites have certain characteristics with respect to housing (e.g., percent owner, percent lacking plumbing) regardless of the income distributions of blacks and whites.

2.    Blacks have the same access as whites with similar incomes to all parts of the housing market.

3.    Blacks and whites have identical income distributions, and blacks are housed any way they choose.

The first dream would equalize housing characteristics for the two racial groups without altering their income distributions; the third dream would equalize the income distributions of the two racial groups and let these altered income distributions guide the selection of housing by the two racial groups. If the second dream were to be realized, the income distributions of the two racial groups would be unchanged, and the market

*Principal Analyst, U.S. Congressional Budget Office (CBO). This analysis is the author's own and should not be attributed to the CBO.

circumstances would be altered so that both blacks and whites would have complete freedom of choice when selecting housing. Two periods are examined: "the Civil Rights Movement" and "since the Civil Rights Movement." "The Civil Rights Movement" is the period 1954-1968 and "since the Civil Rights Movement" is the period since 1968.

## DREAM DEFINITION NUMBER ONE

Equal percentages of blacks and whites have certain characteristics with respect to housing (e.g., percent owner, percent lacking plumbing) regardless of the income distributions of blacks and whites.

A corollary to this definition would be for blacks to have a superior set of housing characteristics to similar whites, regardless of the relative income distributions of the two groups.

The fact that black households are more likely to reside in substandard units than are white households or households of all races belies this dream definition. Housing conditions and ownership statistics for all racial groups have improved over time, however. (See Tables 1, 2, and 3.)

Data from the 1960 Census of Housing reveal a gap between the proportions of blacks and of all races who live in standard housing units when individual measures of substandardness are used. On the criterion of lacking some or all plumbing facilities, black renters were the most disadvantaged group—29 percent lacked some or all plumbing facilities—followed by black owners, 25 percent of whom were similarly housed. (See Table 1.) Only 16 percent and 9 percent, respectively, of renters and owners of all races lacked some or all plumbing. By the criterion of sharing or lacking access to a bath, housing improved considerably both for blacks and all races between 1950 and 1960, although a substantial gap remained between the groups.(1) Crowdedness remained more of a problem for black owners and renters than for others. Thirty-three percent of black renters (versus 16 percent of renters of all races) and 21 percent of black owners (versus 9 percent of owners of all races) continued to live in crowded conditions in 1960.

The year 1960, the midpoint of the Civil Rights Movement, found the percentage of owners among nonwhites and whites at 38 percent and 64 percent, respectively. (See Table 2.) Median household income for non-white owners and for owners of all races were $3,400 and $5,900 respectively. The median ratio of gross rent-as-percent-of-income for nonwhites in 1960 was 26 percent, while for all races it was 25 percent.(2) Median household incomes for nonwhite renters and renters of all races were $2,500 and $4,100, respectively. (See Table 3.)

Although disparities remain, between 1960 and 1983, housing conditions have improved both for blacks and for whites on every measure. The percent of blacks who owned their own homes increased to 42 percent by 1970 and to 45 percent by 1983. Among whites, 65 percent were owners in 1970, and 68 percent in 1983. (See Table 2.)

Two of the major measures of substandardness—lacking some or all plumbing, and crowdedness—also showed improvement for both racial groups. Eighteen percent of black renters and 14 percent of black owners lived in units lacking some or all plumbing in 1970, while only 5 percent and 4 percent, respectively, did in 1983. (See Table 1.) Eight percent and 4 percent, respectively, of renters and owners of all races lived in units lacking some or all plumbing in 1970, while only 3 percent and 1 percent did in 1983.

Since the end of the Civil Rights Movement, crowding also has lessened both for owners and renters. In 1970, 22 percent of black renters and all percent of renters of all races lived in crowded units. By 1983, only 9 percent of black renters and 6 percent of renters of all races continued to live in crowded units.

Median household income for blacks and for all races increased between 1970 and 1983. For black renters it rose from about $4,300 to $8,800, while it rose from $6,300 to $12,400 for all races. Median gross rent also increased between 1970 and 1983. For blacks, it rose from $89 to $266, while for all races it rose from $108 to $315. (See Table 3.) Median house value also rose over the period--for blacks it went from $10,700 to $40,700, while for all races it went from $17,100 to $59,700. (See Table 2.)

Although the gap between the median rents and house values of units occupied by households of the different racial groups was sizable, the median ratios of gross rent-as-a-percent-of-income and of income-to-value were close for all racial groups in both 1970 and 1983. In 1970, median gross rent was 23 percent of income for blacks and 20 percent for all races; in 1983, these figures were 32 percent and 29 percent, respectively. (See Table 3.) In 1970, median value-to-income ratios were 1.7 for blacks and 1.8 for all races; in 1983, they were 2.3 for blacks and 2.4 for all races. (Table 2.)

## DREAM DEFINITION NUMBER TWO

Blacks have the same access as whites with similar incomes to all parts of the housing market.

The continued existence of high levels of residential racial segregation suggests that this dream has not been realized. Residence in segregated neighborhoods may reflect equal opportunity in access to housing if people have voluntarily segregated themselves by race. The historical use of many tactics--racial zoning, racially restrictive convenants on deeds, and steering, for example--to involuntarily segregate blacks, however, makes it difficult to measure the degree of actual black self-segregation. Segregation becomes the opposite of equal opportunity when blacks are forced to reside in segregated areas because of government actions and market machinery that exclude them from other areas--that is, when they are excluded from a large share of the housing supply for which their economic circumstances would allow them to compete. Segregation that is motivated by racial differences and occurs involuntarily also affects the quality of life for blacks when it limits their access to education and employment opportunities.

The 1960s reveal a substantial amount of exclusion and residential segregation of the races. Between 1950 and 1970, the number of blacks living in census tracts that were virtually all-black increased from 3 out of 10 to 5 out of 10. Over the same period, the number of blacks living in mixed neighborhoods--defined as 25 percent or less of black population--declined from 25 percent to 16 percent.(3)

The fact that residential racial segregation continues to exist in the United States seems to be less controversial than the index chosen to measure it. During the Civil Rights Movement, the dissimilarity index reveals a decrease in segregation, while the exposure index shows an increase.(4)

The dissimilarity index measures the percentage of either population that would have to move in order for the percentage distribution by race on each block to equal that of the entire city. If the two populations are distributed identically over a geographical area, the index equals 0 and no households would need to move. If the two populations are distributed with no intersection, that is, no geographical unit has both black and white households, then the index equals 100 and all households would need to move. The black (white) exposure rate to whites (blacks) is defined by the proportion of whites (blacks) in the neighborhood of the average black (white).

The mean dissimilarity index calculated for 109 cities in the United States decreased between the years 1950 and 1970--from 87.3 in 1950, to 86.1 in 1960, to 81.6 in 1970. On the other hand, the exposure index of blacks to whites reflects an increase in segregation (in all regions and for the United States as a whole) between 1960 and 1970. Over the same period, however, the exposure index of whites to blacks indicates increased exposure of whites to blacks--or reduced segregation--for the United States as a whole. These seemingly conflicting trends can be explained by the fact that during that period blacks gained increased access to residential areas primarily through peripheral expansion of existing minority areas.(5) Slower growth in white sectors than in black residential sectors coupled with this expansion pattern could explain this seeming contradiction.

The 1970s are perceived as the decade in which residential segregation became the central issue in the struggle for racial equality.(6) Although only 21 percent of whites surveyed in 1963 felt that fair housing was a major goal of the Civil Rights Movement, 34 percent felt this way by 1977. Only 1 percent of blacks viewed fair housing as a major goal in 1963, while 74 percent did by 1977. In addition, some have viewed fair housing and the end to de facto school segregation as issues of the North while voting rights, employment, and access to public accommodations were issues of the South. The end of the Civil Rights Movement, with its mainly southern focus, also could account for the enhanced interest in equality of access to housing.

Exclusion and residential segregation have remained as real as ever in the years since the Civil Rights Movement. The 216 major metropolitan areas in the nation were 12 percent black in 1970. However, 21 percent of their central cities' populations were black, while only 5 percent of their suburban populations were. By 1980, this distribution was virtually unchanged, with the major metropolitan areas 13 percent black, their central cities 22 percent black, and their suburbs 6 percent black.

McKinney and Schnare have determined that residential segregation increased between 1960 and 1970, but declined between both 1970 and 1980 and 1960 and 1980. By calculating exposure indexes with Census data for 64 SMSAs, they found the degree of segregation to have lessened for each of the Census regions and for the nation as a whole. They infer that, although housing markets today are highly segregated, barriers to integration are breaking down. Tabulations by Taeuber of the dissimilarity index in 1980 (based on these same 64 SMSAs) confirm the findings of McKinney and Schnare for 1970 to 1980 and for 1960 to 1980. The mean dissimilarity index for 1960 was 87.99; for 1970, it was 87.0; and for 1980, it was 80.75.(7)

An enhancement in measuring the equality of access to housing for blacks has been the use of testers. Testers are paired white and black persons given identical socioeconomic characteristics and requirements for residences to use when visiting real estate agents and apartment management offices. Testers make separate visits, close together, to the same property offices. Each makes the same inquiries about availability and prices of residences. Responses given to the black and white testers are later compared.

The use of testers in many markets has revealed that blacks and members of other minority groups do not have equal access with whites to market information. The nationwide Housing Market Practices Survey conducted in 1977 found that both blacks and Hispanics receive less information about available housing than whites in both the rental and sale markets.(8) Discrimination against minorities in the rental market takes place with respect to information on the following aspects of unit availability: whether a unit was available, date of availability, number of units available, number of units offered for inspection, and length of the waiting list.  Real estate sales agents discriminated against minorities when supplying the following information:  whether a house was available in the requested price range and neighborhood, number of houses offered as serious possibilities, and number of houses offered for inspection.

## DREAM DEFINITION NUMBER THREE

Blacks and whites have identical income distributions, and blacks are housed any way they choose.

The fact that the income distributions for blacks and whites continue to differ is the reality that confronts this dream.  The median household incomes on Tables 2 and 3 indicate that blacks and all races have had different distributions of income since the years of the Civil Rights Movement and that they continue to do so today.  The discussion of the reality associated with the previous dream definition revealed that blacks are not yet housed the way they choose, because of discriminatory market practices.

Although median incomes continue to diverge, the median percentages of income spent for rent and the median-to-value ratios for blacks and all races are quite close.  The fact that median rents and median house values were correspondingly lower for blacks than for all races suggests that because blacks rent or buy within their means, they can only acquire a lesser amount (or quality) of housing than households of all racial groups.    Statistics on relative substandardness substantiate this.

As noted above, housing conditions for blacks have improved between 1960 and 1983, but not as much as for households of all races.  Although parity has not been achieved, ownership rates increased by a greater percentage for blacks than for households of all races--from 38 percent to 45 percent for blacks (versus from 62 percent to 65 percent among households of all races).  (See Table 2.)  The percentages of black owner and renter households in units lacking complete plumbing facilities or with a shared bath (or without access to a bath) are single digit numbers in 1983. (See Table 1.)  Comparable figures for households of all races, both owners and renters, also are single digit numbers but are consistently lower than for blacks.

One contemporary problem that can be attributed in part to the lower incomes and limited housing choices of blacks is homelessness.  Two characteristics related to income and housing standards that have been defined as risk factors for homelessness are:  paying in excess of 50 percent of income for housing and/or living in extremely substandard units.(9)

Are blacks at substantially greater risk of homelessness than other racial groups?  Data on household income and changes in household composition between 1960 and 1985 suggest that the existence of sizable subpopulations of black households with certain characteristics may place a higher percentage of black households than households of other racial groups at risk of homelessness.

Tables 4 and 5 show the percentage distributions of household types by race since 1960.  White households--88 percent of all households in 1985--reflect the pattern of all races, with family households a solid majority of all households and married couples the majority of all family households.  Both for all races and whites, however, the proportion of family households, and the proportion that married couples are of these households, have decreased over time.  In 1960, family households were 85 percent of all households, but in 1985, they were 72 percent of all households.  Married couples decreased from 74 percent of all family households in 1960 to 58 percent in 1985.  White married couples dropped from 76 percent to 61 percent of their total family households over the same period.

The picture differs for Black Americans. (See Table 5.) The percentage that family households were of all households declined from 83 to 72 between 1960 and 1985. Over the same period, the percentage of married couples declined from 61 to 37 percent of all family households, and the proportion of female-headed households rose from 19 percent to 31 percent of family households, an increase much greater than the comparable figure for whites.

How do these differences in the distribution of black and white households affect the condition of housing occupied and the risk of homelessness? One cannot say precisely. In general, one would expect family households, especially married couples, to have greater demand for higher quality units than non-family households; income, however, would determine the effectiveness of this demand (i.e., the ability of households to obtain the desired housing). Table 6 reveals that among all races, blacks, and whites, in 1985, married couples had the highest median incomes and therefore the greatest effective demand. Since a smaller proportion of black than of white households is married couples, blacks, collectively, would have less effective demand and therefore, collectively, might live in housing of lesser quality than would households of other racial groups. Thus, since the family composition and income distribution of black households differ from those of either white households or households of all racial groups, one could believe that the median ratios of rent-as-a-percent-of-income and of income-to-value for black households mask greater variance than these same medians for white households or for households of all races. More specifically, the 31 percent of black households headed by females in 1985 with median incomes of about $9,600 could represent a sizable number of households at risk of homelessness if they live in markets in which 30 percent of their incomes, roughly $240 a month, could only acquire substandard housing.(10) (See Table 6.)

**CONCLUSIONS**

From the 1960s to the 1980s, although the housing situation of black Americans has improved with respect to condition and segregation, disparities remain. In addition, it may be true that black households are disproportionately disadvantaged by contemporary problems such as homelessness.

The percentages of black households housed comparably to households of all races continue to approach parity but only over gaps as large as decades. For example, although the 22 percent of black renter households in crowded units in 1970 reflects a 20 percentage point decline from this figure in 1940, it was 1950 when 22 percent of renter households of all races had lived in crowded units! It took 20 years for black renter households to "improve" to the level of residential crowdedness experienced by renter households of all races in 1950. Progess is evident, however; by 1980, the percentage of crowded black renter households equaled the percentage of crowded renter households of all races in 1970!

Thus, the dream and the reality continue to diverge, but the extent of the divergence appears to be lessening by some measures.

TABLE I

Housing Adequacy by Race, 1960 to 1983

| | Owners | | | | | Renters | | | | |
|---|---|---|---|---|---|---|---|---|---|---|
| | 1960 | 1970 | 1975 | 1980 | 1983 | 1960 | 1970 | 1975 | 1980 | 1983 |
| **STRUCTURAL QUALITY** | | | | | | | | | | |
| Lacks Some or | | | | | | | | | | |
| All Plumbing | | | | | | | | | | |
| Blacks a/ | 24.9 | 14.4 | 7.0 | 4.9 | 4.4 | 28.6 | 17.6 | 10.0 | 7.1 | 5.3 |
| All Races | 8.9 | 4.2 | 1.8 | 1.5 | 1.4 | 16.3 | 7.9 | 4.8 | 3.6 | 2.9 |
| | | | | | | | | | | |
| Shares or No Bath | | | | | | | | | | |
| Blacks a/ | 34.6 | 15.3 | 7.2 | 5.1 | 4.7 | 44.6 | 19.2 | 10.8 | 7.5 | 5.8 |
| All Races | 10.6 | 4.8 | 2.0 | 1.7 | 1.7 | 21.3 | 9.2 | 6.7 | 4.3 | 3.6 |
| | | | | | | | | | | |
| **INTERNAL CONDITIONS** | | | | | | | | | | |
| | | | | | | | | | | |
| Crowded b/ | | | | | | | | | | |
| Blacks a/ | 21.0 | 15.5 | 10.9 | 7.9 | 5.8 | 32.9 | 22.2 | 13.2 | 10.0 | 9.0 |
| All Races | 8.7 | 6.4 | 4.0 | 3.1 | 2.3 | 16.1 | 10.6 | 6.7 | 6.2 | 5.6 |

SOURCES: Census Bureau Reports and Annual (American) Housing Survey

NOTE: Figures are percentages indicating the proportion of units so characterized. All races includes blacks.

a: The figures for 1960 reflect data for nonwhites. In the years through 1983, these figures represent blacks.

b: Crowded is defined as 1.01 or more persons per room.

TABLE 2

Affordability for Homeowners by Race and Year

| | Owners a/ (%) | | Median Household Income ($) | | Median House Value b/ ($) | | Median Value/ Income Ratio | |
|---|---|---|---|---|---|---|---|---|
| | Black | All d/ | Black | All | Black | All | Black | All |
| 1960 c/ | 38.4 | 61.9 | 3,400 | 5,900 | 6,700 | N/A | N/A | N/A |
| 1970 | 41.6 | 62.9 | 6,600 | 9,700 | 10,700 | 17,100 | 1.7 | 1.8 |
| 1975 | 43.8 | 64.6 | 9,500 | 13,500 | 18,900 | 29,500 | 1.9 | 2.1 |
| 1980 | 43.9 | 64.4 | 13,600 | 19,800 | 33,500 | 51,300 | 2.3 | 2.5 |
| 1983 | 45.0 | 64.7 | 16,400 | 24,400 | 40,700 | 59,700 | 2.3 | 2.4 |

SOURCES:  Census Bureau Reports Annual (American) Housing Survey, and the
Statistical Abstract of the United States.

NOTE:  All races includes blacks.

a:  Percentage of owners indicates the percentage of units owned by
race.

b:  Median house value is based on estimates by owners.

c:  In 1980, data for blacks represent all nonwhites.

d:  Percentage of owners among whites alone is:  64.4 in 1960, 65.4
in 1970, 67.5 in 1975, 67.8 in 1980, and 67.7 in 1983.

TABLE 3

Affordability for Renters by Race and Year

| | Renters a/ (%) | | Median Household Income ($) | | Median Gross Rent b/ ($) | | Median Gross Rent/Income b/ (%) | |
|---|---|---|---|---|---|---|---|---|
| | Black | All d/ | Black | All | Black | All | Black | All |
| 1960 c/ | 61.1 | 38.1 | 2,500 | 4,100 | 59 | N/A | N/A | N/A |
| 1970 | 56.4 | 37.1 | 4,300 | 6,300 | 89 | 108 | 23 | 20 |
| 1975 | 56.2 | 35.4 | 5,300 | 7,800 | 126 | 156 | 25 | 23 |
| 1980 | 56.1 | 35.6 | 7,500 | 10,500 | 204 | 241 | 29 | 27 |
| 1983 | 55.0 | 35.3 | 8,800 | 12,400 | 266 | 315 | 32 | 29 |

SOURCES: Census Bureau Reports, Annual (American) Housing Survey, and the Statistical Abstract of the United States.

Note: Blacks are included in "all" category.

a: Percentage of renters refers to the percentage of all housing units which are rented.

b: Gross rent is monthly contract rent plus estimated average monthly cost of utilities and fuel when these latter items are paid for by the renter. Both subsidized (welfare agency, relative or friend) and nonsubsidized rent and utilities are included.

c: In 1960, blacks are not reported separately. Consequently, these figures represent all nonwhites.

d: Percentage of renters for whites alone is: 35.6 in 1960, 34.6 in 1970, 32.5 in 1973, 32.2 in 1980, and 32.3 in 1983.

TABLE 4

Household Composition for All Races, 1960 to 1985

|  | 1960 | 1970 | 1975 | 1980 | 1985 |
|---|---|---|---|---|---|
| Households (1,000) | 52,799 | 63,401 | 71,120 | 80,776 | 86,789 |

Percent Distribution

|  | 1960 | 1970 | 1975 | 1980 | 1985 |
|---|---|---|---|---|---|
|  | 100.0 | 100.0 | 100.0 | 100.0 | 100.0 |
| Nonfamily Households | 15.0 | 18.8 | 21.9 | 26.3 | 27.7 |
| Persons Alone | 13.1 | 17.1 | 19.6 | 22.7 | 23.7 |
| Other Nonfamily Households | 1.9 | 1.7 | 2.3 | 3.6 | 4.0 |
| Family Households | 85.0 | 81.2 | 78.1 | 73.7 | 72.3 |
| Married Without Kids | 30.3 | 30.3 | 30.6 | 29.9 | 30.1 |
| Married With Kids | 44.1 | 40.3 | 35.4 | 30.9 | 27.9 |
| One Parent With Kids | 10.7 | 10.6 | 12.1 | 12.9 | 14.2 |
| Male Head | 2.3 | 1.9 | 2.1 | 2.1 | 2.6 |
| Female Head | 8.4 | 8.7 | 10.0 | 10.8 | 11.7 |

SOURCE:   Various issues of the Statistical Abstract of the United States.

Note:   Percentages may not sum to 100.0 due to rounding.

TABLE 5

Household Composition by Race, 1960 to 1985

|  | 1960 | 1970 | 1975 | 1980 | 1985 |
|---|---|---|---|---|---|
| White Households a/ (1,000) | 47,665 | 56,502 | 62,945 | 70,766 | 75,328 |
| | Percent Distribution | | | | |
| Nonfamily Households | 100.0 | 100.0 | 100.0 | 100.0 | 100.0 |
| | 14.3 | 18.3 | 21.4 | 26.2 | 27.8 |
| Family Households | 85.7 | 81.7 | 78.6 | 73.8 | 72.2 |
| Married Couples | 76.0 | 72.5 | 68.3 | 63.2 | 60.6 |
| Male Household Head | 2.3 | 1.9 | 2.0 | 2.0 | 2.4 |
| Female Household Head | 7.5 | 7.4 | 8.3 | 8.6 | 9.2 |
| Black Households a/ (1,000) | 5,134 | 6,223 | 7,262 | 8,586 | 9,480 |
| | Percent Distribution | | | | |
| Nonfamily Households | 100.0 | 100.0 | 100.0 | 100.0 | 100.0 |
| | 17.4 | 21.5 | 24.3 | 28.0 | 28.5 |
| Family Households | 82.6 | 78.5 | 75.7 | 72.0 | 71.5 |
| Married Couples | 60.7 | 53.4 | 46.1 | 40.0 | 36.6 |
| Male Household Head | 3.4 | 2.9 | 2.9 | 3.0 | 3.6 |
| Female Household Head | 18.5 | 22.2 | 26.7 | 29.1 | 31.3 |

SOURCE: Various issues of the Statistical Abstract of the United States.

Note: Percentages may not sum to 100.0 due to rounding.

TABLE 6

Median Income by Household Type and Race, 1985

|  | All Races | Blacks | Whites |
|---|---|---|---|
| All Households | $23,618 | $14,819 | $24,308 |
| Family Households | 28,022 | 17,053 | 29,404 |
| Married Couples | 31,161 | 24,685 | 31,460 |
| Male Household Head | 24,354 | 16,901 | 25,799 |
| Female Household Head | 14,316 | 9,574 | 16,344 |
| Nonfamily Households | 13,798 | 9,571 | 14,391 |
| Persons Alone | 11,884 | 8,360 | 12,327 |
| Other Households | 25,773 | 19,573 | 30,153 |

SOURCE:    Statistical Abstract of the United States 1988.

## NOTES

1.  These discussions generally begin with 1960 but in some cases will refer to 1950 figures to provide context. The data are from the decennial Censuses of Housing in 1960, 1970, and 1980 and from the Annual (American) Housing Survey for the years 1975 and 1983.

2.  John F. Kain, ed., Race and Poverty: The Economics of Discrimination (Englewood Cliffs, NJ: Prentice-Hall, 1969), 115.

3.  James A. Kushner, Apartheid in America: An Historical and Legal Analysis of Contemporary Segregation in the United States (Frederick, MD: Associated Faculty Press, Inc., 1980), 3.

4.  See Annemette Sorensen, Karl Taeuber, and Leslie Hollingsworth Jr., "Indexes of Racial Residential Segregation for 109 Cities in the United States, 1940 to 1970," Sociological Focus 8 (April 1975): 125-133 for results using the dissimilarity index. See Ann B. Schnare, "Trends in Residential Segregation by Race: 1960-1970," Journal of Urban Economics 7 (May 1980): 293-301 for the results using the exposure indexes.

5.  The exposure index used by Schnare is the ratio of actual exposure rates of blacks to whites divided by the exposure rate that would arise if blacks were evenly distributed throughout the metropolitan area. Unlike the dissimilarity index used by Taeuber, the exposure index is independent of the distribution of blacks and whites among census tracts with above- and below-average concentrations of blacks. See Norman R. Cloutier, "The Measurement and Modeling of Segregation: A Survey of Recent Empirical Research," Regional Science Perspectives 14 (1984): 15-32, for an evaluation of the dissimilarity index in this usage.

6.  D. Garth Taylor, "Housing, Neighborhoods, and Race Relations: Recent Survey Evidence," The Annals of the American Academy of Political and Social Sciences 441 (January 1979): 27-28.

7.  See Karl Taeuber, Appendix--a Decent Home: A Report on the Continued Failure of the Federal Government to Provide Equal Housing Opportunity (Washington, D.C.: Citizens Commission on Civil Rights, 1983).

8.  The U.S. Department of Housing and Urban Development recently has launched the first major study of housing discrimination since the 1977 study. The new study, to be completed in mid-1990, will use testers to check for housing discrimination against blacks and Hispanics.

9.  This definition is used by the Maine State Housing Authority in a program it operates with the Enterprise Foundation to improve housing quality throughout the state. See Bureau of National Affairs, The Housing and Development Reporter XV (June 1, 1987), 11, for more information on this program.

10.  The income data in Table 6 reflect all households, some of whom may live in subsidized housing and are, therefore, presumably not living in substandard units. The standard of 30 percent of income was established for federally subsidized housing programs in the 1981 Omnibus Budget Reconciliation Act. Here, the standard is applied to an income figure reflecting tenants of subsidized housing plus tenants in unsubsidized units.

# 11 The Collapse of the Employment Policy Agenda: 1964-1981

*Helene Slessarev*

## INTRODUCTION

This paper examines the ongoing political controversy surrounding the enactment and implementation of anti-discrimination and affirmative action policies in employment. A whole new set of employment policies were enacted during the 1960s, ranging from civil rights guarantees of equal employment to new job training programs for inner-city youth and the long-term unemployed. These new employment policies were enacted by the same liberal coalition that had successfully elected President Kennedy in 1960, enacted major civil rights reform in 1964 and 1965, and passed the Great Society legislation in 1965 that had created numerous other new federal social programs aimed at alleviating inner-city poverty.

The coalition had united firmly in opposition to racial segregation and political disenfranchisement in the South; yet, by the second half of the 1960s, as civil rights organizations shifted their attention to the unequal status of blacks in the North, the liberal coalitions support began to erode. As the American economy entered a protracted period of decline in the early 1970s and jobs became more scarce throughout the economy, the old coalition could no longer agree on a common political agenda. As a result, by the 1980 election, conservative proponents of free market economics were able to gain the political ascendancy.

The result has been an almost complete abandonment of all efforts aimed at providing minorities with full access to the labor market. The Reagan administration ended what had been the largest public employment program since the end of the Second World War, CETA, leaving behind a much reduced and restricted job training program. The minuscule efforts at business and economic or community development have been allowed to wither. However, the most serious erosion has been the abandonment of support of equal opportunity and affirmative action efforts. Lending federal support to the notion of "reverse discrimination," the Reagan administration sought to set aside the civil rights laws that guarantee equal employment opportunities. As stated in the National Urban League's 1987 report on The State of Black America, the implementation of these policies at the very time when increasing job scarcity put blacks at a more severe disadvantage has resulted in "a disproportionate share of the burdens generated by the current negative economic trends to be concentrated among blacks."(1)

By the early 1980s, conservative policy analysts, the press, and Republican Congressmen had successfully discredited many of the existing employment policies making them vulnerable to the political axe of the Reagan budget cutters. The liberal coalition that had spearheaded the enactment of a new set of active employment policies in the 1960s lay in disarray.    Even many liberals had come to accept the conservatives' arguments against affirmative action and jobs programs.    The leadership of the Democratic Party accepted Reagan's call for a restructuring of social priorities and proposed a federal budget that incorporated three-fourths of the Reagan cuts.    Organized labor, the backbone of the New Deal liberal coalition, was in a defensive posture, having suffered both a loss of membership and political power.

## THE LIBERAL COALITION

The liberal coalition of the 1960s had its origins in the New Deal. Blacks first joined President Roosevelt's New Deal coalition in 1936 following the Democratic Party's enactment of relief programs that provided temporary public jobs to significant numbers of unemployed blacks.  These new relief programs brought African-Americans into direct involvement with the federal government for the first time.    Yet, the racial views of many of the New Deal reformers who formulated and administered the relief programs also set definitive limits on the degree to which the federal government served as a vehicle for changes in the racial status quo.  The liberal reformers of this period saw the purpose of the relief programs as being to help all Americans.  The New Dealers saw the future well being of African-Americans as being closely tied to the success of the New Deal reform program.

> The solution to the "Negro problem" ultimately hinged upon the interplay of a number of factors—expanded opportunities and security, the power of education to modify traditional beliefs, the steady rise in black standards, and the eventual decrease in white bigotry.    Within this complex interrelationship there were established limits on the government's activities in dealing with racial questions.  Those limits involved basically the degree to which the white population would accept the inclusion of blacks in New Deal housing, labor, education and health programs.(2)

These reformers assumed that white racism was predicated on the continued lower level of African-American existence.  For them, the key to altering race relations lay in improving the educational and economic status of blacks.

Even as African-Americans were incorporated into the New Deal coalition, they were brought in as secondary partners.  By the end of the Second World War it was organized labor that emerged as the dominant force  in  the  coalition  that  also  included  liberal  organizations representing both Christians and Jews.  Following the merger of the two existing labor federations to form the AFL-CIO in 1956, the new labor federation was positioned to play a central role in the enactment of any progressive social reform legislation supported by the liberal wing of the Democratic Party.  Through its close ties with the leadership of the Democratic Party and its highly efficient lobbying and mass mobilizing capacities, the AFL-CIO became a conduit for policy proposals orginated by organizations lying outside of the established policymaking networks. This gave the AFL-CIO a high degree of veto power over the substance of the post World War II social policy agenda.(3)

African-American interests were primarily represented within the coalition by two older civil rights organizations, the National Association for the Advancement of Colored People and the National Urban League. Both organizations had been founded during the Progressive Era in response to the neglect by white reformers of the particularly oppressive conditions of Black Americans.    Both of these organizations had long established ties to corporate leaders, private foundations, and leaders in the Democratic Party. The NAACP's chief focus had been the judicial dismantling of legal segregation which culminated in the landmark Supreme Court decision, <u>Brown vs. the Board of Education</u> in 1954. The National Urban League was a social welfare organization primarily concerned with placing blacks into jobs.

Much of the upsurge in black activism of the 1950s and 1960s was initiated by a new generation of civil rights organizations such as the Southern Christian Leadership Conference (SCLC), the Student Nonviolent Coordinating Committee (SNCC), and the Congress of Racial Equality (CORE). These new organizations lacked the same close ties to the Party which the National Urban League and the NAACP had forged during the previous decades. Nor did they have the organizational capacity or expertise to translate the demands they were generating in the field into legislative initiatives to be presented in Washington, D.C. In reality only the NAACP possessed that capacity. This meant that none of the organizations at the forefront of the new civil rights mobilizations had the ability on its own to access the national legislative arena. As a result, to press for the legislative enactment of their political demands these new social movements had to depend on the support of intermediary organizations that did possess access to the legislative arena.

Within the liberal coalition, the specific task of organizing support for civil rights legislation was taken up by a broad-based coalition of liberal, labor, religious, and civil rights organizations called the Leadership Conference on Civil Rights. The Leadership Conference had been in existence since 1946 when it formed during the fight for a permanent Fair Employment Practices Commission in the Truman administration. In essence, the Leadership Conference was the organized expression of the New Deal coalition, united in support of civil rights reform.

## THE ENACTMENT OF FEDERAL ANTI-DISCRIMINATION LEGISLATION

President Kennedy did not come into office in 1961 with the intention of tackling the issue of racial inequality. Yet, by 1963 black activism had discredited the southern racial status quo so severely that Kennedy was forced to support legislation ending the southern form of legal segregation and disenfranchisement. While the principal focus of Kennedy's legislation was to end Jim Crow in the South, civil rights organizations also wanted to include an equal employment section in the bill.(4)

Kennedy had not included fair employment in his original bill because he feared it was too controversial and that southern opposition to it would endanger the success of the entire bill.(5) Therefore, Kennedy's initial bill only addressed the desegregation of public facilities, authorized the federal government to participate more fully in lawsuits against school segregation and a number of other requests, including giving the federal government a greater role in protecting voting rights. According to Joseph Rauh, one of the chief civil rights lobbyists for the 1964 Civil Rights bill,

We kept seeing drafts of the bill and no FEPC (Fair Employment Practices Commission)....There was really a division of strategy between the administration and the Leadership Conference and the others who were on the Leadership Conference side. We wanted to put everything in it and then just hold on for dear life. They wanted to put in only the things they thought they could get. In other words, they said we're not going to put in everything and then lose some of it.(6)

The AFL-CIO came to play a decisive role in securing passage of the employment section of the Act. For the first time the AFL-CIO agreed to support a FEPC bill that also included the unions in its coverage. According to Norman Hill, the vice president of the A. Philip Randolph Institute, George Meany's testimony at the Hearings on Title VII and his verbal commitments to support the fair employment legislation was crucial in convincing the administration that Title VII had enough support to overcome southern opposition. "It was through the help and support of the trade unions that Title VII became part of the bill."(7)

Organized labor also supplied a large share of both the financial resources and the staff for the fight over the 1964 bill. In preparation for the fight for Kennedy's bill, Walter Reuther, president of the United Auto Workers, and head of the AFL-CIO's Industrial Union Department, donated office space in Washington, D.C., owned by the Industrial Union Department, to the Leadership Conference.(8)    Three out of five of the chief lobbyists working in support of the legislation came from the AFL-CIO.  Of the five lobbyists working for the Leadership Conference, only Clarence Mitchell from the NAACP represented a civil rights organization that had extensive lobbying experience prior to this effort. Much of the rest of the Leadership Conference's office staff was also composed of staff members from Reuther's Industrial Union Department.(9)

The AFL-CIO was willing to support a Fair Employment title only if its applicability was restricted to future employment.  According to Herbert Hill, then labor director for the NAACP, Meany had been forced to change his position on fair employment by the Democratic Party leadership.  The AFL-CIO and its affiliate unions agreed to support Title VII, but only at a price. "That price was 703H where they attempted to postpone for a generation justice for black workers.  That's the seniority clause which states that nothing in this Act shall be construed as an alteration of seniority rights."(10)  Seniority is a central issue for the labor movement since it establishes a system within the work place to regulate promotions and lay-offs based on length of service. Yet, in establishing seniority systems, many collective bargaining agreements between companies and the unions also served to restrict black workers into separate departments from which they could not bid on jobs elsewhere in the plant.  In that way, the seniority system preserved certain jobs for white workers while freezing blacks permanently into low-wage menial jobs.  Thus, "by overtly or covertly structuring the systems of seniority and promotion on a racially segregated basis, many unions have controlled the level of advancement and wages of black workers."(11)

During the Congressional floor debate on Title VII, its opponents argued that it threatened existing seniority rights and would lead to reverse discrimination.(12)  In a speech on the Senate floor, Senator Lister Hill from Alabama, argued that the pending bill would be "a blow to labor union freedom" and that among other things, the bill would "undermine a basic fabric of unionism, the seniority system, and would make it possible for labor unions to be denied representation rights under the National Labor Act and the Railway Labor Act."(13)

Confident in the limited impact of Title VII, the AFL-CIO responded to Senator Hill's criticisms by stating that "the Bill does not require 'racial balance' on the job.  It does not upset seniority rights already obtained by any employee.  It does not give any race preferential treatment in hiring or in terms of employment."(14)  The comments go on to say, "The AFL-CIO does not believe in righting ancient wrongs by perpetuating new ones....It (the Civil Rights bill) will take nothing away from the American worker which he has already acquired.(15)

The liberal leadership of the Democratic Party also believed the legislation would have only a limited impact.  For example, Hubert Humphrey, Democratic Senator from Minnesota and one of the principal northern liberal supporters of the bill in the Senate defended the bill by saying,

> Contrary to the allegations of some opponents of this Title, there is nothing in it that will give any power to the Commission or any court to require hiring, firing, or promotion of employees in order to meet a racial "quota" or to achieve a certain racial balance. In fact the very opposite is true. Title VII prohibits discrimination.... Title VII is designed to encourage hiring on the basis of ability and qualifications, not race or religion.(16)

Before the 1964 Civil Rights Act finally gained Congressional approval, it was amended a total of 105 times.(17)  Not surprisingly the legislation contains "contradictory and conflicting provisions."(18)  The amendments had seriously weakened the enforcement powers of the Equal Employment Opportunities Commission.    Unlike all other federal regulatory agencies, the EEOC was stripped of all administrative enforcement powers.    Unlike the National Labor Relations Board, the Federal Trade Commission and the Securities and Exchange Commission, the EEOC could not issue cease and desist orders or initiate legal action in the federal courts.  The EEOC was only authorized to make recommendations to the U.S. Attorney General that a lawsuit be filed by the Department of Justice based on the finding of a "pattern and practice" of racial discrimination.

The lack of enforcement power of the EEOC placed the burden of enforcement on individual workers, frequently with the assistance of civil rights organizations and public interest law centers.  Aggrieved workers had the right to initiate suits on their own in federal court, but there was no assurance that victory would bring relief or how much it would cost.  Furthermore, private parties and civil rights organizations did not have the vast resources required to eliminate the extensive patterns of discrimination that still existed throughout the economy.

The passage of the Civil Rights Act of 1964 represented the completion of the southern phase of the Civil Rights Movement.  It was also the highest point of agreement reached within the liberal civil rights coalition.  Within a year, as the Fair Employment section of the Act was about to begin operation, it became evident that there were significant differences within the coalition as to the future direction of the battle for civil rights.  These differences would eventually lead to the collapse of the liberal civil rights coalition and a political realignment, which by 1972 resulted in the AFL-CIO's tacit support of Republican presidential candidate, Richard Nixon.

Organized labor as the dominant force within the liberal coalition had played a crucial role in the fight for the Civil Rights Act, including Title VII, providing much of the funding, verbal support, and lobbyists.  Yet, organized labor anticipated that Title VII would have only limited impact.  The civil rights forces also recognized the limited nature of Title VII, but accepted it as a first step.  For them, Title VII was just the first stage in the elimination of discriminatory employment barriers.

## LABOR RESISTS THE IMPLEMENTATION OF FAIR EMPLOYMENT

With the enactment of Title VII, organized labor soon found itself as the target of growing numbers of complaints from black union members. Discriminatory employment practices against minority and women workers were still extensive within organized labor.  While the AFL-CIO leadership quickly dealt with the most blatant cases, such as those where union bylaws explicitly prohibited blacks from joining, it never anticipated the extent to which many of its other employment practices would now come under attack. Speaking on the AFL–CIO's efforts to end racial discrimination within its own ranks at a meeting of the National Advisory Council on Anti–Discrimination of the UAW in July of 1967, Herbert Hill asserted, "At best there has been a minimal, stragetic accommodation to the requirements of anti–discrimination laws and federal executive orders but this is less than tokenism. The racist pattern remains intact." (19)

Even in the generally more progressive unions such as the UAW, discriminatory employment patterns were still widespread. In early January of 1964 the UAW's Fair Practices Department conducted its own survey to provide the union "with some impressions of the degree of progress being made with respect to the nonwhite membership" of the union.(20) The Department received responses covering approximately one-half of its membership. The survey showed that within the UAW only 12.9 percent of the production workers surveyed were nonwhite, while only 1.4 percent of the skilled trades members were nonwhites. It found that out of 29 states responding to the survey, only 8 had any nonwhite apprentices in training; 20 states surveyed did not have a single nonwhite apprentice. It also found that 94.5 percent of all employees enrolled in either employee in-training programs or employee upgrading programs were white.

There were only 54 nonwhite apprentices out of a total of 1,958 participating in the UAW's joint labor/management programs.(21) The UAW's own employment records submitted to the EEOC in 1966 showed that out of the 61 UAW international officers, board members, department heads and their staff there were only two black men, one Latino man, and two women.(22)

The skilled trade unions which had historically belonged to the AFL had much worse records. These unions still controlled all access to their trades by closed hiring halls which required an existing member's sponsorship in order to be admitted. A 1960 study conducted by the New York State Commission Against Discrimination found that at most 2 percent of the 15,000 registered apprentices in the state were black.(23) The construction unions also limited the total number of new apprentices admitted into training each year so as to guarantee continuous work and high wages for their membership. According to a 1969 NAACP letter to Floyd Hunter, then assistant secretary of HUD in charge of the Model Cities program, the building trades permitted only 3,000 apprenticeship openings in the nationwide construction industry each year and maintained a ratio of 1 apprentice to 8 journeymen.(24)

## THE CIVIL RIGHTS COALITION COMES APART

Contrary to the unions' expectations, the EEOC was quickly flooded with discrimination complaints. Within two days after the Commission went into operation on July 2, 1965, the NAACP filed its first cases. In September 1965, Herbert Hill, then the Association's Labor Director, filed another 214 complaints with the Commission on behalf of NAACP members in fourteen states. All of the unions in the cases were charged with entering into agreements which provided discriminatory separate seniority lines.(25)

Within the first year of operation, the EEOC had received four times as many complaints as had been estimated. According to a report issued by the Leadership Conference, during the first 100 days of its operations, the EEOC had already received 1,383 complaints of which almost 70 percent came from 11 southern states.(26) By 1967 the Commission had received a total of 8,512 cases.(27) Between 1965 and 1967, the United Auto Workers Union experienced a 300 percent increase in the number of complaints handled by its Fair Employment Practices Department. In 1967 it handled 92 formal cases, most of which had been filed through the various state and federal civil rights agencies. This compares to the 23 cases the department handled in 1964.(28)

The flood of new discrimination cases filed by black unionists quite clearly exceeded what any of the union leaders had anticipated. The enactment of Title VII had sent a signal to minority workers that long standing patterns of employment discrimination could now be challenged. The unions responded to the increased volume of cases by refusing to accept the majority of the EEOC's compliance recommendations. In his study of union compliance with the EEOC, Benjamin Wolkison found that the Commission reached agreement with a labor union in only 19 of the 81 cases brought to it. The Commission was unable to achieve compliance by unions in roughly three-fourths of the cases brought to it. The majority of the cases where agreement was reached did not contain certain measures the Commission considered to be essential to providing adequate relief to the charging party.(29)

The majority of cases in which the EEOC did not reach agreement were subsequently dropped. Private suits were initiated in only ten percent of all the cases in which the EEOC had been unable to reach agreement in its conciliation efforts. The large majority of all private party suits were brought to federal courts by civil rights organizations, especially the NAACP Legal Defense Fund. The other route by which cases could be brought to the courts was through the initiative of the Civil Rights Division of the Department of Justice. However, between September of 1967 and September of 1969 the Justice Department filed only thirty-nine cases.(30)  Due to the unions' unwillingness to accept voluntary compliance and the EEOC's lack of enforcement powers, civil rights organizations were forced to pursue other avenues of relief. These organizations proceeded to implement the same dual strategy of protest and legal action that they had successfully employed in the past.

## JUDICIAL EXPANSION OF DEFINITION OF DISRCIMINATION

Spearheaded by the NAACP, efforts were made to use the private right to sue written into Title VII, by encouraging victims of employment discrimination to file suit in federal court. From 1965 to 1971, the ratio of private suits to suits initiated by the Department of Justice was 25 to 1.(31)  It was in the federal courts where the most important legal breakthroughs in the development of class-wide remedies against employment discrimination occurred.

As the courts began to rule on cases brought before them, they interpreted the legislative record of Title VII as meaning that Congress did not intend to freeze an entire generation of black employees into discriminatory patterns that existed before the Act. This orientation led the federal courts to impose increasingly sweeping remedies. In Griggs vs. Duke Power Co., 1971 the court went beyond the earlier school desegregation cases which had insisted on a finding of de jure or intentional discrimination. Here the court ruled that any employment practice which operated to exclude blacks or other minorities that could not be shown to be related to job performance, was prohibited.(32)  The courts began to impose liabilities in cases of de facto employment discrimination.(33)  The courts' earlier experience with the Brown decision had shown them that the lack of specificity in their decisions invited evasion of the law. With these lessons in mind, the federal courts began to move toward a much more precise definition of affirmative action in a much shorter period of time.(34)

Between 1966 and 1972 the federal court decisions on employment discrimination firmly established the use of affirmative action as a necessary remedy. The courts agreed to the implementation of hiring quotas because they were an attempt to compensate for past discrimination;

quotas made it less likely that defendants would discriminate in the future; and made it possible to expunge the discriminatory reputation of the defendants from the minds of blacks who otherwise would be reluctant to seek employment there.  In Quarles vs. Philip Morris the court ruled that the present consequences of past discrimination did fall within the meaning of Title VII.  The courts' decisions in these cases have been far more concerned about eliminating discriminatory employment systems than with the possibility of "preferential treatment."(35)

According to Herbert Hill, who as NAACP Labor Director, literally filed hundreds of discrimination cases in the federal courts,

> From the very beginning the courts went to the underlying principles of the Act and the courts said that 703H notwithstanding, they would have to deal with the present effects of past discrimination.  Until 1977, there is almost a decade of very imaginative, innovative law by the courts where the courts do proceed to order extensive remedies, sweeping remedies that alter the traditional union seniority practices....  For the first time, they in legal terms begin to define the nature of discrimination, and they arrived at the insight regarding the social nature of discrimination—that it was not just deviant malevolent behavior, that these were not random acts of ill will, but rather systematic institutionalized patterns of discrimination.(36)

The courts obviously began to move in a very different direction on Title VII cases than had been anticipated by organized labor during the Congressional hearings.  In their rulings, the courts set aside the compromise on Section 703H in which the AFL-CIO had sought to protect the job status of its current members.  It was this compromise that had formed the basis of the AFL-CIO's strong support for Title VII on 1964.

## MASS ACTION AGAINST JOB DISCRIMINATION

Alongside and tied to legal efforts, there occurred widespread protests against employment discrimination in cities across the country. As early as 1962, prior to the enactment of Title VII, the NAACP called for a national campaign against the construction trades unions which up until then had successfully obtained de facto immunity from compliance with federal, state, and municipal civil rights laws.  The following summer, a coalition of civil rights groups consisting of members from the NAACP, CORE, the Urban League, the Association of Catholic Trade Unionists, and black churches was formed in New York City for the purpose of organizing demonstrations at construction sites throughout the city. During the next eight years similar demonstrations at construction sites took place in dozens of cities, including Cincinnati, Newark, Cleveland, Chicago, St. Louis, San Francisco, Philadelphia, Pittsburgh, Detroit, and Washington, D.C.

The construction industry became a major target because of its long history of lily-white unions, their importance to central city labor markets, and the fact that the construction industry was heavily financed by public funds.  In 1967 the NAACP estimated that the federal government would spend $76.5 billion on the construction of public buildings alone. This money could be used as leverage since Executive Order 10295 signed by President Kennedy in 1962 mandated that all federal contractors comply with affirmative action requirements.  President Kennedy had established the Office of Federal Contract Compliance within the Department of Labor to enforce the Executive Order.  Yet, without mass pressure the OFCC had been reluctant to enforce its sanctions powers against recalcitrant unions.  As was the case with state FEPCs and the EEOC, here again the

existence of an Executive Order and administrative agency set up to enforce that order did not ensure an end to employment discrimination.

In the most fundamental sense, the mass demonstrations at
public construction sites in New York and many other cities
during the 1960s were not only a protest against the discriminatory racial practices of the building trade unions and
contractors, they were also a protest against the failure of
public officials and agencies of government to enforce laws
against racial discrimination in employment, especially on
construction projects subsidized by public funds.(37)

In March of 1969 the Philadelphia black community began a series of
demonstrations at major federal construction sites. The demonstrations
were organized by a coalition of groups including the NAACP, CORE, and
several churches. In response, the OFCC finally issued a new series of
guidelines for minority hiring in the construction industry that came to
be known as the Philadelphia Plan. The Philadelphia Plan required that
contractors establish manning tables that set out requirements for the
employment of a specific number of black workers in each craft at each
stage of construction.

The Philadelphia AFL-CIO responded to the imposition of the Plan by
threatening a work stoppage at construction sites in the city. It also
joined forces with the most conservative Congressional opponents of equal
employment legislation in an effort to stop the implementation of the
Philadelphia Plan. In 1969 Senator Dirksen (R. Ill.) appended a rider to
a Senate appropriations bill that would have barred federal funds for
contracts that contained minimum hiring goals. The arch foes of civil
rights in Congress supported Dirksen and attacked the Philadelphia Plan.
The AFL-CIO lobbied for the Dirksen amendment. At the 1969 annual convention of the Building Trades Department, AFL-CIO President George Meany
issued a denunciation of the Philadelphia Plan, proposing instead that
outreach programs to recruit within black communities be established.
C.J. Haggerty, president of the Building Trades Department, said in an
address before the Carpenters Union convention, "The Philadelphia Plan is
totally unnecessary and entirely unworkable. Its assumption is false at
the outset because it assumes that the building and construction trades
discriminate against minority groups."(38)

When the rider was defeated and Congress for the first time approved
the use of numerical goals and timetables, the AFL-CIO shifted its
tactics. In place of mandatory compliance programs they sought to
institute voluntary outreach and hometown plans. These hometown plans
were negotiated by the U.S. Department of Labor, promising both industry
and union representatives that if they entered into a "voluntary
agreement" there would be an understanding that the Department of Justice
would not bring any legal action.(39) The Department of Labor's goal was
to quiet black protest without pressing organized labor too far. As long
as these plans were in effect, the government was absolved of
responsibility for the enforcement of affirmative action standards.

Between 1967 and 1970, the federal government spent over $4 million
to subsidize Outreach programs aimed at recruiting blacks into union
apprenticeship programs. Yet, these programs resulted in virtually no
improvement in the percentage of African-Americans employed in the
skilled trades. At no point have the building trades shown a willingness
to open their doors to minority workers so that up until the present, the
vast majority of union construction workers remain white. By 1967 and
1968 African-American protest against employer and union discrimination
had spread far beyond just the construction industry. In New York,
blacks organized in opposition to their exclusion from leadership
positions within the International Ladies Garment Workers Union (ILGWU).

The same was true in Chicago where in October of 1968, black workers at a
G.E. Hotpoint plant held a sit down strike, complaining about unequal
treatment in the enforcement of seniority rules, grievances, and hiring
practices.(40)  This came after CORE had announced a national boycott of
G.E. at their July 1968 national convention because of the company's
continued discriminatory personnel practices.(41)

The most militant protest by black workers against continued union
and company employment discrimination originated within the UAW.  The
Detroit Revolutionary Union Movement (DRUM) was first formed by black
workers at Chrysler's Dodge Main plant in Hamtramack, Michigan.  The
majority of blacks in the auto plant supported DRUM's demands for improved safety conditions in the plant and increased black representation
in the union local's leadership since the local had a 60 percent black
membership.  DRUM initially sought to negotiate directly with the
company, bypassing the union altogether.  Later, DRUM ran its own slates
of candidates in local union elections.

The union's incumbent leadership made use of retired workers to
defeat militant black candidates, even though blacks were the majority of
the active membership.(42)  The UAW's leadership bitterly attacked DRUM,
charging that blacks were already well represented in the union's
life.(43)    Although the union's leadership recognized that the auto
companies had denied blacks full access to all jobs in the plants, they
never acknowledged the fact that the union had done very little to change
these conditions.

Nonetheless, significant improvements in the conditions of black
workers in the Detroit area auto industry did occur thereafter.  According to Gould, "It is no coincidence that the most substantial immmrove-
ments in the auto industry—and indeed in the country, for black blue
collar workers—have been in Detroit area Chrysler plants, where one-
fourth of the apprentice work force hired in 1971 was minority."(44)   By
1970, there had also been substantial increases in black repesentation
within the union's structure.  There were now 2 blacks on the 27 member
union Executive Board, 80 black international representatives, several
black department heads, and more black officers in locals with predominantly black memberships.(45)

The combined effect of court rulings, mass actions by blacks against
recalcitrant unions, and the stricter enforcement of affirmative action
regulations pushed organized labor into an alliance with anti-civil
rights forces who were opposed to any further strengthening of equal
employment laws.  By the late 1960s the leadership of the AFL-CIO found
itself in opposition to civil rights organizations in Congressional
debates and court hearings concerning equal employment.  The earlier high
degree of unity among the organizations in the Leadership Conference had
quickly come apart.

**NEW LEGISLATIVE INITIATIVES**

In early 1967 the Leadership Conference decided that it was time to
seek legislation giving the EEOC cease and desist powers.  The Conference
persuaded the Johnson administration to include this provision in its
1967 Omnibus Civil Rights bill.   Initially the AFL-CIO endorsed this
version of the bill, but then "suddenly reversed itself because they
didn't feel that the right of the aggrieved individual to bring suit in
court against management and labor ought to be continued if the EEOC was
to get authority to issue cease and desist orders.   Their position was
'either but not both.'"(46)  The NAACP however, was unwilling to give up
the right of individual suit in exchange for cease and desist since "the
entire history of the development of civil rights law is that private
suits have led the way and government enforcement has followed."(47)
Thus the two key groupings within the Leadership Conference itself could

no longer agree on the future direction of civil rights reform. As a result, there was no Congressional action on the proposal since "Congress quite naturally was not going ahead to do something over which there was so much disagreement by those who usually support civil rights legislation."(48)

In 1971 the Leadership Conference again tried to win cease and desist powers for the EEOC. However, at this point, the Nixon administration refused to support cease and desist, arguing that everything should be handled by EEOC lawsuits. The AFL-CIO demanded the transfer of the Office of Federal Contract Compliance to the EEOC as the price of its support for cease and desist powers. The result was a compromise in which the EEOC was granted the right to sue in court but not cease and desist powers. At the same time, the OFCC was left in the Department of Labor.(49) According to Herbert Hill, shortly thereafter, the "AFL-CIO effected a political rapprochement with the Nixon administration and used other means to eliminate OFCC as a civil rights enforcement mechanism."(50)

## THE EMERGENCE OF THE FULL EMPLOYMENT APPROACH

As black efforts to gain full equality resulted in heightened conflict within the ranks of the liberal coalition, the leadership of the Democratic Party, along with organized labor sought to move the political agenda away from a focus on race to less conflictual issues of general poverty and unemployment. The high visiblity of the Civil Rights Movement had led many Democratic policymakers to acknowledge for the first time that high levels of unemployment and poverty remained in the country's urban centers even during periods of relative economic prosperity. For them, this was primarily a class problem, affecting all poor, white and black alike. From their perspective, continued black poverty was due more to a lack of education and skills than continued discrimination. To a large extent these assumptions were similar to those held by the earlier New Deal reformers. The lack of these skills, more than continued racial discrimination, was seen as preventing blacks from improving their economic status.(51)

In June of 1965, President Johnson delivered a now famous speech at the Howard University commencement in which he stated that "it was not enough just to open the gates of opportunity. All our citizens must have the right to walk through those gates. This is the next and more profound stage of the battle for civil rights. We seek not just freedom but opportunity--not just legal equity but human ability--not just equality as a right and a theory but equality as a fact and as a result."(52) At the heart of the president's speech lay an argument that the next stage of the Civil Rights Movement should not be directed at combating discrimination, but instead aimed at developing social and economic resources. According to Rainwater and Yancey, President Johnson had wanted the speech to serve as a basis for a new consensus on the direction of the Civil Rights Movement. His hope had been to merge the Civil Rights Movement over which the administration had little control with the poverty movement which had orginated within the government and was under its control.(53) They argue that the Howard speech was part of the administration's goal of leapfrogging the movement and rechanneling it "away from the mere passage and implementation of legislation into the area of social and economic change, thereby, reducing the conflict with the movement by cooptation." Not surprisingly, Johnson was unsuccessful in his efforts to step out in front of the Civil Rights Movement. While black leaders recognized the need for economic and social equality for black people, they clearly were not prepared to concede that the problems of discrimination had been eliminated.

The AFL-CIO adopted a similar approach to that of the administration, also hoping to shift the political agenda away from a focus on employment discrimination towards an emphasis on increasing the total number of jobs in the economy.  Full employment was seen as a less divisive issue that could better unite blacks and organized labor. Behind these efforts lay an argument similar to that of the Johnson administration, namely, that with the end of de facto segregation, black inequality had largely become a class question.  From this point of view, black workers' protest against continued exclusion by predominantly white unions was seen as being divisive, and therefore harmful to labor solidarity.

One of the AFl-CIO's primary means of promoting this strategy was its support for the A. Philip Randolph Institute.  For many years Mr. Randolph had been one of the strongest voices within the AFL-CIO demanding equality for black workers.  However, following the 1964 Civil Rights Act, Randolph reversed his longstanding criticisms of George Meany and the leadership of the AFL-CIO, declaring that "he really felt that sufficient progress had been made (on ending internal union discrimination), that there could be an institution founded whose purpose was to work as a partner and ally of the trade union movement on problems of mutual concern to blacks and labor."(55)  Toward this end he founded the A. Philip Randolph Institute (APRI) 1965.  The overwhelming majority of the Institute's funding came from union dues money.(56)

As set out in its statement of purpose, the A. Philip Randolph Institute was established to "instill in the civil rights movement greater understanding of the need for action on behalf of specific economic demands in which the interests of labor and Negro coincide, e.g., minimum wages, extension of the Fair Labor Standards Act, reduction of the workweek, increased public housing, accelerated public works, medical care and anti-poverty programs."(57)  The statement of purpose contained no mention of the need for ongoing efforts to secure equal employment for black workers.  The Randolph Institute was essentially calling for unity between the labor and Civil Rights Movements on the basis of labor's priorities, not those of African-American workers and the organizations that represented them.

One of the very first campaigns undertaken by the APRI in 1966 was the development of a "Freedom Budget."  The first drafts of the "Freedom Budget" were written by Leon Keyserling, the economist responsible for writing the Employment Act of 1946.  Three of the four other members of the advisory committee assisting Keyersling worked for the AFL-CIO.  The chief purpose of the Freedom Budget was to show that the "country is economically and financially capable of eliminating poverty, whatever its international commitments may be."(58)  Essentially the Freedom Budget sought to prove that it was possible to have both guns and butter.

According to Joe Rauh, the Freedom Budget "was a fake....It was an effort to make the Vietnam War look good.  All this period Bayard Rustin was fighting against King talking against the Vietnam War.  But as an agent of the labor movement they were trying to stop King."(59)

The A. Philip Randolph Institute sought to make the "Freedom Budget" the central demand of the Civil Rights Movement.  In a letter to Senator Jacob Javits, A. Philip Randolph wrote "that it is imperative for the Civil Rights Movement that this document become the central program emphasis for the immediate future if we are to avoid considerable frustration and confusion.(60)  Similarly, in his statement at the White House conference  "To Fulfill these Rights" Randolph stated, "I would emphasize that, although the 'Freedom Budget' is essential if Negroes are to have first-class economic and social citizenship, it is not simply a special plea on the behalf of a narrow self-interest of a minority.  For what we propose is nothing less than having Negroes make their full contribution to the creation of a Great Society which will benefit every citizen."(61)

The A. Philip Randolph Institute sought to obtain endorsements for the Freedom Budget from the top leadership of the old liberal labor, and civil rights coalition. Articles in support of the proposal appeared in major labor publications, including The Federationist and The AFL-CIO News. The Randolph Institute distributed 80,000 copies of the popular version of the "Freedom Budget."(62)

Yet, the civil rights organizations responded to the Budget with only lukewarm support. Martin Luther King endorsed the Budget and spoke at the press conference at which it was publically announced.(63) The Congress of Racial Equality (CORE) endorsed it but simultaneously stated its opposition to the premise that the country could afford "guns and butter."(64) John Morsell, the assistant executive director of the NAACP wrote to Bayard Rustin suggesting that the several different budget proposals in existence at the time be consolidated so as to "better serve as a basis for discussion." (65) By October of 1967, Leon Keyserling was complaining to Bayard Rustin about the lack of support for the Budget from the Leadership Conference on Civil Rights.(66)

The "Freedom Budget" was never introduced in Congress. According to Norman Hill, vice president of the APRI, the key reason was that the AFL-CIO refused to support its introduction as a package. Andy Biemiller, who was the legislative director of the AFL-CIO and had also been one of the chief lobbyists for the 1964 Civil Rights Act, was not that enthusiastic about introducing the Freedom Budget as a bill. Norman Hill believes "he was interested in pushing this or that aspect of labor's or AFL-CIO's economic program. But he never really focused on introducing something as comprehensive as the 'Freedom Budget.' Not that there weren't aspects of the AFL-CIO's program that couldn't be subsumed under the 'Freedom Budget.'"(67)

The next serious Congressional debate on full employment did not occur until 1974 when Senator Hubert Humphey (D. Minn.) and Congressman Augustus Hawkins introduced the Humphrey-Hawkins Full Employment Bill. By 1974 the American economy was in the midst of a serious recession. Unemployment was affecting large sections of the working class, including many union workers. Under these conditions, there existed a much greater potential to assemble a broad coalition in support of full employment legislation. However, by 1974, the AFL-CIO's political strength was on decline. Due to its declining membership it did not possess the same national lobbying strength, nor was its clout within the Democratic Party as strong as it had been during the 1960s.

The 1974 Full Employment Bill was also written by Leon Keyserling who had modeled the legislative version of the 1946 Employment Act. The first draft of the Humphrey-Hawkins bill established a legal right to a job for anyone who wanted to work. The bill also had a strong orientation towards equal employment opportunity.(68) The AFL-CIO refused to support this version of the bill, objecting to the bill's guaranteed job provisions. In 1975, the Democratic Party leadership introduced a new version of the bill, this time with AFL-CIO support. The new version had dropped the right to sue for a job along with the emphasis on workers who faced special obstacles to employment. By the time a third draft of the bill was finally passed in 1978, its employment goals had been further modified to a four percent unemployment level, without ever defining "full employment." The fight for Humphrey-Hawkins is the last time that full employment was seriously debated in Congress. President Carter, a Democrat, made no serious efforts to implement the employment goals of the Act.

By the mid-1970s major new legislative initiatives in the field of equal employment and full employment had largely come to an end. Court actions in expanding affirmative action practices continued through 1978. The courts were not affected as quickly as Congress by the collapse of the liberal civil rights coalition.

## CONCLUSION

By the end of the 1960s the reform agenda of the Civil Rights Movement had progressed beyond what other liberal members within the traditional New Deal coalition were prepared to support. As the agenda reached beyond the elimination of legal discrimination, the movement's demands increasingly posed a direct threat to the privileged status of other sectors of society. Specifically, the movement's efforts to realize full employment access for minorities threatened the longstanding assumptions of many white workers that they had a prior right to a job.

Organized labor, as the central force within the liberal coalition, was the critical intermediary between the Civil Rights Movement and the national political institutions, including Congress and the Executive Branch. In this position labor had been able to shape specific legislative outcomes in a way that best suited its own interests. So while they worked for the 1964 Civil Rights Act, including Title VII, they also sought to ensure that Title VII would not have an adverse impact on their own core constituency of white men in the primary sector of the labor market. Thus they sought to protect the status of those workers while simultaneously supporting equal employment legislation for black workers and women who up until then were largely excluded from the best jobs in the primary labor market.

While the AFL-CIO was able to successfully control the legislative agenda so as to protect their members' employment status, they were unable to control the expansion of fair employment coverage once the law went into effect. They were faced with external pressure from two sources--black workers supported by various civil rights organizations and the federal courts. The AFL-CIO exerted little political influence over either of these two groups.

By the late 1960s this pressure posed such a great threat to the traditional status of the AFL-CIO's base that it responded by opposing any further strengthening of the enforcement powers of either the EEOC or the OFCC. In doing so, they united with some of the most conservative opponents of fair employment, who had predicted during the debate over Title VII that its enactment would threaten existing union members' status. The result was the collapse of the liberal civil rights coalition and along with it, the end of any consensus on the future direction of employment policies.

Through its political strength the AFL-CIO had effectively determined the limits of employment reform. The mass activities of the Civil Rights Movement were sufficient to force the Democratic Party to prioritize its demands. Yet, the movement's lack of institutionalized political power left it dependent on the willingness of the Party leadership and organized labor to mobilize their institutional political resources in order to gain the enactment of its demands.

Moving beyond the New Deal policy agenda to a set of social policies designed to completely eliminate remaining barriers to equal access in education, jobs, and housing, required a shift in the balance of power within the liberal wing of the Democratic Party. The conflict within the liberal civil rights coalition after 1964 made it clear that blacks were no longer willing to accept a secondary position within the old coalition. This, however, was unacceptable to organized labor which threatened to abandon the coalition rather than give up its dominant position.

Full employment may be a demand that has the power to unify all the components of the liberal coalition, yet it is an inadequate solution to black employment needs. If it were enacted, it would only guarantee an adequate number of jobs for all who want to work, yet it cannot guarantee equal access to all sectors of the economy. There have been previous periods of full employment in the American economy, during World War II for instance, when blacks still suffered from high unemployment and job discrimination. The solutions to the current levels of high unemployment among blacks lies in a combination of full employment policies and equal access to all jobs. Throughout the 1960s and 1970s these two policy agendas remained separate from each other. In setting the employment agenda for the future it is important to recognize that one will never work without the other.

## NOTES

1. National Urban League, The State of Black America (New York: National Urban League, 1987), 78.

2. John Kirby, Black Americans in the Roosevelt Era: Liberalism and Race (Knoxville: University of Tennessee Press, 1980), 94.

3. David J. Greenstone, Labor in American Politics (New York: Alfred Knopf, 1969).

4. James Harvey, Black Civil Rights During the Kennedy Administration (Jackson, Miss.: University and College Press of Mississippi, 1971).

5. Ibid., 58.

6. Joseph Rauh, interview with author, Washington, D.C. July 25, 1987.

7. Norman Hill, interview with author, New York, July 22, 1986.

8. "Labor Aids Bias Fight," Detroit Free Press, April 4, 1965, 4-C.

9. Charles and Barbara Whalen, The Longest Debate: A Legislative History of the 1964 Civil Rights Act (Cabin John Maryland: Seven Locks Press, 1985).

10. Herbert Hill, interview with author, Madison, August 25, 1986.

11. Herbert Hill, "The Equal Employment Opportunity Acts of 1964 and 1972: A Critical Analysis of the Legislative History and Administration of the Law," Industrial Relations Law Journal 2, no. 1 (Spring 1977): 19.

12. Congressional Record, 88th Cong., 1st session, March 21, 1964, 5820.

13. "AFL-CIO Comments on Lester Hill's Criticism," January 31, 1964, from the AFL-CIO Dept. of Legislation, Box 009, Folder 13, George Meany Memorial Archives.

14. Ibid.

15. Ibid.

16. Hubert Humphrey, Congressional Record, 88th Cong., 1st sess., March 30, 1964 , 6549.

17. Hill, "The Equal Employment Opportunity Acts," 2.

18. Ibid.

19. Herbert Hill memo to Mr. Moon, "NAACP Labor Director to Address Auto Workers National Anti-Discrimination Conference," June 26, 1967, from the NAACP files, Manuscript Division, Library of Congress.

20. William Oliver memo to Walter Reuther, January 16, 1964, from the UAW President's Office, Box 90, Folder 12, Archives of Labor History and Urban Affairs, Wayne State University.

21. Ibid.

22. United Auto Workers EEO-1 Report, Oct., 1966, from the President's Office, Box 7, Folder 11, Archives of Labor History and Urban Affairs, Wayne State University.

23. N.Y. State Commission Against Discrimination, "Negroes in Apprenticeships, New York State," Monthly Labor Review, (Sept. 1960): 952–957.

24. Herbert Hill letter to Mr. Floyd Hunter, Assistant Secretry of HUD for Model Cities, May 2, 1969, from Herbert Hill files of the NAACP, Manuscripts Division, Library of Congress.

25. National Association for the Advancement of Colored People, Press Release, September 7, 1965, from the NAACP files, Manuscript Division of the Library of Congress.

26. Leadership Conference, Internal Memo, 1966. From the files of the Chicago Urban League, Archives of the University of Illinois, Chicago, Box 169, Folder 21.

27. Nijole Benokratis and Joe Feagin, Affirmative Action and Employment Opportunity: Action, Inaction, and Reaction (Boulder, Co.: Westview Press, 1978), 103.

28. William Oliver, memo to W. Reuther, December 30, 1968, from the UAW's President's Office files, Box 91, Folder 9, Archives of Labor History and Urban Affairs, Wayne State University.

29. Benjamin Wolkison, Blacks, Unions, and the EEOC (Lexington, MA.: D.C. Heath & Co., 1975).

30. Ibid., 132.

31. Hill, "The Equal Employment Opportunity Acts," 29.

32. William Gould, Black Workers in White Unions: Job Discrimination in the United States (Ithaca, NY: Cornell University Press, 1977).

33. Ibid.

34. Ibid., 101.

35. Benokratis and Feagin, Affirmative Action, 20–22.

36. H. Hill, interview, August 25, 1986.

37. Herbert Hill, "The Crippled Giant: Organized Labor in Decline,"

*Critical Perspectives of Third World America* 1, no. 1, (Fall 1983): 363.

38. Herbert Hill, *Labor Union Control of Job Training:  A Critical Analysis of Apprenticeship Outreach Programs and the Hometown Plans*, Institute for Urban Affairs and Research,  Howard University, vol. 2, no. 1, 1974.

39. Sanford Kantor, "Blacks and the Chicago Construction Industry: Which Way Now?"  Chicago Urban League Research Report,  September 8, 1965, 18.

40. *The Chicago Daily Defender*,  October 16, 1968, from the files of the Chicago Urban League, Archives of the University of Illinois, Chicago, Box 116, Folder 11.

41. "CORE to Boycott General Electric," *Chicago Daily Defender*, July 24, 1968.  From the files of the Chicago Urban League, Archives of the University of Illinois, Chicago, Box 116, Folder 11.

42. James  Gerschwender, *Class,  Race,  and  Worker  Insurgency* (Cambridge:  Cambridge University Press, 1977), 108.

43. Philip Foner, *Organized Labor and the Black Worker*  (New York: Praeger Publishers, 1978),  416.

44. Gould, *Black Workers in White Unions*, 391.

45. Foner, *Organized Labor*, 421,  January 7, 1970.

46. Joseph Rauh, letter to Walter Reuther,  January 7, 1970, from the UAW President's Office, Box 375, Folder 17, Archives of Labor History and Urban Affairs, Wayne State University.

47. Jack Greenberg, May 4, 1967, Statement before the U.S. Senate Subcommittee on Employment Manpower, and Poverty, from the NAACP files in the Manuscript Division, Library of Congress.

48. Rauh letter to Reuther,  January 1, 1970.

49. Hill, "The Equal Employment Opportunity Acts," 50.

50. Ibid., 51.

51. Henry Aaron, *Politics and the Professors:  The Great Society in Perspective* (Washington, D.C.:  Brookings Institution, 1978), 66.

52. Lee Rainwater and William Yancey, *The Moynihan Report and the Politics of Controversy* (Cambridge:  MIT Press, 1967), 126.

53. Ibid., 273.

54. Ibid., 274.

55. Norman Hill interview, July 22, 1986.

56. Ibid.

57. A. Philip Randolph Institute, Draft Prospectus, from the UAW President's Office, Archives of Labor History and Urban Affairs, Wayne State University.

58. Bayard Rustin, memo to community leaders. "What You Can Do About the Freedom Budget," from the files of the A. Philip Randolph Institute.

59. Rauh, interview July 25, 1987.

60. A. Philp Randolph, letter to Senator Jacob Javits, August 22, 1966, from the files of the A. Philip Randolph Institute.

61. Ibid.

62. A. Philp Randolph Institute memo, March 1967, from the files of the A. Philip Randolph Institute, New York.

63. Martin Luther King, October 26, 1966, Statement on the Occasion of the Introduction of the Freedom Budget, New York City, from the files of the A. Philip Randolph Institute.

64. Floyd McKissick, October 10, 1966, letter to A. Philip Randolph, from the files of the A. Philip Randolph Institute.

65. John Morsell, June 17, 1966, Letter to Bayard Rustin, from the files of the A. Philip Randolph Institute.

66. Leon Keyserling, October 19, 1967, Letter to Bayard Rustin, from the files of the A. Philip Randolph Institute.

67. Interview with Norman Hill, July 22, 1986.

68. Helen Ginsberg, Full Employment and Public Policy: The United States and Sweden (Lexington, MA: D.C. Heath and Co., 1983).

# 12 Black Workers at Risk: Jobs for Life or Death

*Beverly H. Wright*

Since the beginning of the Civil Rights Movement in the United States, Black Americans have made great strides. However, the health status of Black Americans has shown a persistent and distressing disparity in important health indicators when compared to those of their white counterparts. In 1983, the life expectancy of whites reached a new high of 75.2 years, while black life expectancy reached only 69.6 years. This difference in the life expectancy of whites and blacks represents a gap of 5.6 years. The present life expectancy of Black Americans was reached by White Americans in the early 1950s, thus representing a lag of about thirty years.(1)

In 1980, there were 26.5 million blacks in the United States. This represents an increase of approximately 17 percent over 1970 census figures. Approximately 15 percent of the total U.S. population in the 15 or under age category are black. However, by the time they are 64, the relative proportion of the black U.S. population decreases to 8 percent. (2).

## TO WHAT DO WE ATTRIBUTE THE CAUSE OF THIS DISPARITY IN LIFE EXPECTANCY AMONG BLACKS AS COMPARED TO WHITES?

Although many factors are presumed to influence black health status and life expectancy in America today, environmental and occupational exposures are increasingly considered sources of disease and illness.(3) A major demand of the civil rights struggle for Black Americans was equal access to the work place. Black unemployment was seen as a major obstacle to economic stability and progress within the community. Consequently, many black civil rights, business, and political leaders directed their energies toward bringing jobs to their constituents. Ironically, the pursuit of greater job opportunities for blacks overshadowed concern for the safety and health risk related to increased employment within certain job categories. In some instances, a right to have a job also came to mean a right to die due to job exposures.

There are approximately 100 million workers in America. Each year 100,000 die from occupational diseases while nearly 400,000 new cases each year are reported.(4) Approximately 9 million persons each year suffer from severe work-related injuries.(5)

Blacks, however, have a 37 percent greater chance of suffering an occupational injury or illness and a 20 percent greater chance of dying from an occupational disease or injury than do white workers. Black workers are also twice as likely to be permanently disabled by work-related diseases than their white counterparts. Approximately one and one-half million or fifteen percent of the black work force are permanently or partially disabled due to a job-related injury or illness.(6)

This paper investigates the effects of hazards in the work place on the health (i.e., general health status) of Black Americans.(7)    Specifically examined is the extent to which the life expectancy of blacks can be explained by occupational or job categories as opposed to only "intrinsic" (i.e., diet, smoking, drinking, etc.) racial or cultural differences between blacks and whites.  Also investigated are the effects of the Civil Rights Movement on black labor force participation and the resultant health status of black workers.

Black workers in the United States represent more than 12 million people and constitute a major segment of this nation's work force.  The black work force comprises 12 percent of the total number of employed individuals in the United States and represents 30 percent of all unionized workers; they constitute the highest proportional percentage of unionized workers in this country.(8)

Since the establishment of the Occupational Safety and Health Act of 1970, improvements in the general safety and health of workers have been made.  Particularly in the area of the identification of hazards and the establishment of controls for toxic and cancer-causing agents, substantial improvements in the work place environment have been advanced.  Blacks and other minority workers, however, have not benefited from these improvements to the degree that white workers have.  Among this highly unionized group within the work force, the injury, disease, and death rates are disproportionately high as compared to their white counterparts in certain industries.

For example, higher rates of illness and injury were found among black as compared to white workers in a 1946-1950 study of the chromate and bichromate industry.  Black workers were concentrated in the industry job category that exposed workers to high levels of chromate dust.  They also suffered higher incidences of damage to the nasal cavity.  Forty-one percent of the black workers at the plant as compared to sixteen percent of the whites worked in the most hazardous dry end of the processing.  It is believed that this overexposure to chromium-bearing dusts caused the increase in deaths among black workers at the plant.(9)

Black iron and steel foundry workers were also found to have higher rates of high blood pressure and some heart diseases than their white coworkers.  Higher death rates from hypertensive heart disease and stroke were found for black steel masons (twelve times as high) than for white steel masons.(10)

Three cases of rare neoplasm angiosarcoma of the liver in 1974 were reported in workers exposed to vinyl chloride.  A black worker was the first patient to exhibit this rare cancer.  The connection between cancer and exposure to vinyl chloride had been known since 1934.  Federal standards were developed shortly after the discovery of this case to reduce worker exposure to this carcinogenic substance. (11)    These and other reported findings seem to suggest that race and occupation combine to place some minorities (especially blacks) in "double jeopardy" of loss of life and susceptibility to disease and injury.  The question thus arises, why is it that black workers have fared so poorly in the area of job health safety?

Many theories are offered to explain diseases.  However, "social causation" theorists, such as Hall, assert the idea that "we cannot understand disease incidence without looking at the social context in which people live and die."(12)  This most interesting and useful theoretical approach explains possible relationships among disease-causing agents as well as contributing factors within those relationships.  From this premise, Hall, in a study of health in inner cities, identifies three causes for diseases among low-income, inner-city minorities: (1) physically-induced, (2) socially-induced, and (3) genetically-induced disease.  All three causes provide insight into reasons why low-income, inner-city minorities (and other inner-city residents) contract disease at a much greater rate than the more affluent urban, suburban, and rural resident. Hall's model is easily adapted to the questions of this research effort and works well in explaining why black workers are at greater risk of injury, disease, and death than are white workers. Three causal explanations for the excess risk of injury, disease, and death among black workers are advanced in the literature. (1) Socially-induced diseases are those that result from social rather than physical, genetic, or environmental causes. Most importantly, these illnesses are often beyond the individual's control. For example, one of the ramifications of race may be sources of disease. In the case of black workers, consequences of race could include job discrimination and job placement, as well as numerous other stressors. (2) Physically-induced diseases (in this research also including genetics) are those that result from physical rather than environmental or social causes. Physically-induced diseases are those that occur because of intrinsic, racial, or cultural factors such as unhealthy diets and habits. Genetic factors are also classified as physical inducement of disease. Hall, however, does not include genetic inducement with physical inducement of disease. Stereotypes and myth about minority groups, as well as genetic differences between races, have often been used as sources of disease and as justification for singling out some groups for differential treatment. For example, in the case of black workers, the myth concerning their ability to withstand hotter temperatures has been used as justification for their being assigned to the extremely dangerous coke ovens within the steel industry. Certain cultural habits, such as diets and smoking are also used as explanations of disease and injury in black workers. (3) Environmentally-induced disease, for the purposes of this research effort, are separated from physically-induced disease and are discussed separately. Environmentally-induced diseases are those that result from environmental rather than physical or social causes and are caused by the quality of the environment in which we live. These include our homes, communities, and work environments. Most often, environmental exposure is involuntary and individuals lack specific information on the hazards associated with their environments. For example, in the case of black workers, shipyard workers in coastal Georgia were found to have a disproportionately high lung cancer death rate. This incidence of cancer was shown to be related to job exposure.(13)

## SOCIALLY-INDUCED DISEASES

Socially-induced diseases result from social rather than physical, genetic, or environmental causes. Stress and stress-related illnesses are identified as socially-induced diseases. They can occur "from physical and pyschological responses to a variety of social as well as pathological factors over which people have varying degrees of control."(14) Stress and stress-related illnesses represent a major health problem among Black Americans since their origins are often due to social factors beyond the individual's control.(15) Hypertension is a stress-related disease and is primarily seen as one that is socially-induced. Only ten percent of all hypertension occurs because of a secondary effect of problems such as pituitary or adrenal tumors.(16) An examination of hypertension among Black Americans and a review of stress-related diseases within certain industries where significant numbers of black workers are employed further illustrate the volatile position of blacks in the work place.

Hypertension is defined as elevated blood pressure and is a major cause of organ damage and death in humans. It is believed to be the "body's response to its need to accommodate faster breathing and heartbeat in response to stress and other factors."(17) Approximately 25 to

30 million Americans are hypertensive.(18)    Hypertension rates for Black Americans of every age are nearly twice as high as those for whites.(19) Approximately six million of the 25 to 30 million Americans who suffer from hypertension are black.    Hypertension death rates are approximately 3.8 to 3.2 times higher for black males than for white males.    The rate for black females is 3.9 to 4.8 times higher than the rate for white females in the South Atlantic and Southeast Central regions.    These regions have the highest reported U.S. mortality rate for black males and females.(20)    Heart disease, which is hypertensive-related, accounts for more deaths a year than any other single category.    Black Americans experience in excess of 26,169 deaths each year from hypertensive-related diseases.    Although these statistics suggest an inherent or genetic propensity to hypertension among Black Americans, hypertension rates for blacks who are not Americans and who reside in other countries are significantly lower than for whitesin those same countries.(21)

Explanations for this increased risk of hypertension and related diseases among Black Americans range from cultural habits (i.e., eating, drinking, smoking) to psychological stressors due to discrimination or genetics.    A social factor contributing to this increased risk that is generally overlooked is stressors in the work place.  To what extent is stress or stress-related disease due to occupational environments?

Available data lend support to the contention that occupational environments play a far more important role than is presently realized in the causation of stress-related diseases. Studies show that working conditions within certain industries contribute to the increased incidence of stress-related mortality and morbidity. Black workers are also more likely to be employed in stress-related job categories within these industries than are white workers.

For example, studies of both iron and steel foundry workers and laundry and dry cleaning industry workers show an increase in the incidence of stress-related mortality and morbidity among blacks as compared to white workers.(22)    Black iron and steel foundry workers are concentrated in the most hazardous of jobs within that industry--the coke oven operation.    The job involves a process that releases dangerous gases and dust particles, including carcinogens, and exposes the workers to extreme heat.    These conditions increase the risk of stress-related diseases and death.    Laundry workers are also exposed to a number of hazards on the job, including excessive heat, which can cause exhaustion, cramps, rashes, and heat strokes. Dry cleaning workers are exposed to many different solvents and heat from pressers.  Working conditions and exposures in these industries where significant numbers of blacks are employed increase the risk of stress-related disease and death among black workers. These data seem to suggest that the social practice of discriminatory job placement has resulted in the assignment of blacks to extremely hazardous jobs that are also stress-inducing.  Consequently, black workers as compared to white workers disproportionately suffer from stress-related illnesses and death.  Discriminatory job placement based on race in America has had a negative impact on the health of black workers in these industries and on the general health status of blacks in America.

## PHYSICALLY-INDUCED DISEASES

Physically-induced diseases are those that occur because of intrinsic factors such as diets, smoking, or genetics.  Even more significant is the fact that the individual's behavior and/or characteristics are seen as the primary cause of disease.  "Victim blaming" is often the end result.

In the area of occupational health and safety, a number of "victim blaming" arguments are advanced to explain the higher injury and death rates of nonwhite workers.  The basic argument, however, is that "modern industrial working conditions are so safe that if a worker gets hurt or sick it must be his or her fault and not the fault of the industry."(23) Consequently, the lower life expectancy and higher incidence of cancer and death rates incurred by nonwhite (especially black) workers is often attributed to either bad habits or genetics.  For example, Paul Kotin resurrected the "hypersusceptibility worker" notion that shifts the focus from "what chemicals cause cancer to what people get cancer."(24) Kotin's argument begins with the reasonable assumption that "all biological organisms, including humans, vary in their response to external stimuli such as toxic substance or carcinogens."  Based on this assumption he then asserts that management has a "right" to select sturdier workers for riskier jobs.  This viewpoint supports management's "right" to continue discriminatory job placement practices that already exist in some industries.  For example, in the iron and steel industry one study showed that ninety-one percent of all workers in the coke ovens were black and were exposed to (among other things) extreme heat.(25)  The industry justifies this practice on the basis of the myth that "they [blacks] absorb heat better."(26)  Similar practices based on myths were found within the electronics industry where "dark skinned" minority workers were regularly assigned to jobs using caustic chemicals because skin irritations resulting from job exposure are not as pronounced on dark skin as they are on white skin.  Consequently, "dark skinned" workers will have fewer complaints than their white counterparts whose skin irritations are more noticeable.(27)

A second blame-the-victim tactic shifts the responsibility for occupational injury and death from uncontrolled exposure in the workplace to the workers' own insidious lifestyle.(28)  For example, management often assigns the cause for the high incidence of lung cancer found among workers in some industries to smoking habits rather than to overexposure to dusts and chemicals in the workplace.  The facts are that smoking definitely increases the susceptibility of workers exposed to dust and chemicals (i.e., for example, asbestos, rubber, and steel workers), but the risk to nonsmoking workers in such industries is also greater than that of persons who do not work in such environments.(29)

Black males have the highest reported incidence rate for all cancers combined and have a particularly high incidence of lung cancer.  In fact, the death rate of lung cancer among blacks is about twenty times higher than it was forty years ago.  Although smoking certainly accounts for some of the increase in lung cancer among black males, this alarming increase cannot be attributed to smoking alone.  The excess risks are more likely due to environmental factors including occupational exposure. Only recently are we beginning to uncover occupationally-induced cancer problems that have existed for years.  Present data reveal that a significant number of black workers in specific industries have been assigned to the most hazardous jobs that also exposed them to numerous now known carcinogens.(30)  The degree to which excess risks of lung cancer in black males may be attributed to occupational exposure is reflected, for example, in the fact that the highest incidence of lung cancer among Black American males is in Pittsburgh, Pennsylvania.  This fact is not surprising when one realizes that a significant number of black males in Pittsburgh are employed in the most hazardous jobs in the steel industry, which exposes them to known carcinogens.

"Blaming the victims" is an industry management tactic that is used to justify inaction in areas of occupational health and safety.  Myths or racist stereotypes are often used to camouflage discriminatory job placement practices resulting in the purposeful exposure of black workers to hazardous work conditions.  Equally insidious is the "victim blaming" tactic employed by industry that blames occupational illness and death on intrinsic, racial or cultural characteristics including alleged genetic deficiencies.  This rationale then absolves the industry of any blame for disease or injury rates among workers.

## ENVIRONMENTALLY-INDUCED DISEASES

Environmentally-induced diseases are those that occur due to exposures in the environment. The work environments of some industries have already been shown to be extremely hazardous for workers, especially black workers. Not surprisingly, cancer rates for blacks are increasing at epidemic rates, and black workers experience disproportionately high cancer incidence and death rates.

Although in 1949 the reported cancer rate for blacks was 20 percent lower than the rate reported for whites, by 1967 the number of deaths from all cancer increased twice as rapidly among blacks as it did among whites. Presently, black males have the highest reported incidence rate for all cancers combined. Blacks are experiencing a growing cancer epidemic with a 25 percent increase in the cancer rate over the last 10 years. The American Cancer Society data show that the cancer mortality rates of blacks and whites were practically the same 30 years ago.(31) However, cancer death rates in whites have subsequently increased by 10 percent while the rate for blacks has astoundingly increased by 40 percent. Many factors have been cited as possible contributors to the high incidence of cancer among blacks. Here again, smoking, diet, and genetics are included. The relationship between occupational exposures and cancer has received only minimal attention by the scientific community. However, available data tend to support the relationship between the work environment and the incidence of cancer among workers.

The exposure of black workers to many of the chemicals that are now known as carcinogens began in the early 1900s when large numbers of southern blacks migrated to urban industrial areas to work. The status and nature of the jobs, however, were no different from those relegated to them in the South. Black workers were hired for the worst jobs. These most often were the most strenuous and hazardous jobs that also exposed them to chemicals that are known to cause cancer.(32) Studies of industries where large numbers of blacks have worked in jobs using or producing carcinogens suggest that this exposure is responsible for some excess risk of cancer among black workers.(33) For example, a study of 6,500 rubber workers in a large tire manufacturing plant in Akron, Ohio, found that 27 percent of the black workers in the sample, but only 3 percent of the white workers, had worked in the compounding and mixing area. The compounding and mixing area is located at the front of the production line where workers are exposed to dusts, chemicals, ingredients, and vapors that contain toxins and is the most dangerous location in the plant. Black workers in this area showed elevations in cancers of several types as compared to whites, including respiratory and prostate cancer.(34) The cities of Toledo, Cleveland, and Akron, Ohio, have major rubber producing and fabricating plants; these cities also have significantly high prostate cancer rates for blacks.(35)

A study of 59,000 steelworkers or 62 percent of all U.S. males working in basic steel production was conducted from 1953 through 1962.(36) The area of greatest hazardous exposure in this industry is the coke oven operation. Workers are exposed (among other things) to dangerous gases and dust particles, including the carcinogen Benzo (a) Pyrene. The Study revealed that 89 percent of nonwhite coke plant workers were employed at the coke ovens while only 31 percent of white workers were employed in that area.(37) The findings of the 1953-1962 study revealed that nonwhite workers (mostly black) in the coke plant experienced double the expected death rate from malignant neoplasms. In fact, all of the excess for nonwhite coke plant workers was due to cancer of the respiratory system. Although only slightly over 7 respiratory cancer deaths would have been expected among nonwhite coke plant workers,

25 deaths from this cause occurred among those employed at least 5 years in the coke plant. The comparable number of expected deaths for whites in this area was 8.4 with only 7 actual deaths.(38) Exposures to carcinogens and toxins were greatest among workers employed in full time "top side" jobs in the coke plant. Nineteen percent of nonwhite workers compared to only three percent of white workers were employed in this capacity. Significantly, almost all of the excess death rates from lung cancer were due to death of men employed in full time "top side" jobs at the coke plant. The lung cancer rate among nonwhite full time "top side" workers was 8 times greater than expected, 19 versus 2.2. (39)

Other illustrations of industry exposure of black workers to possible cancer-causing agents include the following:

1.  The National Cancer Institute conducted a study of laundry and dry cleaning workers and found that blacks had higher death rates from cancer of the liver, lung, cervix, uterus, and skin.(40)

2.  A 1978 cancer mortality study of coastal Georgia residents found black shipyard workers to have a lung cancer death rate two times higher than expected.(41)

3.  A 1946 U.S. Public Health study of chromate workers found that the respiratory cancer mortality rate for all workers was 29 times higher than expected. However, the actual to expected respiratory cancer death ratio was 14.29 for whites and 80.00 for blacks.

These data suggest that the excess risk of cancer that exists for black workers as compared to white workers may be due to greater exposure of black workers to carcinogens in the work place. Moreover, the placement of blacks in greater numbers than whites in the most dangerous jobs in certain industries is the primary reason for this overexposure.

**CONCLUSION**

There are numerous factors that contribute to the health status of Black Americans. Occupational exposures, however, have received little attention. In fact, statistics on occupational safety and health are generally lacking, and race-specific data are even harder to find. However, black workers represent over 15 percent of the total work force in nearly 33 occupational categories. Unfortunately, a large percentage of the black work force remains overrepresented in low-pay, low-skill, high-risk blue collar and service occupations. Moreover, blacks are concentrated in certain industries, many of which have above average injury and illness rates. They are, for example, overrepresented in laundry and dry cleaning, tobacco manufacture, fabric mills, smelters, hospitals (as orderlies and attendants), and service industries. Available data on job placement patterns within certain industries strongly suggest that black workers are intentionally placed in the dirtiest and most hazardous jobs in certain industries. Generally, black workers are relegated by discriminatory employment practices into the least desirable jobs. Historically, racist attitudes or practices have exacerbated resulting health and safety problems. For example, the Gauley Bridge disaster (1930-1931) in West Virginia was responsible for the disability of 1500 workers and the death of 500 mostly black workers. They were recruited to tunnel through a mountain with a high silica content. Overexposure to this substance usually causes a chronic lung disease. In the Gauley Bridge incident, 169 black men literally dropped dead on the spot and were hurriedly buried on the spot. The workers who earned about thirty cents an hour were not told of the known hazards or given protective breathing devices. The disaster was not uncovered until 1935 and resulted in an amendment to the West Virginia compensation law, but not soon enough to benefit the dead, disabled, or family members of the Gauley Bridge disaster.(42)

Similarly, in 1969 the textile industry denied the evidence that exposure to cotton dust could cause byssinosis or "brown lung" disease. The general sentiment of the industry on this matter was reflected in an editorial in the industry's journal: "We are particularly intrigued by the term 'byssinosis,' a thing thought up by the venal doctors who attended the last International Labor Association meeting in Africa where inferior races are bound to be inflicted by diseases more superior races defeated years ago."(43)

In 1987, black workers are still relegated to the dirtiest and most hazardous jobs within certain industries. There is evidence to support the contention that working conditions in certain industries employing significant numbers of blacks are contributing to the increased incidence of injury, disease and death among black as compared to white workers. Moreover, there is a great disparity between the general health status (as represented by important health indicators such as life expectancy, incidence of disease, and death rates) of Black Americans as compared to whites. Available data, although limited, suggest that occupational factors play a significant role in the causation of major disease and health problems among Black Americans. That black workers are at "special risk" of loss of life and susceptibility to disease and injury because of discriminatory job placement practices is strongly supported by these data. A job should not be a death sentence. However, black workers, due to their race and resultant discrimination are relegated to jobs with increased risk of injury, disease, and death. Race and occupation place blacks in "double jeopardy" of loss of life and susceptibility to disease. The effects on the general health status of Black Americans is ominous and is even more distressing in light of the "inaction" on our government's part to address this problem. Even more disturbing is the fact that there is much evidence to support the notion that blacks are generally not aware of the dangers in their work environment.

In sum, arguments that place the blame for the excess risk of injury, disease, and death of black workers on physical factors (such as their "hypersusceptibility") or those that place the blame for the excess risk of injury, disease, and death of blacks in general on instrinsic factors (such as diet, smoking, and genetics) are generally not supported by the evidence. These data suggest that it is unlikely that physical or genetic characteristics are solely the blame for the increased health risk among Black Americans. In fact, it seems much more likely that environmental causes, including the work environment, contribute far more to this increased risk of injury, disease, and death among Black Americans than has been realized. Environmental pollutants and occupational hazards are increasingly identified as sources of death and disease among Black Americans. However, blacks were involved in civil rights struggles during the peak period of the environmental movement, roughly during the late sixties and early seventies. Many of the key environmental issues of this period (e.g., wildlife and wilderness preservation, energy and resource conservation, regulation of industrial pollutors) were not high priority items on the civil rights agenda. Social justice, political empowerment, and equal access to education and employment were at the heart of blacks' struggle for parity with the larger society. Blacks were demanding equal access to the workplace. Civil rights advocates and boosters of unrestrained business development were closely aligned on the issue of jobs.

In a desperate attempt to improve the economic conditions of their constituents, many black civil rights, business, and political leaders directed their energies toward bringing jobs to their constituents. In many instances, this was achieved at great health risks to black workers and the surrounding communities. The promise of jobs and a broadened tax base in economically depressed communities are often seen as acceptable tradeoffs to potential health and environmental risks. This scenario has proven to be the rule in economically depressed and politically oppressed communities in this country (especially in the South) and their counterparts around the world (especially in the Third World). Workers are often forced to make personal sacrifices in terms of job security and job safety. The work place in this case is an arena where unavoidable tradeoffs must be made between jobs and work place hazards.(44) If workers want to keep their jobs, they must work under conditions which may be hazardous to them, their families, and their community. This practice amounts to "environmental blackmail" and is equivalent to economic bondage.(45) Black workers are especially vulnerable to job blackmail because of the threat of unemployment and their concentration in certain types of occupations. Fear of unemployment acts as a potent incentive for many blacks to stay in and accept jobs they know are health-threatening. There continues to be considerable overlap between the agendas of black civil rights advocates and those of economic boosters (both groups call for more jobs). However, the 1980s have seen the emergence of a small cadre of blacks who also advocate environmental issues as civil rights. An alliance has been forged between organized labor, blacks, and environmental groups as exhibited by the 1983 urban environment conference workshops held in New Orleans.(46) Environmental and civil rights issues were presented as compatible agenda items by this coalition. Environmental protection and social justice are not necessarily incompatible goals.(47)

Black communities, especially in the South, are just beginning to integrate environmental issues into traditional civil rights agendas. The jobs vs. environment argument is now being challenged as black organizations broaden their definition of civil rights to include air and water quality, hazardous wastes, and other environmental issues. Finally, black communities need to incorporate environmental safeguards into their agendas for economic development. The promise of jobs may provide short-term solutions to economically depressed black communities. However, health and environmental risks can often overshadow the benefits associated with hazardous low-paying occupations.

**NOTES**

1. U.S. Department of Health and Human Services, Report on the Secretary's Task Force on Black and Minority Health (Washington, D.C., 1985), 2.

2. Ibid., 51.

3. Nicholas Ashford, Crisis in the Workplace: Occupational Disease and Injury, Report to the Ford Foundation (Cambridge MA: MIT Press, 1976); Morris Davis, "Occupational Hazards and Black Workers" Urban Health (August 1977): 16-18; Samuel Epstein, Lester Brown, and Carl Pope, Hazardous Waste in America (San Francisco: Sierra Club Books, 1983); Morris Davis, "The Impact of Workplace Health and Safety on Black Workers: Assessment and Prognosis," Labor Studies Journal 4 (Spring 1981): 29-40; Richard Kazis and Richard Grossman, Fear and Work: Job Blackmail, Labor and the Environment (New York: The Pilgrim Press, 1983; Robert Bullard and Beverly Wright, "The Politics of Pollution: Implications for the Black Community," Phylon 47 (March 1986): 71-78.

4.    U.S. Council on Environmental Quality, Environmental Quality: The Tenth Annual Report (Washington, D.C.: GPO, 1980), 22; Ray Elling, The Struggle for Worker's Health: A Study of Six Industrialized Countries (New York: Baywood Publishing Co., Inc., 1986), 19.

5.    Congressional Quarterly, Inc., Environment and Health (Washington, D.C.: CQ Inc., 1981), 105.

6.    Urban Environment Conference, Inc., Taking Back Our Health (Washington, D.C.: UEC, Inc., 1983), 1-6.

7.    See also Davis, "Impact of Workplace Health and Safety," 29-40.

8.    Ibid., 29.

9.    Urban Environment Conference, Inc., 1983, 4; Davis, "Impact of Workplace Health and Safety on Black Workers," 32; W. M. Gafafer, Health of Workers in Chromate-Producing Industry (U.S. Health Service Publication, 1970), 192.

10.    Davis, "Impact of Workplace Health and Safety," 29-40; H. Rockett and C. Redmond, "Long-term Mortality Study of Steelworkers, X, Mortality Patterns among Masons," Journal of Occupational Medicine 18 (August 1976): 541-45.

11.    J. L. Creech and M. N. Johnson, "Angiosarcoma of the Liver in Manufacture of Polyvinyl Chloride," Journal of Occupational Medicine 16 (March 1974): 150-51; Davis, "Impact of Workplace Health and Safety," 32.

12.    Ellen Hall, Inner City Health in America (Washington, D.C.: Urban Environment Foundation, 1979), 13.

13.    William Blot, "Lung Cancer after Employment in Shipyards during World War II," New England Journal of Medicine 21 (September 1978).

14.    Hall, 29.

15.    Joseph Eyer, "Hypertension as a Disease of Modern Society," International Journal of Health Services, 5 (October 1975): 547.

16.    Hall, 29.

17.    Ibid, 31.

18.    Richard Williams, Textbooks of Black-Related Diseases (New York: McGraw-Hill, 1975), 4-16.

19.    Jay Weiss, Psychological Factors in Stress and Disease (San Francisco: W. H. Freeman and Co., 1976), 12.

20.    Hall, 32.

21.    Ibid., 32.

22.    H. Rockett and Carol Redmond, "Long Term Mortality Study," 541-45; Aaron Blair, "Causes of Death among Laundry and Drycleaning Workers," American Journal of Public Health 69 (May 1979); 509; Davis, Impact of Workplace Health and Safety," 33.

23.   Samuel Epstein, The Politics of Cancer, (San Francisco:  Sierra Club Books, 1978), 395.

24.   Ibid., 395.

25.   Ibid., 55.

26.   Davis, "Occupational Hazards," 17.

27.   Ibid., 17.

28.   Epstein, The Politics of Cancer, 396: Davis, "Impact of Work-place Health and Safety," 33;  Urban Environment Conference, Inc., Taking Back Our Health, 5.

29.   Epstein, The Politics of Cancer, 366; Urban Environment Confer-ence, Inc., Taking Back Our Health, 5.

30.   Davis, "Occupational Hazards," 17; Davis, "Impact of Workplace Health and Safety," 33; Epstein, Brown, and Pope, Hazardous Waste in America, 396.

31.   American Cancer Society, Cancer Facts and Figures:  1986 (New York:  The Society, 1986), 13.

32.   Davis, "Impact of Workplace Health and Safety," 33-36.

33.   Urban Environment Conference, Inc., Taking Back Our Health, 5-6;  Davis "Impact of Workplace Health and Safety," 34;   Hale, Inner City Health in America, 19-28.

34.   A. J. McMichael, et. al., "Mortality Among Rubber Workers: Relationships to Specific Jobs," Journal of Occupational Medicine  18 (March 1976):  184.

35.   Ibid.

36.   Lloyd Williams, "Long-term Mortality of Steel Workers, I, Meth-odology," Journal of Occupational Medicine 11 (June 1969):  301.

37.   Williams, "Long-term Mortality Study of Steelworkers, V, Res-piratory Cancer in Coke Plant Workers," Journal of Occupational Medicine 13 (February 1971):  55.

38.   Ibid.

39.   Ibid., 59

40.   Blair, 509.

41.   William Blot, et. al, "Lung Cancer after Employment in Ship-yards," New England Journal of Medicine 21 (September 1978):  620-24.

42.   Davis, "Occupational Hazards," 17.

43.   Ibid.

44.   D. Nelkins and M .S. Brown, Workers at Risk:  Voices from the Workplace (Chicago:  University of Chicago Press, 1984).

45.    Kazis and Grossman, Fear at Work, 15-16.

46.    Stephanie Pollack and Jo Ann Grouzucak, Reagan, Toxics and Minorities (Washington, D.C.:  Urban Environment Conference, Inc., 1984).

47.    Denton Morrison and Riley Dunlap, "Environmentalism and Elitism:  A Conceptual and Empirical Analysis," Environmental Management 10 (July/August 1986):  581-89.

# 13 "Where Do We Go from Here"

*Vincent Harding*

I want to express my appreciation to all of you, all of us who have participated in this conference at a variety of levels. It has been clearly a very rich and powerful experience and those who sat up here and those who sat there have all contributed to its power. I want also to thank especially Frank Smith, who just introduced me, and the NOAH (New Opportunities at Hofstra) program which he directs. If one takes any part of the human experience seriously and grabs hold of it and goes deep down with it, one comes up with an understanding of what it means to be human and one can start with our art, with our dance, with our religion, with our folklore, or with our great struggle of freedom. This conference is another lesson in how much power and depth and tremendous wisdom there is in the study of the black experience in America, and I want to thank Frank and the NOAH young people for their part in the organizing and facilitating of it. I also want to dedicate this talk to them, partly because of the profound experience I had a few summers ago as a result of the discussions with them of my book, There Is a River, in which these young people raised some of the most important questions about the meaning and purpose of the book I have ever faced with anybody, and partly because of the wonderful compassion which they showed when I was hospitalized very unexpectedly.

Now what I would like to do is take the responsibility for helping to close it off. And maybe what I would like to call this is really a set of reflections on what we have been doing and thinking and feeling and wanting and hoping and trying to figure out. What I would like to suggest is that this is a good time at the end of the two days to perhaps quiet ourselves a bit more and focus ourselves, and ponder a bit about what it is we have been about other than another academic conference. One cannot talk about the human struggle for freedom and justice anywhere and simply make it academic. It has never been simply academic, and it never will be simply academic, but those who are academic are very wise to study it.

I would like us to spend some time prodding each other and being prodded and looking at our situations as closely as we can, looking at our personal situations, looking at our collective situation just as we have already begun to do. It seems to me that at the end of a gathering like this, of such great import, it is absolutely necessary to know that this is simply one step toward others, and that the next obvious step for us in this kind of arena and in this time in the life of ourselves and of our nation and of our world, is to face the familiar question; the question that Martin King made most famous in the title of his book twenty-one years ago, "Where do we go from here?" It is a marvelous question simply because it recognizes that it is a question, and because

it recognizes that deep at the bottommost level it is not simply a personal question, it is a collective question as well.  Where do we go from
here?   Remember, those of you who saw the book when it came out, or have
seen it since that time in libraries or on your own shelves, remember the
title of the book didn't stop there.  It's very important to remember the
title of the book was Where Do We Go from Here: Chaos or Community?.   I
think that puts it most adequately.  Where do we go from here: chaos or
community?   I want to dedicate this question especially to the young
people who are here at the conference, that is, of course, the ones who
are slightly younger than I.

Where do we go from here?  I think that one of the places that we go
is to recognize that what we have experienced over these last two days is
that the conference has really helped us to redefine and to keep redefining the title of the conference itself.  And I would throw out a title
that is really more nineteenth century than twenty-first century.   I
would say that what we are talking about here is The Modern Black
Struggle for Freedom, Justice, Equality, and Transformation; and then I
would go on with the title, A Struggle We Gladly Share with all Others
Who Are Truly Committed to Freedom, Justice, Equality, and Transformation.  That is what I think is part of what we are doing.  I think that
where we have been going is to discover again that the Civil Rights Movement, what we call the Civil Rights Movement, was simply one necessary,
powerful, creative phase of that larger struggle for freedom, justice,
equality, and transformation.   Civil Rights is just a piece of it, a
necessary piece, but not the whole story.

Where do we go from here?  What I am suggesting is that we go on, if
we are alive, constantly redefining what we are about.  The title of the
conference begins with, "Dream and Reality," so we begin by asking what
is the dream of the movement, what is the reality of the movement?  By
now, at the end of the conference, we can ask intelligently what we have
been talking about.  That is a good place, when it is all over to ask
that question.  What I think we have been talking about is the recognition that when we say reality what we understand is that reality is not a
frozen given, that reality is not set in concrete that you have to accept.  No, that is not reality at all.  Reality is what we create, reality is what we create out of our courage to dream and to act on our
dreams.  That is what reality becomes.  One of the greatest of our revolutionary philosophers, Franz Fanon, made it very, very clear in Wretched
of the Earth when he said, paraphrasing him now, that every generation,
though they came out of relative obscurity and nobody has ever heard of
them in Queens or Harlem or Bedford Sty, that every generation coming out
of relative obscurity is called upon to create a new reality or to say "I
can do it, baby;" that the choice is ours to get in and work on creating
a new reality or betray the mission of our foreparents, every generation,
and this one is no exception.

So where do we go from here?  We go not only to redefine what
reality is about but we have been trying to redefine the dream itself,
and what so many people have said today and yesterday is that it is very
important that we realize that the 1963 march on Washington statement
that is in our program is only one statement of one part of our great
dream.   Martin King's statement is only one part of one aspect of our
great dream of the freedom movement, and we love it, we cherish it, we
are very glad for it; but it is not sufficient to express what the dream
of this movement is all about.

I would rather begin back before World War II.  I would rather begin
with another great black dreamer, a Harlem brother by way of the Mid-West
and Mexico. I would rather begin with Langston Hughes as a way of filling
in the meaning of the dream.  I would rather begin in 1937, when Langston
was a radical and writing out of the experience of social struggle.  At
that point, he wrote the poem that ends with these stanzas:

O, let America be America again--
The land that never has been yet--
And yet must be--the land where every man is free. (1)

You see that is what we mean by reality: we are going after something
that has not yet been. We are not handed America, here, love it or leave
it. No, that is not for us. We say, "Yes, love it enough to struggle to
change it." That is what we are talking about.

The land that's mine--the poor man's, Indian's, Negro's, ME--
Who made America.
Whose sweat and blood, whose faith and pain,
Whose hand at the foundry, whose plow in the rain,
Must bring back our mighty dream again. (2)

Sure, call me any name you choose, like "communist"; the steel of
freedom does not stain from those who live like leeches on the people's
lives. We must take back our land again. Do not join the leech crowd,
take the land back from those who want to live that way. Oh yes, I say
plain, America was never America to me but notice Brother Langston never
stops with complaining, you see complaining, complaining, white folks
this, that; America this, that--that is never enough. Oh yes, I say it
plain, America never was America to me, and yet I swear this oath;
America will be an everliving dream, an everliving seed; its dream lies
in the heart of me. We, We, We, the people must redeem our land; buy it
back, win it back, take it back; must redeem our land, the mines, the
plants, the rivers, the mountains, and the endless plains, all the
stretch of these great green states. We the people must make America
again and again and again in every generation. If you get tired after a
while, you are not ready yet, unless you also know how to get new breath,
and we will talk about that in just a moment. Langston gives a beautiful
statement of the dream. We could have gone back to DuBois, we could have
gone further back to Ellen Watkins Harper, we could have gone back to
David Walker. Whereever there have been strugglers for justice and truth
in American society, the dream coming out of the black struggle for
freedom has always been there. And what Langston says is the fundamental
truth,

First in the heart is the dream--
Then the mind starts seeking a way (3).

So where do we go? We go within us, at least part of the time, to
try to check out what the dream is that we have for America; are we just
folks who complain about other people's version of America? What is our
version? What is our vision, what do we believe America should be like,
look like; and if we do not dream it, you may be sure that somebody else
will be on the job and we may not like their dream so we better be about
it, about it deep within us; that is the role of We the People. I think
that is where we have to go to recognize that it is the role, not of the
professionals, not even of the folks who are running for president and
running away from president. What we have got to recognize is that the
handling of the dream, the shaping of the dream is our responsibility to
vision, to organize, to work; that is our responsibility.
So where do we go from here? We go back before 1963 and we go on
past 1963, we go on, as David Garrow and others were saying this morning,
to remember that Martin did not get stuck in the March on Washington,
Martin kept marching. That was not a "lay down after you finish" march,
that was a "march to get ready" march.   John Lewis said at the march
that we have to just march all through this country, all around this
country until justice is done.(4)  So Martin within a few years was

marching deep into the heart of the communities of the poor, had been
drawn deeply by his own sense of compassion into the communities of the
poor, and as a result of that was dreaming some very powerful dreams.
For instance, if we go on beyond 1963, we hear Martin King saying that
our movement is much more than a struggle for the rights of Negroes;
rather our movement is forcing America to face all its interrelated
flaws: racism, poverty, militarism, and materialism. (5)   Martin was
saying that the black freedom struggle is exposing the evils that are
deeply rooted in the whole structure of our society.  It reveals systemic
rather than superficial flaws, and it suggests that radical reconstruction of society itself is the real issue to be faced by 1966 and 1967.

Radical reconstruction of society itself is the real issue to be
faced.   If you go forward with Martin, you hear him saying by 1967,
something is wrong with capitalism.  Anybody who stands with the poor
honestly comes to that conclusion--anybody.  Malcolm came to that conclusion.  Now if you want to live apart from the poor you can have all sorts
of wonderful rationalizations for free enterprise, where people are free
to be poor.  But if you stand with the poor, if you experience their
homes and their houses, and what they have to live through and go
through, then you come to the conclusion which King came to--something is
wrong with capitalism as it now stands in the United States.   We are
listening to all of you who think Martin King is some kind of simple-
minded integrationist, we are not interested in being integrated into
this value stucture.  Power must be relocated.  All right, it sounds almost like Malcolm, doesn't it?   And to make very clear that if we keep
going forward, what we recognize is what our sister from Africa recognized, that Martin was an international human being.  Now you see, that
should not be surprising.  Anybody who says they are spiritually oriented, anybody who says they are a child of the living God, means that they
recognize that the living God has all kinds of children around, and none
of them is more valuable than any other of them.  So none of them has any
right to say it's all right for them to be poor as long as we can have
three cars, I mean they just like being poor.  That is not living a God-
child relationship.  None of us has any right to be pointing missiles at
some of God's children, saying, well I know it is my sister and brother
but they are communists.   Martin King tried to walk his talk and tried
to be consistent about being a child of God, and therefore he said that a
storm is rising against the privileged minority of the earth from which
there is no shelter in isolation or in armament.(6)  The storm will not
abate until a just distribution of the fruits of the earth enable men and
women everywhere to live in dignity and human decency.   The storm is
rising from the privileged minority of the earth.  Do not let some of us
think that just because we are colored, that that does not mean us too,
if we are living in the heart of the center of the privileged minority
country of the earth.

King went on with a kind of hope which was endemic to the man all of
his life.  He concluded that statement about the storm by saying that the
American Negro may be the vanguard of a prolonged struggle that may
change the shape of the world as billions of deprived shake and transform
the earth in the quest for life, freedom, and justice.(7)  Now watch out,
every time folks shake the earth in the quest for life, freedom, and
justice, there is going to be a call to you young people, there is going
to be a call that says:   Be all that you can be.  Grenada, Nicaragua,
maybe South Africa:   some of us are going to have to decide where do we
stand.

Where do we stand?  Where do we go from here?  Becoming more and
more mature, more and more adult, which does not mean smoking cigarettes
and drinking liquor; that is not how you become mature and adult.   It
means taking responsibility for your life and where you really stand and
what you really believe.

Where do we go from here?  I think that we need to go at least to the point of trying not just to praise them (Malcolm and Martin), not even to argue about which of them should be praised more, because that is not the point at this point.  I think we have to at least go so far as taking their vision and their lives seriously; not just making rhetorical statements about Malcolm: my hero; or Martin: wonderful leaders; but by asking how seriously we take these brothers and what they were saying at the end of their lives.  I think where we go from here is also to look at them and take seriously the fact that neither could have gone as far as he went unless he had found some very deep spiritual resources on which to call: we would think of them as different resources.  Malcolm, the child of Allah; Martin, Jesus' boy; maybe that is not as different as we think.  The fact is that both of them went down deep below the surface to the fountains of human renewal and drank deeply there because they knew they had a long race to run.  Where do we go from here?  At least look at them, look at where they went for renewal and let us ask ourselves where we are going to get the strength to go on.

Where do we go from here?  I think if we listen to our brothers and listen to the sisters and brothers who have spoken here, we might realize that the title of this conference that we have been playing with is very, very tricky; there is a fundamental tension between a vision of equality in the United States as it is and a vision of transformation based on the dreams within us.  A vision of equality in the United States may end up to be too narrow a vision, too narrow certainly to fit in lots of the street folks that we know; we may need to open up our dream to a dream of transformation.  Let me give you an example of what I am talking about.  If we are dreaming only about equality and equal opportunity, then when we walk up to the White House and go down into the basement where Henry Kissinger used to live and where Admiral Poindexter used to live, we may come out nice and proud.  Down in the basement is the head of National Security, security advisor for the president of the United States.  We look and we see a colored man at the desk and we are proud; look at that, a general: a black general in the basement of the White House just where Mr. Kissinger used to be.  If all we are thinking about is equality, we will be happy for that.  We are equal to Kissinger, we are equal to Poindexter.  We are equal to any three-star general in the army.  But then if we come up out the basement, and we follow our black three-star general around, we see some of the folks he is travelling with such as Eliot Abrams, who can not even talk to Congress anymore because he has been lying to them for the last five years about Central America.  If we follow him around, we see Colin Powell, General Powell—equal General Powell—going down with Abrams to Central America to talk to the Central Americans, to talk to them as they are trying to work out their problems on their own initiative.  We hear equal General Colin Powell saying essentially, "Listen y'all, don't mess with us; we are big and bad up there in the U.S.A., and if you don't do things the way we want them done, if you don't eliminate those Sandinistas one way or another, don't expect any help from us, understand that."  In other words, we are finding out that he is as equal as a bully, and if that is what we want, then we have to watch out.  Is that what we want after we have been bullied around all of our generations?  Equality in the America that we know today may not be an adequate vision.  Compare him to a Frank Smith who comes in to Hofstra University and does not spend all of his time saying, "Oh Hofstra, thank you so much for letting poor me in; I am now equal; Oh yes, Hofstra, I appreciate you so much."  No. Frank says, "I know where I came from, and I know who's out there where I came from, and I want to be about transforming them and transforming this university so it can deal with them."  Not equality of opportunity; if all Frank wanted to do was be equal, our folks would be in sad shape.  Frank is saying in his little basement, you know, desk, "I want to do something about changing the situation for the benefit of the humanity of both my students and this university." Very, very different vision.

Where do we go from here? I think it is to realize that at this point in history the basic tension is no longer between integration and separation, that is an old argument now. The basic tension especially for people like us in this room is now between integration and transformation. Think about it please. One way leads us to Colin Powell; the other way leads us to Ben Chavis, to Diane Nash, to Sonia Sanchez, to Bob Moses, and to people who have worked for twenty-five years to change this society, change themselves, and have not accepted the given assumptions, the given reality of the society. This is a hard saying but I believe that Martin meant us to be mature enough by 1990 to deal with the hard path, not just cry because he died; but ask why he died, and what does it have to do with our living.

Where do we go from here? I think that one of the most fascinating places we can go is back in the 1960s again and carry back to the 1960s our present concern for the black crime rate in the black community. You know, of course, that black people constitute forty percent of folks who were murdered in this country. All right, and you know we are not anything like forty percent of the population in this country; and you know, of course, that no longer are we mostly afraid of white folks killing us; in most black communities we are much more afraid, when we are honest, of us killing us. Why? We have to ask that question and one of the answers is that we have provided, we, us, of every age, of every occupation, of every gradation of color, that we have provided very few alternatives for a lot of our young folks. If you go back to 1961, 1962, 1963, and you read the criminal records of Albany, Georgia, and Birmingham, Alabama, and Jackson, Mississippi, the story is very clear: in every community where there was an active struggle for freedom and justice going on, the black crime rate went down to almost nothing. How is that for fighting crime? Where do we go from here? To deal with interesting questions like that, we go to hear somebody who was quoted to us today and because we still have a lot of work to do with our educational system; most of us did not know the name when we heard it. Somebody interestingly who came from Euro-American background quoted to us one of the great black philosophers of the twentieth century, William Stewart Nelson of Howard University, who was one of the great Gandhian scholars, who indeed went in the 1930s to march with Gandhi in the Indian freedom struggle and then came back to this country to hope and pray and mostly write about how we need a Gandhian movement in this country. What we need to think about and where we need to go is to remember how William Stewart Nelson struggled for more than twenty years, finally in 1955 getting very tired and saying that after twenty years of trying to promote this idea, he did not believe there was a Gandhi for Black America. What we need to do is realize that that was Rosa's year and that was Martin's year; and that was E.D. Nixon's year; and that was Joanne Robinson's year; and that was the year of fifty thousand Black Gandhis of Montgomery. But this brother had kept going for twenty-five years believing that was what we needed, and no one else, not many other folks, paid any attention to William Stewart Nelson, but he kept going, going, and going. Where are the long distance runners among us?

Where do we go from here? Well, I have an answer, not just a question. I think if we want to go from here and find some of the folks who are going to be on the case for a long time, all we need to do is look around us. Booker T. Washington had a questionable metaphor that he always liked to use and that was, "Let down your buckets where they are." My feeling is, if we look around us, we have some folks right in this room who are going to be the ones for the next period of time ahead. Now I don't know what their year is, and they probably don't know what their year is either. It sure is not 1955, but it might be 1995 or even 1989.

We've got young people here, young people and maybe even some more mature adults who will begin to study very, very hard; study very, very long, begin to question and challenge, and like DuBois, struggle to change American foreign policy so that there will never be another Grenada, so that there will never be this kind of business with trying to strangle our young revolution in Nicaragua, so that we will not have to worry about black young people being sent to South America to save the free world.  There are going to be folks here who are going to be working on that.  There are going to be some folks here, I think, who are going to be challenging American militarism like Martin King, at its roots, challenging so much that they might even say to themselves, "No, I am not going, and I am even going to encourage other people not to register sometime, just to keep the system on its toes."  There are going to be some people who are as concerned as King about American militarism that they are going to look around Long Island and say, "Does this community have to depend upon defense contracts the way that it does; is that the only alternative for life on Long Island?"  There are going to be some folks who are going to be asking embarrassing questions, they are going to be going all around their own black and Hispanic communities and they are going to be saying, "Do our young men really have to come to the point where the only work they can get is being trained how to put down other folks, that the only paychecks they can get are the paychecks that come out of the U.S. military?"  King said that you cannot be a truly compassionate country as long as you are spending so much of your money and time and energy figuring out how to kill people.(8)  And some of us who are young here are going to be raising that question first within ourselves and then within our society and saying, "Where do I go, where do we go from here?"  What are the alternatives to capitalism as we know them?  Do people have to be automatically ground out of the system in order for some other people to succeed or can there truly be a common-wealth?  Some of us are right here, some of us are going to be lawyers, some of us right here are going to be lawyers, not lawyers whose big job is to make money and have three BMWs, but whose big job is like C.B. King, like Arthur Kinoy, like Marian King, like Haywood Burns, like Bill Kuntsler, like lots of other folks whose main job is justice, justice, justice, before money.  Some of us folks are going to be lawyers like that.  Some are going to be teachers, some are going to be teachers like Frank Smith, some are going to be teachers like Brother Vincent who was up here before telling us about his experiences as a teacher.  Some of them are going to be remembering what Harris Wofford said earlier this afternoon.  Harris was a fascinating brother, and I have no hesitation about calling him brother.  Harris said, "There was a part of America that I had totally shut out of my life as I was growing up, there was a part of America that I had totally shut out of my life."  Now of course black folks don't do that, do they?  Hispanic folks don't do that, do they?  Of course, it is true, we do because some of it is too painful for some of us to bear [we think] but if we are not going to bear it, who is?

Where are we going from here?  We are going to get the courage to open up our eyes to a lot of things that are very painful, but which will not be addressed until some of us face them and deal with them.  Remember, remember that we are talking about King, we are talking about Malcolm; those brothers never shut their eyes to anything.  So I am looking to this gathering and gatherings like it for the organizers who are going to come forth to redeem the land.  I am looking for the civil engineers and the economists who are going to be learning to make the mind safe, not only how to make the mind safe, but also how to make the wealth of the mind go to the people who need it.  I am looking to a gathering like this for new biologists and botanists because it is they who will rescue and redeem the plants that are being so badly poisoned by our greed.  I am looking for new ecologists and new organizers to redeem

the rivers from their pollution because they will know that if you do not
redeem the rivers, you are killing your great-grand children. So I expect that that is where I am going from here, I am going to look for
folks who are really serious about giving themselves to serious work. So
when Harris Wofford asked what America would be like if we had twenty-
five more years of King changing, moving; if we had had twenty-five more
years of Malcolm changing, developing, if we had had twenty-five more
years of Ruby Doris Smith changing, moving; when he asked that, I said,
"Well, that's really not the main question, the main question is an
answer." Look around you, there are folks here who have got lots more
than twenty-five years to develop. I see you, some of you have thirty
years, some of you have forty years, some of you have fifty years, some
of you have even more years than I do, maybe sixty years, to grow and to
change. I see Jonathan, I see Leslie, I see Christopher, I see Christine,
I see Michelle, I see Claudia, I see all of Frank's young folks, and what
I know is that these folks know how much they have been loved and cared
for. I see you, I know you have a long time to go, and I am for you;
that is where I go from here. I go with you, and now I realize and I
think, we realize that a conference like this opens up the options to us.
    Where do we go from here? No, Martin, not just chaos or community;
I think we have got three options when we are serious and honest with
each other about where we go from this kind of experience. We can go
right on to where America seems to be wanting to go and that is to social
chaos where nobody is responsible for anybody else, sometimes even in the
same household. That is one option, social chaos. A second option that
Martin didn't talk about but which he knew about is the option of para-
noid individualism and personal isolationism whether hiding in religion;
hiding in money; hiding in sex; or hiding in drugs; but essentially
hiding from everybody else and living a life only for ourselves. Social
chaos or personal chaos; committing social suicide or personal suicide.
But I think there is always the third option: the option of the compassionate community: that is the hard option. That is the option that a
lot of people believe is unrealistic. Well, King said that if that does
not become our reality, we are all going to be burning up soon.
    Where do we go? Some of us, maybe more than I realize, at least
some of us, are going to give our lives and our skills and our resources
of every kind to continue the struggle that made it possible for us to be
here. Some of us are going to carry on the tradition that our foreparents and other folks' foreparents began for us. Some of us are going to
go on trying to reshape the modern black struggle for freedom and
justice, for equality and transformation. And some of us have already
discovered it: that it is a struggle that we can gladly share with all
others who are truly committed to freedom, to justice, to equality, to
transformation.
    Where do we go from here? To create a new reality, of course, to
create a new reality based on a new vision, based on a new people that is
made up of many peoples, to struggle for a new society starting with me,
you, me. Here we come, Malcolm; here we come, Martin. Open the way,
Ruby Doris, Ella Baker, we are on your path. That's where we go from
here.

**NOTES**

    1. Langston Hughes, "Let America Be America Again," lines 62-64,
in America in Poetry, ed. Charles Sullivan (New York: Harry N. Abrams,
1988), 185.

    2. Ibid, lines 65-69.

    3. Langston Hughes, "Freedom's Plow," lines 9-10, in Hughes,

Langston, The Langston Hughes Reader (New York: George Braziller, Inc., 1958), 131.

4.    August 28, 1963.  "All of us must get in the revolution--get in and stay in the streets of every city, village and hamlet of this nation, until true freedom comes, until the revolution is complete."  Printed in Joanne Grant, Black Protest:  History, Documents and Analysis, (Greenwich, CT:  Fawcett Publications, 1968),  377.

5.    Martin Luther King, Where Do We Go from Here: Chaos or Community? (New York:  Harper and Row, 1967), 132-35.

6.    Ibid., 169-71.

7.    Ibid.

8.    Ibid., 188.

# Index

# About the Editor and the Contributors

JACK BLOOM is the author of <u>Class, Race and The Civil Rights Movement</u> published by Indiana University Press in 1987. He holds a Ph.D. from the University of California at Berkeley and is currently Associate Professor of Sociology at Indiana University Northwest. In the summer of 1988, he was Visiting Associate Professor at Warsaw University in Poland. He has also written and lectured on class and ethnic conflict in Kenya.

RHODA LOIS BLUMBERG is Professor of Sociology at Rutgers University and specializes in Racial and Ethnic Relations, Women's Studies, Social Movements, and Complex Organizations. She received her Ph.D. from the University of Chicago and held a Fulbright-Hayes Research Scholarship in India in 1966-67. She has written a number of books, including <u>Civil Rights: The 1960's Freedom Struggle,</u> and <u>Indian Women in Transition: A Bengalore Case</u>.

JULIAN BOND was recently a Visiting Professor at Harvard University. He was an active member of the Student Nonviolent Coordinating Committee. Having been elected three times to the Georgia House of Representatives, but barred from taking office, he served four terms beginning in 1967 after the Supreme Court of the United States ruled that the legislators had erred in not permitting him to take office. In 1968 he was nominated as Vice President of the United States at the Democratic convention, but withdrew his name because he did not meet the age requirement.

ROBERT D. BULLARD is a visiting scholar and Associate Professor of Sociology in the Energy Resources Group at the University of California at Berkeley. He was previously on the faculty at the University of Tennessee at Knoxville. He is the author of numerous publications on the African-American Experience including <u>Invisible Houston: The Black Experience in Boom and Bust.</u>

GEORGE E. DICKINSON is Professor and Chair in the Department of Sociology and Anthropology at the College of Charleston in South Carolina. He has taught at Morehead State University in Kentucky, Memphis State, Pennsylvania State University at University Park, and a number of other universities. In addition to his work on the behavior and attitudes of adolescents, Dr. Dickinson has a number of publications in the area of death education and attitudes toward dying. The Sociology of the Family and the Sociology of Death and Dying are two of his principal areas of research and publications.

GERALD ANTHONY FOSTER is presently Vice President for Academic Affairs at Virginia Union University in Richmond, and previously held the position of Dean of the School of Arts and Letters at Hampton University in Hampton, Virginia.  In addition to teaching and college administration at Hampton, Pace, Fordham, and City University of New York, Dr. Foster held administrative posts for the New York City Department of Human Resources, (Youth Division), and the Westchester Community Planning Council.  He has presented papers and published in the areas of Community Planning, Sociology of the Family, and Minority Youth.

DAVID J. GARROW was awarded the Pulitzer Prize for Biography for his 1986 publication of Bearing the Cross:  Martin Luther King Jr. and the Southern Christian Leadership Conference.  He received his Ph.D. from Duke University in 1981; has been on the faculty at the University of North Carolina at Chapel Hill and is currently a Professor of Political Science at the Graduate Center of the City College of New York.  He was senior advisor for the award winning TV documentary, "Eyes on the Prize," and has authored several other books on the Civil Rights Movement and Martin Luther King, Jr.

VINCENT HARDING author of There Is a River, Must Walls Divide, and The Other American Revolution, is on the faculty of the Iliff School of Theology at the University of Denver.  He holds a Ph.D. in History from the University of Chicago.  In the early 1960s, Dr. Harding worked full time in the black freedom movement and in 1968 became director of the Martin Luther King, Jr., Memorial Center.  He was also coordinator of the CBS series, "Black Heritage."

WILHELMINA A. LEIGH holds a Ph.D. in Economics from Johns Hopkins University and is currently Principal Analyst for the Congressional Budget Office with oversight on housing legislation.  She has worked for the National Urban League, HUD, and the Department of Labor.  She was an Assistant Professor in the City Regional Planning Program at Harvard University between 1977 and 1981.  She has a number of publications, mainly in the area of housing.

HELENE SLESSAREV holds the title of Employment, Affirmative Action, and Policy Evaluation Specialist in the Research Department of the Chicago Urban League.  She holds a Ph.D. from the University of Chicago.  Her research and publications are mainly in the area of employment policy and job training, as well as the impact of retrenchment in employment on racial tensions.

JEANNINE SWIFT is an Associate Professor of Economics at Hofstra University in Hempstead, New York.  She received her Ph.D. from MIT and is the author of two books, Agrarian Reform in Chile and Economic Development in Latin America.

RONALD L. TAYLOR holds a Ph.D. in Sociology from Boston University and is Associate Professor of Sociology at the University of Connecticut at

Storrs.    He has published a number of works on psychosocial development among black children and teenagers, as well as among black male workers.

MICHAEL H. WASHINGTON specializes in Urban Educational History in the United States with emphasis on the black educational experience during the twentieth century.  He is currently an Associate Professor of History at Northern Kentucky University and was the founder of the Afro-American Studies program at that university.  He has written a number of articles in the area of the black struggle for quality education, as well as on other topics.

BEVERLY H. WRIGHT is Assistant Professor of Sociology at the Wake Forest University in Winston-Salem, North Carolina.  She previously worked as a counselor and later as assistant director of the Educational Opportunity Program at the State University of New York at Buffalo.  Since receiving her Ph.D. from SUNY, Buffalo, she has written and lectured in a variety of areas, including racial and personal self-esteem, blacks and the environment, and achievement motivation.

**Hofstra University's**
**Cultural and Intercultural Studies**
*Coordinating Editor, Alexej Ugrinsky*

Franklin D. Roosevelt: The Man, the Myth, the Era, 1882-1945
*(Editors: Herbert D. Rosenbaum and Elizabeth Bartelme)*

The Stendhal Bicentennial Papers
*(Editor: Avriel Goldberger)*

Faith of a (Woman) Writer
*(Editors: Alice Kessler-Harris and William McBrien)*

José Ortega y Gasset: Proceedings of the *Espectador Universal* International
Interdisciplinary Conference
*(Editor: Nora de Marval-McNair)*

George Orwell
*(Editors: Courtney T. Wemyss and Alexej Ugrinsky)*

John F. Kennedy: The Promise Revisited
*(Editors: Paul Harper and Joann P. Krieg)*

Lyndon Baines Johnson and the Uses of Power
*(Editors: Bernard J. Firestone and Robert C. Vogt)*

Eighteenth-Century Women and the Arts
*(Editors: Frederick M. Keener and Susan E. Lorsch)*

Suburbia Re-examined
*(Editor: Barbara M. Kelly)*

James Joyce and His Contemporaries
*(Editors: Diana A. Ben-Merre and Maureen Murphy)*

The World of George Sand
*(Editors: Natalie Datlof, Jeanne Fuchs, and David A. Powell)*

Richard M. Nixon: Politician, President, Administrator
*(Editors: Leon Friedman and William F. Levantrosser)*